Bo
Fa
F

D0228872

The Undiscovered Country

The Undiscovered Country

Journeys Among the Dead

CARL WATKINS

THE BODLEY HEAD
LONDON

Published by The Bodley Head 2013

2 4 6 8 10 9 7 5 3 1

First published in Great Britain in 2013 by
The Bodley Head
Random House, 20 Vauxhall Bridge Road,
London SW1V 2SA

www.bodleyhead.co.uk
www.vintage-books.co.uk

Addresses for companies within The Random House Group Limited can be found at:
www.randomhouse.co.uk/offices.htm

The Random House Group Limited Reg. No. 954009

A CIP catalogue record for this book
is available from the British Library

ISBN 9781847921406

The Random House Group Limited supports the Forest Stewardship Council (FSC®),
the leading international forest-certification organisation. Our books carrying the FSC label are
printed on FSC®-certified paper. FSC is the only forest-certification scheme endorsed by the
leading environmental organisations, including Greenpeace. Our paper procurement policy
can be found at www.randomhouse.co.uk/environment

Maps by Darren Bennett
Typeset in Dante MT by Palimpsest Book Production Ltd,
Falkirk, Stirlingshire
Printed and bound in Great Britain by
Clays Ltd, St Ives PLC

CONTENTS

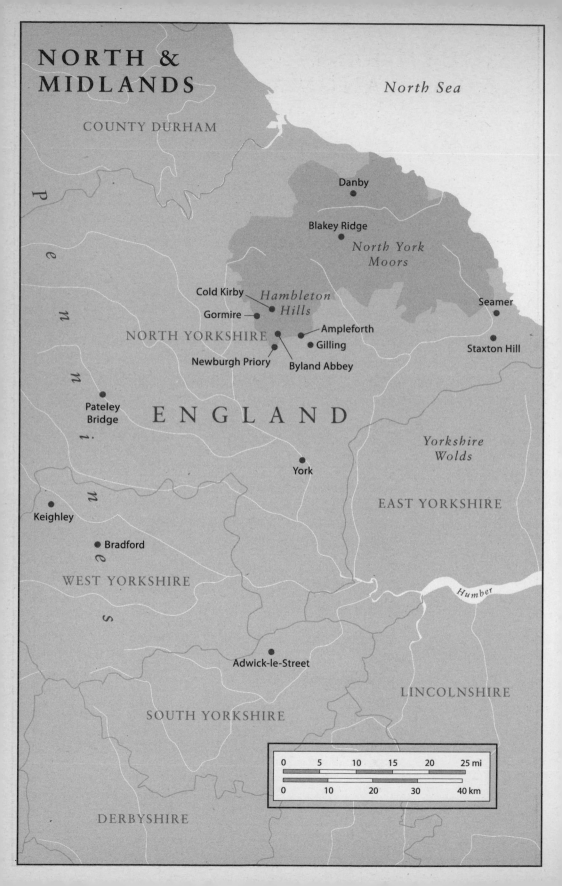

NORTH &
MIDLANDS

North Sea

COUNTY DURHAM

Danby

Blakey Ridge

North York Moors

Cold Kirby *Hambleton Hills*

Seamer

Gormire

Ampleforth

NORTH YORKSHIRE Gilling

Staxton Hill

Newburgh Priory Byland Abbey

Pateley Bridge

E N G L A N D

Yorkshire Wolds

York

EAST YORKSHIRE

Keighley

Bradford

Humber

WEST YORKSHIRE

Adwick-le-Street

LINCOLNSHIRE

SOUTH YORKSHIRE

| 0 | 5 | 10 | 15 | 20 | 25 mi |
| 0 | 10 | 20 | 30 | 40 km |

DERBYSHIRE

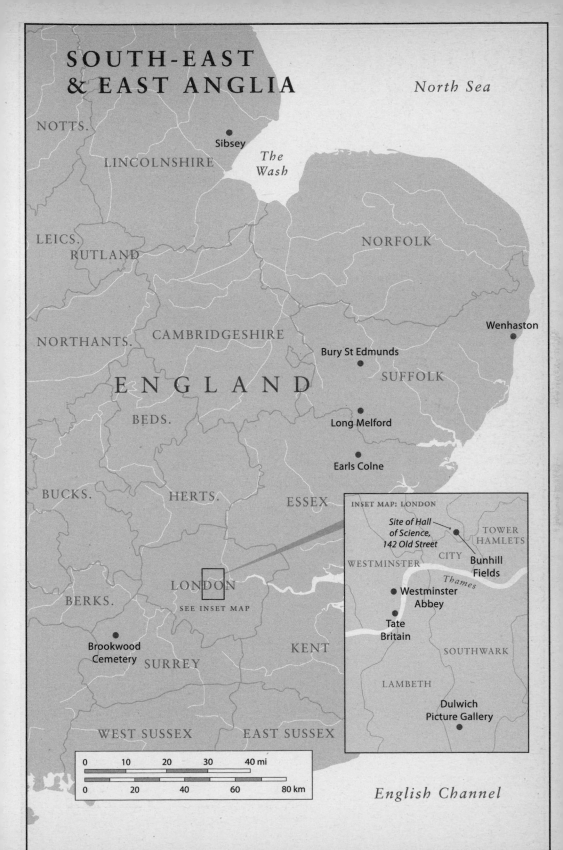

SOUTH-EAST
& EAST ANGLIA

North Sea

NOTTS.

LINCOLNSHIRE

Sibsey

The
Wash

LEICS.

RUTLAND

NORFOLK

NORTHANTS.

CAMBRIDGESHIRE

Wenhaston

ENGLAND

Bury St Edmunds

SUFFOLK

BEDS.

Long Melford

Earls Colne

BUCKS.

HERTS.

ESSEX

INSET MAP: LONDON

Site of Hall
of Science,
142 Old Street

TOWER
HAMLETS

CITY

Bunhill
Fields

WESTMINSTER

LONDON

SEE INSET MAP

Thames

BERKS.

Westminster
Abbey

Tate
Britain

Brookwood
Cemetery

SURREY

KENT

SOUTHWARK

LAMBETH

WEST SUSSEX

EAST SUSSEX

Dulwich
Picture Gallery

| 0 | 10 | 20 | 30 | 40 mi |

| 0 | 20 | 40 | 60 | 80 km |

English Channel

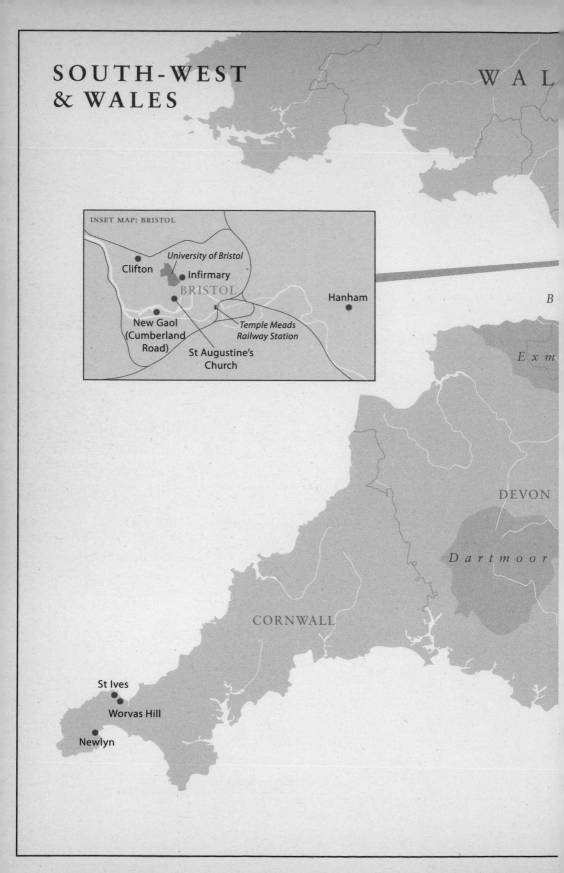

SOUTH-WEST & WALES

W A L

INSET MAP: BRISTOL

Clifton

University of Bristol

Infirmary

BRISTOL

Hanham

New Gaol
(Cumberland
Road)

*Temple Meads
Railway Station*

St Augustine's
Church

B

E x m

DEVON

D a r t m o o r

CORNWALL

St Ives

Worvas Hill

Newlyn

WALES

HEREFORDSHIRE

GLOUCESTERSHIRE

*Cotswold
Hills*

Glyntaff

Llantrisant   Cardiff

Bristol

SEE INSET MAP

Bath

WILTSHIRE

Bristol Channel

ENGLAND

Tidworth

oor

SOMERSET

*Salisbury
Plain*

Sampford
Peverell

HAMPSHIRE
*New
Forest*

DORSET

Dorchester

English Channel

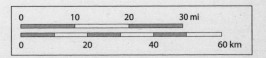

0	10	20	30 mi
0	20	40	60 km

PICTURE ACKNOWLEDGEMENTS

Colour illustrations are reproduced by kind permission of:

Alamy: Photograph of the Wenhaston Doom painting (© C. B. Newham); Illustration of William Price as Druid (© Mary Evans Picture Library); Photograph of the Tomb of the Unknown Warrior (© Angelo Hornak); All Saints Church, York: Detail from the 'Apocalypse Window'; Bridgeman Art Library: *The Great Day of His Wrath* by John Martin, engraved by Charles Mottram (1807–76) (Private Collection/© Christopher Wood Gallery, London); Imperial War Museum: Photograph of the Unknown Warrior's coffin, Westminster Abbey; St Ives Museum: Photograph of the Knill Monument, Worvas Hill, Cornwall; St Mary's Church, Bury St Edmunds: Photograph of John Baret's tomb (© F. R. Wilkinson MBE); Tate Museum: *The Plains of Heaven* by John Martin (© Tate, London 2012); The Trustees of the Dulwich Picture Gallery: *Venetia, Lady Digby, on her Deathbed* by Sir Anthony van Dyck (© Dulwich Picture Gallery, London).

PROLOGUE

A large painting draws in viewers at an exhibition in Tate Britain. Most stand before it curious, some transfixed, others a little uncomprehending. The painting is of a landscape but not a landscape as that genre is conventionally understood. It is on a massive scale, measuring some thirteen feet by nine, but the subject is more striking than the size, for this is no pastoral idyll or romantic fantasy. It is a painting of destruction on a cosmic scale. An earthquake shakes mountains out of their places. Lightning rives boulders from the tops and sends them down into the valley. A city totters, fragments and falls inwards. Reds, oranges and blacks dominate; everything is darkness and fiery light. Getting closer, the painting folds the viewer in and, as it does so, pulls the gaze towards tiny human beings in the shadows, some in rich clothes, others naked, some crying out, others trying to hide in rocks and caves, all fragile and grabbing at the disintegrating earth. The key to the painting is a scriptural verse: 'For the great day of his wrath is come and who shall be able to stand?'[1] It comes from the last and easily the strangest book of the Bible, Revelation, a vision cast in poetic, almost hallucinatory, language of how the world would end. This painting, *The Great Day of His Wrath*, was no ordinary piece of art. It was a prophecy in paint.[2]

The idea of the painting was, then, an ancient one but the painting itself is not ancient. It is the work of a relatively modern man, John Martin, who painted it in the early 1850s – an age of railways, wireless telegraphy, steamships, heavy industry. Martin had been born at East Landends near Haydon Bridge in 1789 as the industrial transformation of Britain was under way. He walked the hills as a boy, fearing the mine workings with their reputations for ghosts and hobgoblins and filing away in his memory impressions of sublime nature. Rather later, as he strayed further afield, he encountered blast furnaces, illuminated by night with liquid fire; they inspired his palette of colours when he created his vision of the last things. Martin's mother bequeathed her religion to him. She counted among her ancestors Nicholas Ridley, Protestant, bishop and a martyr who had been burned to death slowly at Oxford in 1555 when his pyre did not catch light properly.[3] She was a descendant worthy of him in her zeal, and her piety was fierce: she believed in the devil's angels and a fiery hell, a place, she told her son, where the blasphemer and the swearer would ultimately be consigned. John's three brothers, older than him, were brought up in the fervour and turned into eccentrics. William, the eldest, was a frustrated inventor. Richard was practical, a soldier who fought in Wellington's army against Napoleon. Then there was Jonathan, a preacher, visionary and madman – he was condemned to Bedlam after he almost succeeded in burning down York Minster. Only the timely arrival of a powerful pumping engine from Leeds saved the great church from the flames. The older Martin brothers were full of millenarian speculation. They wondered about the end of the world, anxious that it might come in their own day, and John listened and absorbed it all.

When he put brush to canvas half a century later, *The Great Day of His Wrath* was one image in a sequence of three. Revelation, the book at the heart of apocalyptic talk, laid out in detail how the end would come and John Martin tried to put the essence of the story into two further paintings. They also hang in Tate Britain. The second is less arresting than the first. It shows the judgement of the living and the dead. Christ is enthroned in the upper middle of the painting surrounded by white-robed elders and angels. In that portion of the painting stillness prevails. Below there is turbulence. The drama is explained in a pamphlet, a fragile thing only six inches by four inches, which forms a

'Descriptive Key' to the 'Grand and Solemn Pictures'. Mass-produced for the original exhibition using cheap paper, very few copies have survived.[4] It explains that peoples from the four corners of the earth have been summoned and now 'nation meets nation in an unusual brotherhood'. As the living gather together, the dead, too, have been raised from their graves; all are separated: sheep from goats, good from wicked, blessed from cursed. On the right-hand side, an angel holding the trumpet that has announced the judgement looks down, observing the scenes that play out in the landscape of the Bible but which are also full of features of Victorian England. For not only different peoples but also different times would meet in this moment of cosmic unity. In the distance the armies of the Antichrist are vanquished as they try to lay siege to the people of God on Mount Zion. In the foreground, the damned gather in the valley of Jehosaphat, bathed in what remains of the sun's light. The land around them crumbles away and they lose their footings; hills disintegrate, cities collapse and a steam train, trailing smoke and carriages, falls into the chasm. Among the lost souls are the rich and the powerful: a crowned king, a bishop in full pontificals, a Catholic, sprawled in the foreground. All wicked things, explains the pamphlet, pass away in the end times – avarice and pride, pomp and hypocrisy, pretended faith and false sanctity, fake humility and the 'hideous engines and vain trophies of war'.

On the left-hand side of the painting are the saved, men and women of all estates: painters, philosophers, divines, holy martyrs, virtuous queens, innocent children, ordinary people, 'all who have benefited mankind and served the cause of Christianity' united now 'in brotherly love'. Some are knowable – John Milton and William Shakespeare; there are Protestant heroes too, counterpoints of the damned bishop, the medieval heretic John Wyclif and the stirrer of the Reformation, the German monk Martin Luther. Faintly visible in the distance 'in illimitable space' is a celestial city which waits for the blessed, a place lighted not by sun or moon but by the glory of God. To the far left is a grassy path, winding through trees, a way out of the dying world onto the *Plains of Heaven*. This is the final painting. Built around the Bible text 'I saw a new heaven and a new earth', mountains rise far away in a haze while in the foreground the inhabitants of heaven gather among flowers. The painting brings life to the scriptural promise that 'God shall wipe away all tears from their eyes, and there shall be no more death, neither sorrow nor crying . . . for the former things are passed away'. And 'he that sat upon the throne said "behold, I make all things new"'.[5] All this, too, made sense to John Martin, his family and Victorian men and women who came to see the paintings in the 1850s. The pamphlet guide explained the judgement scene quite fully but, for the other paintings, it was deemed sufficient to list illustrative quotations; the Bible was familiar enough for at least a basic understanding to be taken as read.

The essence of the Christian prophecy John Martin painted had been brought to England by St Augustine and his missionaries in 597. Endlessly elaborated and reconceived, read, preached and for some of the time figured in art, it had become fixed in the imaginations of Christian men and women down the generations. It formed an essential element in a body of knowledge about not only how the world itself would die, but how each man and woman within it would die. It held out the prospect of judgement for all, of the eternal fires of hell to the unregenerate and new life to those who embraced Christ, souls that would rise to inherit a new world. This story, central to the Church's message, modi-fied, refined, sometimes quarrelled over, was shared by the people of Christian Britain for 1,300 years. And it was still alive – very much alive – in the mid Victorian England that John Martin set out to please with these, his last and greatest works. And please Martin did. The paintings were almost instantly famous. The railways, which by the 1850s criss-crossed much of England, carried them to most major towns, beginning with those of the north-east and then London in 1855. Crowds queued to see them. Viewed by gas lamps in darkened rooms, they became more phantasmagoria than art, cinematography before cinema, seeming almost to move in the shimmering light. Mass-produced engravings spread the images even further afield. They appeared in homes, church halls, school rooms. The *Descriptive Key* gave advance notice of the impressions to be made 'in the most costly manner' and of a quality 'commensurate with the importance of these grand subjects' so that the public could order their own copies. Nourished on the Bible, pulpit preaching and Sunday school teaching about heaven and hell and judgement, and still exposed to wonder tales about the invisible world, the paintings made sense to most who saw them; many still interpreted them not as poetic images licensed by art but as painted prophecies, approximations of things that would surely come to pass.

Long after Martin's death, the paintings were, for a time, forever on the road or rails, touring almost every major city of the British Isles; their fame spread overseas during the 1860s and 1870s and they were packed off by steamship to the United States and Australia. Their appeal seemed as durable as the prophecy they captured. But then, quite suddenly, the spell seemed to break, and not only because the terrible glamour of the paintings began to wear off. The painting of heaven was still admired beyond the 1870s – and it continued to be put on display – but the others were shuffled into storage. Eventually the allure of the *Plains of Heaven* began to fade as well. It too was hidden away. A later owner of the paintings wondered about showing them again to the public, confessing 'some feeling that the religious element that in my youth was so strong in our midst, has, in a measure, passed away'.[6] By the 1930s the triptych was almost forgotten; the paintings sold for a pittance, one even being cut into pieces to cover a screen.

It was not simply that artistic fashions had shifted in the late Victorian decades, beginning the paintings' slide into obscurity, although that was one part of the story. It was also that the cultural chemistry that powered the early enthusiasm was altering. John Martin had been born into a European world in transformation; the Bastille was stormed within days of his birth and the

French Revolution set in motion, but as he ended his life, a second, very different, revolution was under way, a revolution not of politics but of the imagination. For in the century or so after his death in 1854, the beliefs that had underpinned the popularity of his art faded. The idea of the resurrection of the body, that all would one day stand before Christ, that many would be cast into a fiery hell for eternity, even that there was a tangible place called heaven, all began to slip away. The fate of the paintings is more than a metaphor for this change; it is intimately related to the crumbling of a vision of the other world that had held sway for generations. And when the paintings were retrieved and set again on a gallery's walls in the 1970s, they were resurrected as art and not prophecy.[7] Startling, overwhelming, garish and more than a little kitsch, the restored triptych had become an artefact testifying to ways of thinking about this world and the next that had fallen away. Clues to a vanished world – now the alienness of the vision, not its familiarity – drew the viewers in. Today this is still how most people engage with them. Rapt but uncertain, they are sent back to the modern key and catalogue to make some sense of what they see.

That altered relationship between viewer and painting high-lights the scale of the imaginative revolution wrought since the paintings were first put on show. It is as if the men and women of the modern age are separated from their Victorian forebears by chasms as deep as those John Martin envisaged in the last days. Emptying pews, closure of churches, diminishing numbers of baptisms and marriages in church are commonplaces in a modern narrative of dechristianisation, elements in a story of cultural change that has seen the hold of Christianity over imaginations weaken in Britain during the twentieth century, and more surely so since the 1960s.[8] Modern Britain is a place of many faiths and none, a place where religious narratives about how to live and how to die have lost much of their power, where many pick and mix spiritualities from an array of ideas far more cosmopolitan in its make-up than in John Martin's day.

Looking back at the past from this vantage point, what stands out is a grand continuity, a past, stretching from the advent of Christianity until perhaps the late Victorian era, in which the people living in the British Isles, in the very broadest of terms, shared a vision of their own end and that of the world. Making sense of those people and their beliefs from that same vantage point can be no easy task. Thomas Browne, a seventeenth-century scholar, an archaeologist before archaeology, surveyed funerary urns and ashes deposited in ancient Britain and meditated on the faith of those who practised the rites. As he struggled to make sense of it, he saw that 'the religion of one seems madness unto another'. Many of us now are a little like Thomas Browne as he gazed at his mysterious pots; we look back on Britain's past – the comparatively recent past – and can make little sense of the beliefs that we see at work there.

In trying to enter that world, there are still points of contact. Few might now accept the narrative of the last things that John Martin's paintings offered, a narrative of judgement, hellfire and heaven, but two-thirds of the population of Britain still believe in the soul. As many as four in ten believe in the of ghosts and around half hold that there is some kind of life after death, a figure seemingly quite stable since the Second World War.[9] Residues of older visions are still there in the way people speak and structure their thoughts about the dead, too. Most are still cremated or buried according to Christian rites. Words about peace and rest, promises of a better place are expressed on cards attached to funeral flowers or printed in newspaper memorial notices. Some people talk to the dead. Some hold that dead loved ones watch over them. Votive lights set in candle racks in many churches and cathedrals suggest the dead are still in mind and notes pinned to prayer boards seek prayers for them, sometimes ask for help from them. Memorial announcements in newspapers sometimes address the dead as if they might be able to read the page; memorials on the internet sometimes speak to the dead as if they were there, somewhere, still within reach. In the modern world it is almost as if death is an obstacle to communication a little like distance, just as susceptible to being shrunk by an electronic miracle. 'Hellfire and harps' have all but vanished from these interpretations.[10] But there is still an idea that at the end of life there might be a place of bliss and radiance, stillness and freedom from pain; a place where children gone before their time become angels and there is hope of meeting again. The Russians capture something of this fuzzy hopefulness of modern heaven with their own expression. They call it 'Another Light'.[11]

This book begins with people and paintings at an exhibition in a country that seems to be in the business of dispensing with organised religion. But it works with the grain of beliefs and emotions around the dead that are often enduring. It is a modest bid to raise the dead, or some of the dead, and to make them come back to life briefly in stories made out of their lives. The critics, for the most part, did not much care for John Martin's paintings even if the public did. This was, they sneered, art to please the 'ignorant eye', ignorant, that is, of what made art great. It is fitting then that this is not, for the most part, a book about establishment figures, about elites and their beliefs or even about churchmen and abstract theologies. It is a book about how ordinary people in the past – people a little like those who queued to see John Martin's paintings in 1855 and those who view them still today – imagined the dead. It travels through this world to uncover the next, unravelling the stories behind places and artefacts and people that appear along the way. It travels through time, from the Middle Ages, when ordinary men and women can first be coaxed to speak to us directly from reticent sources, to the edge of the modern world, the immediate aftermath of the Great War, when ordinary men and women come more sharply into focus in letters and memoirs and photographs. It tells no single story for there is no single story to be told. This is, then, a book of many stories, pictures in words, set before the reader for contemplation.

I

THE STRANGE ISLES

In the south aisle of St Mary's Church in the East Anglian market town of Bury St Edmunds an effigy lies flat on its back on a tomb chest, resting there as it has done since the mid fifteenth century. The figure is not, as is more conventionally the case with tombs, a representation of a living person. It is a carved corpse, half clothed, skin stretched tight as a drum over bones that almost protrude, face set hard in a rictus, the nose crumbled away, the work of decomposition already begun. The effigy is not only an image of a dead human being, it is a reflection of the onlooker's future too. It confronts the viewer in the starkest fashion with his or her own eventual fate. Inscriptions laced round the figure make this plain. One scroll reads, 'From earth I came and onto earth I am brought, This is my nature, for of earth I was wrought.' Another: 'He that will sadly behold one with his eye, May see his own mirror and learn for to die.' A card near to the tomb announces that it is of a man called John Baret, a prosperous Bury merchant who lived through the first two-thirds of the fifteenth century and died in 1467. He worshipped at St Mary's and years before his death he commissioned his cadaverous tomb, gazing on it from his pew and meditating on his own end. Then, when his end came, his stone corpse continued to look down on its dead self thanks to many little mirrors set in the roof above the tomb. They are still there, dulled by time but occasionally catching a glint of light.[1]

Today John Baret's effigy cuts an incongruous figure in the

church bustling with worshippers, visitors, guides and helpers. It exerts a grim fascination over tourists, bespeaking a kind of medieval comfortableness with the things of death, a readiness to gaze on death, which is remote, alien to modern sensibilities. And yet they know that his tomb's message is for them, too. People are as fragile in their flesh and blood now as John Baret and his generation, and the tomb's messages have not lost all of their power. They turn away from it, sometimes with a shudder. These facts of life and sensations in the face of death bridge the half-millennium that separates us from them. Yet in most ways, the life John Baret lived and the way in which he conceived its ending are almost impossibly hard to envisage at such a great distance.

When the historian Thomas Carlyle came to Bury in the nineteenth century he wondered if he could ever make sense of the town's medieval inhabitants.[2] The ancient ruins of the great monastery of St Edmund that once dominated the town stuck out like 'a broken, blackened shin-bone of the dead ages', its stones uncommunicative about the lives once lived inside them. Written records scarcely helped him because they said little of inner things; to him the people of that part of the past, the great age of faith, seemed utterly remote. So very rarely, mused Carlyle, 'some real human figure is seen moving' and then they were only half seen, as if in a wintry twilight. Standing by John Baret's tomb, the problems that beset Carlyle have not gone away. There are no diaries, memoirs or boxes of letters to reveal how the people of John Baret's Bury lived, how they died or what they thought about death and the dead. Most of them are destined to be figures forever imprisoned in Carlyle's wintry twilight. But John Baret emerges with a little more clarity and sharpness of definition than most. He can be summoned to life not only through the traces on his tomb but, paradoxically, because of the very precision with which he prepared for death. His unusually voluminous will allows the man carved in stone to live again, flickeringly, in the imagination.

A Figure Half Seen

John Baret's Bury was no backwater. Some four or five thousand souls filled its late medieval streets.[3] It was among the wealthiest towns in Suffolk and Suffolk was one of the wealthiest counties of England, its prosperity founded partly on cloth manufacture.[4] This was a place full of fine houses and in the 1460s many were being rebuilt in the latest style, jettied upper floors stretching out over the streets, new chimney stacks freeing them of fug, more and smaller chambers arranged within, refinements that were all conducive to comfortable living. But this was a place of poverty too. The poor lived in the shadow of fine houses belonging to the rich. The fifteenth century was a hard economic time and many were sinking on Fortune's Wheel even as some men rose. So this was a place of anxiety as well as pleasure; anxiety for the impoverished who wondered how they would live and anxiety for the rich who feared for their souls when they died. At the heart of the town, the abbey of St Edmund sailed through it all. The abbey had given the town life. The plan of the central streets – still a neat grid today – had been the handiwork of an early abbot and the abbots still ruled their creation in the 1460s, though riots and rebellions had seen the monastery's grip on the town's affairs weaken. The abbey's life sprang from its saint: the bones of Edmund, the martyr-king killed by the Vikings in the ninth century, lay in a reliquary there. They still pulled in pilgrim crowds eager that their souls be relieved of sins or broken bodies mended by his miraculous intercession.

Even King Henry VI had made the journey to the shrine. On the day of his visit in 1434, aldermen in scarlet, burgesses and ordinary townsfolk assembled to greet the king on Newmarket Heath, there to be touched by what limited glamour this most unprepossessing king could muster. John Baret would have been in his thirties or early forties by then, for he was born some time between 1392 and 1400. He was the son of Geoffrey and Joan Baret; Geoffrey, a man of some small property in the town had ties to the abbey, serving Abbot Cratfield who had appointed him keeper of his fishponds at Babwell in 1391. The family was already rich enough for the young John to have made a good marriage to a woman called Elizabeth Drury. This was not likely to have been a love match. She was the daughter of a knight, Sir Roger Drury of Rougham. The Drurys brought age-old aristocratic sparkle to the union and to the Barets, a family on the rise, while John Baret brought hard cash. He also brought a nose for business to their partnership, especially cloth business, and it was from this branch of manufacture that he made his money. The comfortable life this bought John and Elizabeth shines out from his will. Lists of possessions seem endless. There were tables, testers, cupboards, coffers, cushions, coverlets, curtains, featherbeds, pillows, pewter pots, pans, sheets, blankets, brasses, basins, tubs and other 'ostilmentys' too many to itemise.[5] Things mattered to Baret. They were parcelled out as mementoes to friends or bequeathed to family with care. Many were described with loving precision. He had a 'covered, chased silver salt-cellar'. There were candlesticks of laton 'whereon is written "Grace me Govern"', his motto. The 'best spoons' were singled out and so too were cloths painted with images, most likely religious ones, that had been hanging in the hall. In a world where most had little, possessions filled John Baret's life. His house was a mansion with many rooms in which to put them. It stands today – now 3 Chequer Square where it hides inside a Georgian rebuilding – but the will reveals in passing that it once had a hall, study, 'white chamber', a chapel, parlours and sundry other chambers, kitchens, outhouses and storerooms. This was, emphatically, a rich man's house. And, in local terms, a powerful man too. For his will and tomb reveal that he had risen in the world to wear the abbot of Bury's livery and the collar of the Lancastrian kings.[6]

The Barets worshipped a short walk from Chequer Square at St Mary's where John's tomb stood, waiting. It was one of the town's two parish churches. Still imposing, its grandeur testified to the wealth, piety and self-confidence of the townsfolk who built and beautified it. A great medieval hammerbeam roof floats above the nave, borne aloft by angels that would once have been brightly painted. Grave slabs, some medieval, lie underfoot, and pockmarks in the stone suggest where brasses were once inset, calling to mind the dead of the parish. Windows were set with stained glass, walls plastered with pictures of Bible stories. Niches and alcoves were filled with statues of saints painted so as to stand out in a church lit by rushlights and candles. Latin liturgies under way at the several altars filled the space with sound. The air was heavy with incense and there may have been a sicklier tang, too, from bodies buried in the church precincts but not always well sealed in their long homes. All around the church was a steady to and fro of parishioners at their own devotions. On Sundays and feast days the parishioners converged on the church for mass. Gathered in the nave, they watched as the priest consecrated wafer and wine, transformed them into the flesh and blood of Christ and in so doing renewed the sacrifice Christ had made for sinful beings on the cross. Mass reminded all how Christ had suffered and died for them, conquered death itself through his resurrection and ransomed all who were alive to his message out of hell. This was the central, saving rite of the medieval Church.

On these and other occasions, John Baret would have received discomforting messages too, messages that called into question the riches he had spent a lifetime accumulating. For it was easier for a camel to pass through the eye of a needle than for a rich man to enter the kingdom of heaven. Preachers drove that message home – the camel, one felt constrained to remind, was 'a terrible and great beast' – and it was captured in stained glass and painted mural, in plays of Bible stories; it could not be escaped.[7] In hell there was only stink and darkness, the 'horrible sight of devils, dragons, worms and serpents', sorrowing, weeping, wailing, gnashing of teeth, 'hunger and thirst irremediable'.[8] If all the leaves of the trees of the earth were turned into tongues they would not be able to tell of its pains.[9] The danger of landing there was great for a merchant like Baret. Not only riches but also the way they were acquired might block the way to heaven. Tales from the pulpit reminded congregations about this. Some hit close to home. In one, a dead merchant haunted the dreams of his former business partner. The ghost said that he was damned 'because we grew rich at the expense of many' who they had deceived 'in the sale of wool'. When the sleeper woke he was traumatised. Communion wafers choked him. The sight of a crucifix terrified him and he shielded his eyes. There was no place in the Church, no place in heaven, for a man made wealthy by sharp practice.[10] Living the faith, attending mass, confessing sins at least annually to the priest, taking communion from his hands at Easter, paying his tithes and giving generously to the Church could all help John Baret on the way to salvation. But as he grew old, earlier wheeling and dealing clearly preyed on his mind and he looked to his will as the last chance to make amends. One man in particular, Edmund Tabor, was to be recompensed for the wrongs John Baret had done to him. In this, Baret was far from unusual. The will was the place to set things right with God and man, to pay debts and especially to discharge debts to the Church that might otherwise put the soul in peril.

But the business of death in the Middle Ages entailed much more than setting wrongs right. In his mind's eye – very much a merchant's eye, watchful, accounting – John Baret saw with precision what must happen when he was dead and laid it all out in unusual detail. His funeral was to be *spectaculum* and *speculum*; a spectacle in which John Baret would be remembered and a mirror in which those who came to see him off could discern their futures. The two were connected. For as people remembered Baret and saw themselves in his bones, they might be moved to think and pray for him as they hoped others, in time, would pray for them. So he planned intricately for the funeral. He laid out money for black gowns, which friends and kin were to wear. There were payments for children dressed in surplices and for chanters skilled in the singing of pricked song, for subdeacons, deacons and priests, the last each to receive fourpence in a purse.[11]

He wanted attendants – men in black and women in white – to hold torches and provided for numerous candles, signifiers of salvation and practical aids; for lights kept evil spirits from the body. The scale of it all was designed to proclaim that a man of substance was dead. Even the officiating priest would double as an advertising hoarding: his vestment, 'ready made against the time' in white cloth and fine gold thread, was worked with John Baret's coat of arms and a 'remembrance' of his motto, 'Grace me gouerne'. Many outside the church's walls who could not come to the funeral were co-opted as John Baret's mourners too. Every bedridden man and woman would have tuppence, the prisoners in the gaol their 'bread, meat and drink' and each 'lazar' in the leper house pennies and a loaf of bread. At the centre of all this funereal commotion would be the still figure of John Baret. Encoffined, encircled by candles, bells tolling, his charitable giving would work like gravity. It would draw everyone in the town, on this his funeral day, into orbit around his corpse.

And even when the funeral was over and the people had gone, John Baret still planned to have an abiding presence in Bury. In the year after his demise, every week, on the day of the week on which he had died, there was to be a 'mind'. The St Mary priest would put on his white-and-gold vestment again and say 'a mass of our lady', 'rehearse' John Baret's name, saying De profundis for him, his father and mother and all Christian souls, and then offer up a requiem mass for them all. On the 'yearday' – the anniversary of Baret's death – he envisaged an even grander ceremony: the whole panoply of the funeral was to be reprised, with chimes, lights, money and bread, the only difference this time being the necessary absence of his corpse, for this would now be closed up in its tomb.

Spectacle, yes; but all this was a sound investment too, an investment in John Baret's post-mortem future. The canny merchant was calculating even as he prepared for death, for, when he was gone, money could buy him one thing that he still needed: prayer. The special masses chanted for him by the priests, the intercessions of all the town's poor folk, the prayers of his friends and neighbours and fellow burgesses would all help him on his journey through the other world. With solemn ritual and hard cash working on feelings of friendship and fellowship among the townsfolk, John Baret insinuated himself into collective memory. He would etch his name on the fabric of the church and town too. The tomb itself cried out for prayers. It was loaded not only with pleas to God to be merciful, to blot out his many iniquities, to find a place for him in heaven, but also appeals to friends, family, neighbours and well-wishers. Looking on the sack of skin and bones carved on the lid, the living should pity and help him. Above all, they should pray for him – 'Wherefore ye people in way of charity, With your good prayers I pray you help me.' One day everyone would be as Baret is today – 'for like I am right so shall ye all be' – and they too would need help.

As they squared up to death, medieval men and women drew on that fellow feeling: the helpless dead needed the living as they travelled into the next world and medieval men and women could, and should, lighten the darkness of the dead by their prayers. An indulgence enshrined another, perhaps more mercenary, contract between living and dead. Indulgences were commonplace in late medieval England and promised remission of some of the punishment due for one's own sins, so long as one had confessed them, and were issued by the Church in return for a good deed. But Baret's was a rather special kind of document. He wanted it to be pinned up so 'it may be read and . . . exhort the people to pray for me' since it affirmed that those who did so would find their own suffering reduced in the next world in recompense.[12] Even as they travelled out of Bury, the townsfolk would not escape the memory of John Baret. He planned to rebuild its Risbygate. There he would add a statue of the Blessed Virgin Mary to watch over the gate and an inscription bearing his own name.[13] Not only in their devotions in church but in their daily comings and goings, the townsfolk were encouraged to remember him. Baret's ambition was of a piece with the piety of his time, for prayers were not things only of church-time. Devotions bled into everyday life, at home, at work, on the move. And even as people got on with their lives, they were exhorted to remember the dead. This was piety with a practical edge. Gates, roads, bridges were all the sorts of things that merchants liked to provide. Keeping them in good repair was a fitting gesture by those eager to grease the wheels of trade. In death, money left for the same purposes earned gratitude from their peers and acquired a numinous dimension too. For what better call to mind could there be of a soul on the threshold of a new frontier, travelling in the next world, than a memorial at a bridge, roadside or town gate?

To the Strange Isles

When death finally came for John Baret he would likely have been prepared. The signs of death were well known; commonplace diagnostics even rendered them into verse so that people could remember them and make ready. When eyes were misting, lips turning black, mouth gaping, heart trembling, spittle running, hands shaking, those at a bedside knew that it was time to fetch the priest.[14] Baret was steeped too in teaching about the last things. He had probably meditated on his little tract, *Disce Mori*, Learn to Die; the rhythms of the deathbed were familiar things, for people in the fifteenth century seldom died alone or sequestered from company but fortified by friends and neighbours gathered in prayer.[15] John Baret would have watched others die. Now the candles burned for him. One was placed in his fingers while he had enough strength to hold it, a symbol of Christ 'light of the world' who gave 'clear light unto the soul by the dark way and unknown by the which he shall walk'.[16] Family, friends and neighbours gathered and prayed at the deathbed. This solidarity mattered because this final crisis of John Baret's life was a cosmic drama too. Worlds, visible and invisible, collided in these moments. Demons made a last great effort to win the soul, tormenting and testing, they drifted through his dreams and waking delirium. They crowded about the bed, 'disfigured, foul and loathsome', gazing with terrible eyes 'as they had been two basins, glowing and burning as fire' or 'with sparks of fire spitting out of his mouth', all of them 'so foul that no tongue can tell nor heart think [of] the abominable and disfigured shape of them'.[17] They drove Baret to doubt Christ's mercy, to despair at the Church's works in a last desperate attempt to snatch him to hell. Prayers and blessed candles, invocations of saints and angels, banished them.[18] A priest held a crucifix before Baret's eyes and he held Christ in his mind, thinking on the cross and the wounds Christ suffered for humankind. He thought of Mary and her pity at the foot of the cross and he reached out for her help in this final crisis of his life.[19] Even as the priest offered consolation, he had last questions too. Did John reject heresy? Did he wish to die in the true faith of holy Church? Did he truly repent of his sins? Was he 'in charity' with his neighbours, and if not would he settle his debts and compose his quarrels with them? Only when these questions were satisfactorily answered did the priest absolve his sins and anoint his body, touching eyes, ears, nose and mouth with oil. With this all that could be done had been done. John Baret, it was to be hoped, would now be able to die a 'good death'. He waited between worlds.

A few miles south of Bury St Edmunds, across undulating Suffolk countryside, is the village of Long Melford. This place makes a little more sense of the man who lay dying in Bury St Edmunds in 1467. Long by name and long by nature, the village is strung out up the High Street, which rises gradually, flanked by houses, shops and inns, many in Georgian brick, others of Tudor and medieval timberwork, until it ends at an eminence on which the church sits. 'Church' does not do justice to a building that resembles a modest cathedral. Inside, flooded with pure light, are the bones of the Cloptons, friends and relatives of John Baret who made something of a mausoleum of the church. They, and their neighbours, also rebuilt the nave, tower and chancel in splendour and had appeals for prayer cut into the stone of its outside walls and inscribed near the window arches for which they had paid. Remembered in his will, the Cloptons were to have keepsakes of Baret. There was, among other things, a spoon in beryl, silver and gilt for Mistress Clopton and a ring for Sir William, the son of Sir John Clopton who had paid for much of the work in the church. This ring was more than a memento since John Baret hoped that Sir William would ensure that the will's provisions were enacted, for this powerful local figure was one of his executors.

But these kin ties are not the main reason for travelling to Long Melford. The Barets and Cloptons were tied together by something more than blood, business and that silver ring. John Baret and Sir William's father both had connections to a famous man too. His name was John Lydgate. Born a few miles away in another Suffolk village, Lidgate, in about 1370, this second John became a monk of Bury. His star rose in the world thanks to his verse; favoured by the future Henry V and high society around him, he put into poetry not only epic history but everyday sentiment and ordinary experience.[20] He wrote of life and love and faith and he reflected on mortality too. 'Feblysshed' in old age, suffering 'unwieldy joints' and 'cloudy sight', he remembered his youth as a springtime among honeysuckle and primroses when he ran without a bridle, stealing apples, neglecting prayers, missing mass, hating school and fearing only the rod. Standing at the other end of his life's span, having long since turned to Christ, he mused on death, the 'uncertain passage'.[21] His work and its mortuary themes clearly appealed to the Cloptons; his poetry runs round the cornices of a Long Melford chantry chapel dedicated to prayer for the soul of Sir William's father. During the fifteenth century, at the junction of nave and chancel in the main body of the church, there also hung great stained cloths with images from a picture-story he had popularised. This story too had a mortuary theme: it was called 'The Dance of Death'.[22]

The tale was simple and grim. Death, a crumbling corpse, summoned the living who could not refuse him. Neither the king's majesty nor the physician's medicaments could save them. The sergeant found himself 'arrested'. The labourer, whose hard life had made him long for eternal rest, wanted to follow his plough again when Death eventually came, glad to suffer in wind and rain, but there could be no reprieve. A child 'full young and was born yesterday' gurgled for mercy and could scarce form a word, but was not spared. The rich burgess – and here Lydgate's verse moved closer to home – could be as 'strange, devious and contrary' as he pleased but all the 'houses, rents and treasure' accumulated through cunning would not help him. Death could not be bought off or cheated. Men and women of all estates must dance and die. Metaphors shifted but the message remained: man was a flower 'amorously flourishing', which faded swiftly at the frost; human life was but a puff of wind. The warning was not lost on Sir William. He had paid for the stained cloths illustrating the story and he lavished money on Long Melford church against the day when he must step out with Death. And the story had not, of course, been lost on John Baret either. He had chosen a cadaverous tomb. While he was alive, it would be his mirror, reflecting the image of his future self. This was how Lydgate conceived his tale of dancing corpses: 'And have this mirror ever in remembrance', he warned those who read the poem, 'Before your mind, above all things, To all estates, a true resemblance, that worms' food is the end of your living.'

In this little knot of connections are some of the reasons why John Baret chose to be buried in a cadaver tomb with mirrors set in the roof above.[23] But his piety was not unrelievedly grim. There is another John Baret to set beside the cadaverous one. On the tomb chest there is a little image of the man as he had been in life. He wears the collar of the Lancastrian kings. He is swagged with his mottos. The tomb celebrates worldly power and glamour and money even as it worries about these things. The tomb today is muted stone. This seems of a piece with a dour kind of piety. But then it was brash in bright paint. Even in the crowded church space, with its pious noise, drifting incense, gaudy paintings and clamour of brasses and inscriptions, Baret's stone corpse would have cut something of a dash. And he wanted it to. He paid to re-engineer parts of the church round his final resting place. He was keen that sight lines be opened up so that no one could miss him when they came to worship at St Mary's. This was partly because he wanted to arrest the eye and solicit prayers. But it was also because he wanted to be remembered as the great man he had once been. Death might be the great leveller but he could not quite bring himself to believe it. And being remembered for what he had been mattered all the more because John and Elizabeth were childless. Medieval men and women hoped to live on, as many modern ones do, in their children. The Cloptons would; John and Elizabeth Baret would not. The tragedy of their lives was to have won great riches and then to have none to carry the family name down the ages. The plums of the estate went to more distant kin; Baret worried that some fool or idiot might get his hands on his property when he had gone and squander it all.[24] So viewed from Long Melford, John Baret's choice of a cadaver tomb begins to make sense, even as the tomb itself turns into a thing of contradictions. In that, too, there is a point of contact between the ancient and modern worlds. Medieval men and women were as strange in their contra-dictoriness as modern ones are.

Places of Marvellous Pain

At John Baret's deathbed when all vital signs were gone, when no sound could be heard from his heart and a glass held over his mouth showed no mist, a window was opened to let the soul loose. The soul was breathed out with that last deep gasp of air. Artists showed it as a tiny naked figure leaving the mouth, some-times winged by angels or snatched at by devils depending on the

dead man's fate. The passing bell was rung at St Mary's to warn
the parish that one of its own was dead. The body was laid out
– women's work and some wills, though not Baret's, left money
for them to do it.[25] A vigil was kept by family and friends while
his body lay at home and then, shrouded, 'chested', set on a bier,
John Baret made his last journey to the church in which he had
worshipped. The intricate mechanism created by his will began
to operate, conveying his body to the grave and his soul into the
next world. But what of his soul's fate? Where did it go?

Answers to these questions are to be found in a village called
Wenhaston. The journey there runs east through High Suffolk.
This was, and is, verdant country. While the fens to the north were
known for venting their 'poisoned air' in summer and 'cold exha-
lations and mists' in winter, these parts had an equable climate
and good soil. In the sixteenth century from their loams 'uprose
the grain that filleth purses' but in the fifteenth century the
economy was more a patchwork of arable land and pasture.[26] The
money that sprang from this business helped build grand churches
like Long Melford's in many villages and small towns. Cobbled
out of flints from fields because there was little decent building
stone, their scale still bespeaks wealth.[27] Wenhaston, lying just a
few miles from the sea and now only a scatter of cottages, was in
the fifteenth century part of a thriving commercial landscape that
John Baret must have known well. His father hailed from Cratfield,
a dozen miles away, and there were Barets at nearby Walberswick
on the coast. That bustling port would surely have figured in the
family's mercantile calculations. It was a major harbour trading in
wool, fish and other commodities, having stolen the place of nearby
Dunwich when that town was consumed by the sea during a
succession of storms. Wenhaston itself was close enough to
Walberswick to be caught up in its prosperity, profiting too from
wool, fish and the produce of the wood pastures of this part of
Suffolk. The church, although outwardly unprepossessing by standards set elsewhere in the county, still benefited from rebuilding in
the late fifteenth century.[28] Its greatest treasure comes into view

only after unlatching the door. Then the visitor is transported into the medieval afterlife. Rough-painted on boards, some five metres across and two and a half metres high, on the wall facing the door, is a Doom – an image of the end of time. It depicts Christ's return, sitting on a rainbow and flanked by saints, the dead rising naked from their graves and waiting for judgement, hands clasped in prayer. Guided by the same verses of scripture, the anonymous medieval artist painted on these boards the story that John Martin rendered in the middle of the nineteenth century.

In the Middle Ages, Dooms like this were commonplace, customarily located, as this one once was, in the chancel arch of the church where they served as prominent reminders to parish-ioners of the last things. That the Wenhaston Doom has survived is a remarkable piece of luck. For having been whitewashed in the later sixteenth century, the apparently nondescript boards were earmarked for destruction during refurbishment of the church in 1892. Set outside in the churchyard for burning next day, it rained during the night and while the whitewash was carried away by the rain, the oil-work underneath was insoluble.

Right at the heart of this painting there is an image of what waited for John Baret immediately after death, the psychostasis or the weighing of souls. Faithfulness and virtue were measured against sins to determine the soul's fate, whether bound ultimately for heaven or for hell.[29] The Archangel Michael holds a pair of scales. A soul – a tiny, naked, vulnerable figure – sits in the left-hand pan and holds up its hands in prayer. Its wicked deeds, in the shape of two demons, weigh down the right-hand pan. A large devil – Satan himself, perhaps – lurks in the wings, ready to snatch any who fail the test to hell. Dooms like this one rendered abstruse theology in everyday terms. At Bartlow in Cambridgeshire, Michael weighed souls using a wooden beam and baskets woven from fenland rushes. All could grasp the meaning of this kind of image. In many depictions, a saint intervened in the drama to help the sinner. Most commonly this was Mary. None was better placed to plead with Christ than his mother. Mary was the

Mediatrix, the Empress of Hell, the most powerful of intercessors. In art, she might be shown pulling down one side of the scales used in the weighing so as to cheat Satan of a soul or tossing her prayer beads into the pan to tip the balance in the soul's favour. John Baret had been devoted to her, paying for the reredos of her altar in St Mary's Church to be repainted and setting aside money in his will so that her statue there could have a new and 'goodly' crown of metal gilt or nicely worked wood. When he died he would look to her for help.

Weighed and not found wanting, helped by Mary to pass the test of the psychostasis, there was still the matter of John Baret's imperfections. The God of the Middle Ages was not all mercy. He was characterised too by justice and he would not let the minor offences that John Baret had neglected to confess during life pass, nor would he allow more grievous sins, duly confessed to the priest in a spirit of sorrow, to go unpunished. Undeserving of hellfire, John Baret's soul was not pristine enough for heaven. It must first be cleansed. The place for this was purgatory. Since the middle of the thirteenth century the Church had affirmed that during the in-between time separating individual death from the world's end, souls were purged of their sins in fire. This would be the lot of most of the dead, for most were neither damnable nor pure. The utterly unregenerate who felt nothing for their sins would be cast into hell. The saint might make a journey straightways to heaven. The rest would be plunged in fire until they were clean. Scripture had little to say on the subject but a kind of logic suggested the existence of suffering hereafter which fell short of damnation, for surely the sorrowful sinner deserved punishment but one that was not eternal? The Church had also accumulated a wealth of evidence in the form of visionary experiences which indicated the existence of places where torment was temporary.[30] These visions described the perilous journey that John Baret's soul must make.

The visions were not always from long ago or faraway places. Some were quite recent and local. In 1206 a peasant called Thurkill from Stisted in Essex became famous after he toured the purgatorial places. Falling into a catatonic state and seeming dead to the world, his soul threaded its way through the afterlife led by St Michael. He came back only when his anxious wife fetched a priest and he forced holy water down the man's throat, causing him to choke, splutter and return to his senses. Many others had claimed to make such journeys since Thurkill's day. Their stories spread easily. Visions were retailed by preachers from the pulpit and, for those who could read and afford them, in manuscript books. Many were fantastically lurid. Sinful souls were impaled on spikes. They were plunged in boiling cauldrons. Some were 'fried in the fire as if they had been a fish in hot oil'; others were endlessly drowned and resuscitated and drowned again in pools skimmed with ice or eaten by monsters which excreted them whole so that they might be devoured afresh.[31] Mountains 'as red as blood' and stinking rivers filled the other world. Everywhere there was darkness and fire of incomprehensible intensity. Purgatory fire was to earthly fire as earthly fire was to its mere image in a painting; it burned fiercely but gave no light and never consumed its human fuel. In purgatory, punishments were fitted to the crime. Gluttons were eaten by adders and toads.[32] Hot lechers were frozen in an icy wind. The slothful were nailed down in fields, unable to move. Backbiters were strung up by their lying tongues. The covetous were broken on wheels. Usurers were forced to drink molten gold. The proud tumbled from the heights into a burning pit. Thieves boiled in vats of molten precious metal. Murderers were butchered on blocks. The poor had had their purgatory in this world and might move with more dispatch through the fires of the next but the wealthy and powerful were singled out and detained. Their fine clothes now ignited and blazed endlessly.[33] 'What', one writer enquired of souls of the rich in purgatory fire, 'profits it you now, your great pomps and clothings . . . chains of gold, precious stones, wide and superfluous sleeves, by the which superfluities you sought honours and exaltations in the world?'[34] Now these accoutrements dragged them down into the flames.

Yet 'the pain of purgatory', as one writer explained, 'is full of good hope and of grace'.[35] Each moment the soul trapped there inched closer to heaven. Their hope – of cleansing, which led to salvation – was sometimes symbolised by saints and angels presiding in purgatory – though demons – 'which presenteth themselves in horrible figures' – could usually be seen even if they were not always stage-managing the torments.[36] Progress was suggested too by the colour-coding of souls. Those mired in sin were black as pitch, those soon to quit purgatory for heaven glowed bright; those in the midst of purging were grey or speckled black and white.[37] The soul in purgatory was a traveller passing through, not a permanent resident; for all the horror, there would be release.

And yet there could be no complacency. Not used providently for the good of the soul, John Baret's riches would make him 'fat for the fiend's larder'.[38] This is why he planned such elaborate exequies. The prayers of the poor and charitable deeds done in his name would help him because these things would speed him through the pains of purgatory. They would be like cooling water poured on scalded flesh. Most of all, masses celebrated by priests could help him in his trouble. The mass recreated Christ's sacrifice. Its mystery saw bread and wine turn into Christ's body and blood as the priest spoke the formula of consecration over them. Enormous power for good was liberated in those moments. And some of it could be directed towards a specified need. Most commonly in the late Middle Ages, special masses were used to help a soul in purgatory, alleviating its torment, shortening its pains. So Baret wanted all of these things – prayers, charity and masses – in abundance when he was gone. Itemising them in his will, he did everything he could to make sure that he got them. For a great fear of the dying was that they might be forgotten. A tale much repeated in preachers' books and manuals explained the fear. The story turned on a pact between two monks, each of whom had promised to say mass immediately for the soul of the one who died first. When death came for one, the other was confronted almost instantly by a terrible blazing ghost. The ghost identified himself as the dead friend and called the living man an 'inhuman and cruel fellow', for he had, he said, been abandoned in purgatory for twenty years.[39] The survivor was mystified. He told the ghost, 'Your carrion is not yet buried.' The dead man's body was scarcely cold. He was even now on his way to say mass for him. Purgatory fire was so agonising that a few moments in the flames felt like decades.

The story suggests why Sir William Clopton was given the silver ring. John Baret needed him more than any other. As executor he would set the provisions of the will in motion. Only then would the sudden burst of prayers, charity and masses designed to launch John Baret on his way to eternity take effect. If Sir William needed reminding of his obligations, a battery of stories existed to remind executors of their crucial duties. Sometimes the negligent met angry ghosts, sometimes they were tormented themselves in the other world when they died. Others suffered punishment in the here and now. One tale told how the soul of a knight killed in Charlemagne's service was abandoned by a friend. He preferred to keep the dead man's horse rather than selling it to buy alms and prayers. But it did the unfaithful friend no good. He was seized by demons who carried him up into the air before dropping him so that he was dashed to pieces on rocks.[40] Leaving the dead without help was a dreadful deed. Trapped in pain 'a hundred thousand double that of this present world', they would be left to shift for themselves and make an inexorably slow passage through the fire.[41] The ring was much more than a memento, it bound the living man to the dead one; its gift formed a sacred trust.

The many medieval stories of the other world, with all its fearful solidity, mystify the modern reader. How could such claims be made? Some of the alleged visionaries were already figures lost in the mists of time by the fifteenth century. Some dated back to the age of Bede. But some testimony was fresh. There were flesh-and-blood men and women in John Baret's day who claimed to have stepped into the other world in their dreams.

Edmund Leversedge was a Somerset native. Born in Frome and buried close by his mother's grave in Westbury in 1496, he left money to the image of Mary in the church, a guild which would pray for him and the Carthusian monks. When he made those provisions he thought he knew what death would bring, for he had already been there once, touring the other world in a dream. He had travelled in the spirit through a twilight place which he thought was purgatory and then approached a brilliant luminescence, heaven, he assumed, from which voices came and ladders descended but which he could not enter. Instead of going up, he went down again and resumed the flesh armed with his strange news.[42] Believing, in the Middle Ages, might be seeing for a man like Edmund. He would have gazed on images like the Wenhaston Doom and would have been heard preaching about other-worldly fire, convinced that this might be his eventual lot. He would have talked through his sins, and their consequences, with his priest. He may even have read stories of women and men who had visited the world beyond the grave. Small wonder that a man or woman's dreams could be populated by such things.

There was ample space in the medieval world for purgatory too. It might be out there on the world's edge, in its interstices, or just beneath its surface. But it was there. The earth's edges were mysterious and the possibility that places existed where justice was meted out to the dead was plausible. Word came to England of mountains in the Mediterranean which spewed fire and where souls were heard wailing or of floes of burning rocks in Iceland which seemed to exude from the other world. From Ireland came still more detailed tales of a marvellous cave through which purgatory could be entered. Located beneath a church on Station Island in Lough Derg, St Patrick's Purgatory had been shown to the saint during his missionary endeavours among the Irish. There, it was believed, the crust thinned and worlds touched. With God's grace, a pilgrim might enter purgatory briefly while still alive. Many made the pilgrimage in the hope of being cleansed but when an Italian, Antonio Manini, entered in 1411 he was disappointed. The office of the dead was read over him and then he waited alone for the gates of the other world to open. Nothing happened. He saw only darkness. But disappointments like Antonio's did not invalidate belief; God simply had not granted Antonio the grace of entering purgatory in the flesh. He would have to wait, as most did, until he died in order to experience it. Purgatory was still out there, somewhere, in a little-discovered world. And, crucially, those imprisoned behind its gates were still within reach of the living and made claims upon them. The dead detained amidst its dark fires and glaciers were not completely dead – not yet. They could, as John Baret knew so well, still be helped in their trouble with prayer.

Woundes Fresch and Rede

In the Wenhaston Doom, Christ returned in majesty. Seated on a rainbow, he is flanked by a fading sun and moon, signs that the world is dying, and he appears not as the dying man of the crucifix but the terrible judge.[43] To his left are the special dead, the saints, Mary prominent among them. Below them the ordinary dead are in the act of rising from their graves. A king, pope, cardinal, queen and humble parishioners are resurrected. Peter, holding a golden key to the gates of heaven, greets them in the dress of a bishop. On the edges of the painting, framing it, there are glimpses of eternal things. To the left, the saved climb a flight of steps leading to heaven. To the right the damned, chained and herded by spiteful, spiny, horn-blowing demons, are swallowed by a hell-mouth. A pair of figures, one of the saved and one of the damned, look out from the painting; meeting their gaze, the onlookers were obliged to ponder their own fates. Some people were laid in the ground with metwands – measuring sticks – as tokens of this moment of evaluation.[44] Most were buried reverently in the conviction that their bodies would be needed again, laid out on an east–west alignment ready to greet Christ who would come from the east. The Creed, which late medieval parishioners were supposed to know by heart, declared that when God decided to 'deem the quick and the dead' then 'souls shall return again to our bodies'. 'We shall', the Creed affirmed, '[be] the same and none other than we are now'.[45] So the dead rose in their *own* renewed bodies. Making the point in a different way, an angel in a fifteenth-century doom-play told the dead to 'rise and fetch your flesh'.[46]

In this spirit, the dead of the Wenhaston Doom, rich and poor alike, clamber from their graves, breaking out of top-knotted shrouds. How, exactly, the risen dead would look was an open question. Most expected to look rather like their earthly selves, and the Wenhaston figures rise as individuals, their identities still very much intact. Whether the damned and saved would be visibly different was a trickier issue. At Wenhaston they look alike but some authorities held that the dead might be marked by their destiny as soon as they re-emerged from the grave. 'Much marvel', thought one writer, 'shall there be between the bodies of them that be damned and of them that be blessed.'[47] The bodies of the saved would possess 'clarity, subtlety and agility'. The damned 'shall be black . . . stinking and horrible and so deformed that no earthly heart may think of it'. That the dead would already know their fate as they came to judgement was the message of another Doom. This one, at Chesterton in Cambridgeshire, showed a demon hauling a body out of the grave, staking a claim even as it was in the business of resurrection. All this made a sort of sense. The soul had, after all, already been weighed in the balance at death. Those found wanting knew they were lost; the repentant had been purged in purgatory fire and knew they were saved. The fate of the dead was clear, though only now, as they stood before Christ, would they really understand it. Mystery plays, in which the drama of the end of the world was played out in the streets of major towns with painted hell-mouths and smoking cauldrons, portray saved souls who know their happy estate. They thank God 'that in this manner made us to rise, body and soul together clean' – 'clean' because they had been purged already in purgatory fire.[48]

So the last things would come to pass. In St Mary's Church, Bury St Edmunds, John Baret's tomb would split as he resumed the flesh. No longer skeletal or cadaverous, he would wear again his own regenerated body. But what did a man like John Baret expect to feel? At the heart of the Wenhaston Doom there is a cross-shaped space. Here the Rood group was fixed to the boards, a cross with Christ hanging on it which was framed by two other wooden statues: Mary, the suffering mother at the foot of the cross, and John the Evangelist.[49] This dead body, Christ's dead body, was at the heart of medieval dying. Gazing at it hanging on the crucifix, the onlooker was reminded of Christ's Passion, his sacrifice for mankind, his triumph over death and his promise of eternal life. In the Doom scene, Christ was there again. Alive, in majesty, he was still marked by the nail and spear wounds suffered in the name of ordinary sinners. Living but still bleeding, he was king and judge. Nor, according to many depictions, would he be alone. Around him would crowd the poor. Transfigured now from powerless to powerful, the poor would be Christ's doomsmen, joining him in the act of judgement. Christ was in the poor and those who had disregarded them had recrucified him.[50] On doomsday, tomb broken open, flesh fetched, shroud discarded, a newly risen John Baret would stand before the judge. Christ would 'show him his wounds that he suffered for us' and, as he gazed at them, self-knowledge would crystallise in sensation. For while the blessed would be filled with thankful joy, the wicked who had 'despised the price of the precious blood' would recoil in horror.[51] Their predicament was terrible: 'above them an angry judge, below them the horrid abyss, on the right their accusing sins, on the left the hordes of demons . . . inside their burning conscience; outside the world on fire'.[52] John Baret's hope that at this moment he would go the right way was worked out in his will, expressed in his tomb. He gave charitably, wanted prayers, endowed masses, sought saintly intercession. He gazed on his own dead body, rendered lifeless in stone, meditating on death before he was dead, hoping for resurrection to eternal life. And he more than hoped for this, he planned for it too. In leaf upon leaf of his will he tried to rule the future. Prayers and masses would ring out in his name down the ages. He would be remembered, perhaps, until doomsday itself. But this was not to be, or at least not to be in the way he intended. For within a hundred years or so, the Wenhaston Doom was whitewashed and replaced with the royal coat of arms, the Rood prised from the boards, the almsdeeds, prayers and masses he planned extinguished and purgatory's fires prematurely quenched.

2

SPIRIT OF HEALTH OR GOBLIN DAMNED

We step out of the Wenhaston church into another world by way of a medieval book, a book of ghost stories. It translocates its reader, conveying him or her from the Suffolk of John Baret, from arable fields and windswept flatlands, to higher, wilder terrain, a moor-edge location in North Yorkshire where the ruins of Byland Abbey, a Cistercian monastery, stand. The open country of the Vale of York lies to the south of this place but the moors rise steeply above it to the north. Although modest in height, they attract early winter snows, which make them a world unto themselves when the valley below is green. To medieval eyes this landscape was not beautiful but terrifying. Long before the abbey was built, the Venerable Bede thought these 'steep and remote hills' more suitable for 'dens of robbers and haunts of wild beasts than for men'.[1] Generations later, Bede's successors agreed. The monks who colonised the moors in the twelfth century entered 'a place of horror and vast solitude' but they did so by choice, alighting on the place precisely because this was wild country where minds could be bent to God free from distraction. In the event, the desolation sometimes proved too much; the monks who founded Byland moved their community from 'Old' to 'New' Byland, migrating down from the moor to the vale where there was a little more shelter and the weather was more clement.[2] There they continued the struggle inwardly for their own salvation and for that of all Christians, living among angels, saints and spirits, in a world where, for them, the invisible was as real, more real, than visible things.[3]

At some point, probably in the early fifteenth century, one of the monks began to collect ghost stories. The heyday of the monasteries was in the past then. Outbreaks of plague and other epidemic disease had whittled away numbers at Byland and fewer recruits came forward to take their places. By 1400, a dozen or so monks were rattling around the cloisters. It was a good place to tell ghost stories and, as the abbey emptied of monks, the land round about was still full of spirits. It was a good place, too, to hear stories that people in the neighbourhood were telling. Monasteries were not sealed off from the world; however much isolation had been the ambition of the founders, stories, including ghost stories, readily reached the ears of monks and those told by old, trustworthy men, the reliable repositories of local lore, were likely to be taken seriously.[4] Stories about apparitions could not lightly be set aside and, since the chronicle of Byland warned that things not written down 'slip away and wither as the sin of forgetfulness triumphs', there was reason to commit them to writing.[5]

And someone did just that, setting them down, in a hardly legible hand, in a manuscript volume that is otherwise unremarkable. A late medieval copy of Cicero, it is the kind of book that many monastic libraries of the time possessed. The writer will be forever anonymous; all that can be known is that he was a monk, a white-robed Cistercian, and both he and the book belonged to Byland. The thought-world he evokes is unfamiliar even though his stories pre-date John Baret's death by perhaps only half a century. For Baret death seemed carefully scripted, obedient to a rich merchant's plans, his mortuary provisions laid out in terms that the church approved. Here, from the vantage point of the moors, new dimensions of belief about death and the dead are opened to view; the medieval dead become more frightening, less tied up in theology, more elemental, almost as if they had taken some of their qualities from the landscape they were reputed to haunt.

On a dark night, in the early years of the fifteenth century, a tailor named Mr Snowball was travelling alone from Gilling towards his home in Ampleforth. He was a well-off man, rich enough to have a horse and to own a sword.[6] The tailor's journey was perfectly ordinary and neither it nor Mr Snowball need have left any trace in the record but for the events said to have taken place that night. The Ampleforth road would have been inky dark then – it is inky dark even now – but it was a major route in the Middle Ages nonetheless, noted in an early charter as well-made and wide.[7] The same charter records that the road went by way of a little stream called the Holbeck. Here the tailor's troubles began. He was startled by a sound – it was as if ducks were babbling in the beck – then a raven flew at his face. It began to circle him and so he dismounted, the bird perching on the ground a short distance away and eyeing him. Now he could see that this was no ordinary raven as sparks of fire showered from its wings. Snowball drew his sword and held it out by the hilt in front of him so that it formed the shape of the cross and enjoined the creature, whatever it was, to do him no harm. The raven did not retreat. Instead it flew straight at him, striking him in the side and causing a wound. The tailor struggled to his feet and tried to fend off the bird but he could not deflect it. Desperate and terrified, he called on it in God's name to reveal what it was and then the bird began to change shape before his eyes. First it took the form of a dog, a chain round its neck, then, as Snowball begged it in the name of the Holy Trinity and the blood of Christ to say what it wanted, it transformed again, this time into the form of a man. The body was ghastly. It was 'thin and horrible', resembling 'the pictures of the dead kings'. These were figures traced on church walls, calling to mind a story about a hunting trip in which three living kings met their own dead selves, a warning to them that all earthly power and riches and glory would soon pass away.[8]

Now as the tailor looked on in terror, the man, or what was once a man, the almost living image of the kings, spoke. It was as if his innards were burning and he formed his words 'in his entrails, for he did not speak with his tongue'. He was a ghost and he was in agony. He had sinned grievously and had been excommunicated, cast out of the Church. In this condition, he had died and now found himself earthbound, caught between death and life. The tailor must go to the priest who had pronounced the sentence of excommunication and get it revoked then, with this done, he must have twenty masses sung for the dead man's soul. Once freed from excommunication, these masses would release him from torment, but while still under sentence he could make no progress and the masses would do him no good. The tailor swore to do as he was asked; the ghost said he would appear again when the deeds were done. The two did not leave each other on easy terms. The tailor was in danger as the ghost made plain. If he broke his promise then he would be cursed: his flesh would shrivel and his skin fall away. There were other ghosts wandering the moors and the tailor must beware of them because having entered into a pact with one ghost he might now be vulnerable to the approaches of others. He must arm himself against the terrors of the night by carrying a gospel book and keeping the name of Jesus always on his lips. He must also take care not to look on the light of wood fire for to see one after seeing a ghost might be mortally dangerous. The tailor for his part worried that the ghost would haunt other travellers while he was busy trying to help him. So he conjured him, speaking words of power, telling him that he was to be confined to the Holbeck until their next meeting. The ghost begged him not to do this. So the tailor relented and constrained him to haunt the dry slopes of Byland Bank instead. Then living and dead man finally parted.

Why did seeing a ghost not only fray the nerves but leave percipients physically weak? Why did ghosts fear water? Why was it dangerous to look on a wood fire after seeing a spirit? Much of this lore will be forever unintelligible. Only scraps survive in manuscripts like the Byland book and even there the monk passed over some things quickly without explaining them. Perhaps they puzzled him too. Or perhaps they were such well-known features of belief that they needed no elaboration: the audience would understand immediately why they mattered. A German monk, Caesarius of Heisterbach, had an answer to the final question about the danger from a wood fire.[9] He said that seeing fire after seeing an evil spirit placed the percipient in jeopardy because of the sharp contrast between spiritual darkness and physical light. The Byland ghost did not explain why he gave his advice about seeing fire, whether the reasoning was the same as that of Caesarius or belonged to some deeper, older lore; in any event, Snowball took the advice on trust and did not respond as if it was a surprise. Whether from shock or because he failed to heed the ghost's cautionary words, after the haunting Mr Snowball was ill for days.

Once he had recovered he did exactly as he was told. He went first to the priest who had excommunicated the man. From him he received a letter of absolution which released the soul from its sentence. He then went to seek advice on what he should do next, travelling to see a churchman, a man named Richard of Pickering, who explained that the letter should be buried in the ghost's grave. This done, the tailor went lastly to the friars in York and paid for them to have masses said for the dead man's soul. Ready to meet the ghost again, Snowball took precautions, gathering charmed things that would keep him safe during the encounter. As he prepared for the rendezvous, a neighbour offered to come along on the expedition but then, as the time approached, nerves got the better of him and he backed out and so the tailor travelled alone. On reaching the appointed place, he drew a circle. He kept the gospels and other sacred texts near to him and laid four cloths on the edge of the circle, each inscribed with words of power written on them and one bearing the name 'Jesus of Nazareth'. He stood inside the circle and waited for the ghost. It soon came. Again, it took on the shape of a dog but then, when it was conjured, it turned into a man 'of great stature, thin and horrible'. For all his terrifying appearance, the ghost was pleased: he had hovered nearby as the tailor buried the absolution in the grave and his troubled spirit was much helped by it and the singing of masses. On Monday, he said, he would pass 'into everlasting joy with thirty other spirits' whose earthly torments were also at an end. The two then parted for the last time and the tailor travelled back to Ampleforth along the edge of the moors. His sensitive eyes now saw many ghosts. One was a hunter who wandered the moors forever sounding a hunting horn. Another was a priest who had been more interested in the pleasures of the chase than the needs of his flock. A third was a man who had killed a pregnant woman, and walked in the shape of a bullock. It followed the tailor for a time and he conjured it to speak in every way he knew. None of them worked; it made no answer. Drawing closer he discovered the reason. The little bullock had no eyes, no mouth, no ears. It was doomed to walk until Judgement Day.

Dead Men's Tales

The Church had not invented ghosts – belief in them long ante-dated Christianity – but medieval churchmen were comfortable with them. Priests had crafted a framework in which ghosts might haunt, explaining them as souls from purgatory. They readily told improving stories about charred, blackened or burning souls wandering out of the next world discoursing on their misdemean-ours, pleading for masses, warning the living to mend their lives or face the same fate.[10] Sermons had long been peppered with apparitions like these, testifying to the malignancy of sin and the power of prayer. These were morally neater, altogether more sanitised stories than the tale of Mr Snowball. But the sorts of ideas they contained were in the writer's thoughts as they recorded the local story as he, or another member of the community around the same date, also scribbled notes about sin and confes-sion into the blank leaves at the end of the book of Cicero. These observations formed a prism through which the monk and his peers saw the stories they heard in and around the moors, a means to give them a theological shape and form. The dead, they thought, wandered the banks and becks of the moors because of their sins; their stories, however strange, might be moralities, warning the living about how they should live and how they should die. Sins not properly confessed, corn stolen from a landlord, even slipshod ploughing, all landed souls in post-mortem trouble. One ghost seized hold of a labourer in broad daylight and the two thrashed about in a field while the other workers fled. A canon of Newburgh in life, the dead man had filched the prior's silver spoons and, though not caught, the prior had excommunicated the nameless thief. Where man could not detect a crime, God would see and judge; the canon's soul would have no rest until the buried loot was restored to its rightful owner.

Even the ghosts of children walked if they died outside the faith. One was seen by his father. The man was travelling with a party of pilgrims and, when taking his turn keeping the watch 'against night-fears' while the others slept, he witnessed a procession of the dead. All save one of the ghosts rode on mortuaries, the beasts given as death duties to the Church. The last soul was obliged to crawl. Conjured by the percipient, the ghost said he was the man's son. He had been buried unbaptised. He had no mortuary on which to ride to salvation. For without baptism, no one would be saved; its waters washed away the sins with which every human being was born and, uncleansed, a child's soul was forever separated from God.[11] So dreadful was this prospect that midwives were told not to spare the mother in childbirth but 'to undo her with a knife . . . for to save the child's life'.[12] Even the laity could administer this sacrament and must know the words so that they could baptise a child *in extremis*. So, the little ghost's father named his son in the name of the Holy Trinity. The child stood up and marched behind his elders, a sign that he had joined the ranks of the saved.

These were a monk's tales, shot through with the Church's concerns about sin and punishment. But they were also stories for the winter fire of a labourer's cottage, told by ordinary people fearful of a sentence of excommunication, grieving over a child who had died unchristened, ready to summon up anxieties about the dead and to pass the dark hours before bed with a tale about ghosts. These men and women lived hard lives in cruck-built wooden long houses cheek by jowl with their beasts. By the fourteenth century the luckier and richer of them might have houses of stone. They come alive now in objects left behind and turned up by archaeologists – distaffs, candle-holders, fire-covers – things they used to earn a living and keep out the cold of the moorland night.[13] Something of them can be conjured out of the Byland book, too; for their preoccupations were imprinted on its stories. In the telling of such stories of supernatural vengeance, the opportunist thief, the dishonest servant, the farmer on the make might be given pause for thought. For if they were not caught in this life, they might be punished in the next. So too the greedy relative eyeing up an inheritance. Agnes de Lond had no rest because she had cut off her children, leaving her land to her brother instead. She troubled him after death, telling him to give the property to the rightful heirs so that she might have peace. But he would have none of it. So Agnes warned that she would walk until he died but then he would take her place. The moment for setting things right would then have passed; he would walk until the end of time.

This was a world full of ghosts, full of gossip about ghosts. Tittle-tattle was spiced by supernatural terrors as people wondered who might be walking after death and why. An abiding fear of the Byland monk was that in telling the stories he poured fuel on the fires of scandal. He carefully concealed the identities of some of the ghosts; in other cases he fretted about having revealed them. He seems to have been freer and easier with stories about people who lived further afield. Ecclesiastical court cases occasionally popped up in the record to bear out his anxieties; for talk about ghosts could be a cause of dissension. Lately, in 1397, a woman in the diocese of Hereford had even been dragged before a church for saying that her father haunted around his grave at night.[14] Even the gentry were not above such things. So much is clear from a bundle of documents known to historians as the Armburgh Papers. This little archive was concerned principally with a long-running legal dispute. It opened with a short summary of the case as it stood in the mid 1440s. Most of this is dry legal stuff but in the midst of it, the writer notes the fate of one of his adversaries, a man named Richard Baynard. 'He', the author explained gleefully, 'went a-hunting with my Lady of Bergavenny [and] suddenly he fell down and died.' This, he observed, was 'without housel and shrift'. In other words, he had died a bad death, without the last rites. But then the writer added something more, for soon 'he walked and yet does and has done much harm, as it is openly noised and known in the country there about'.[15] Baynard's soul was restless, so the gossips said, and that might be made into a handy political weapon when people were ready to think that wicked dead could wander.

James Tankerlay's Ghost

From Byland Abbey, at the foot of the moor, an old road runs hard by the scarp slope up onto the tops. A few miles from Byland, on the western flank of the Hambleton Hills, is Cold Kirby. The name is apt. The cottages and farms that form the hamlet, facing each other, generously spaced along the main street, are swept by a bitter wind in winter. They comprise a settlement with ancient roots but the church is quite modern; like many on the moors it was rebuilt in the nineteenth century. Inside, on a laminated card, curled slightly from the damp, is a legend about a medieval priest which leads from the nineteenth-century church into the Middle Ages. The story, originally from the Byland book, is about a man called James Tankerlay. It says that Tankerlay had served the parish of Kirby, although he had not, it seems, always served it well.[16] Despite being a priest, he had kept a woman as his concubine in flagrant contravention of the Church's law. When he died he was still afforded the privilege of burial with the monks in their graveyard at Byland. But James Tankerlay would not rest. He began to rise from the grave each night and walk the moors. One night he wandered further afield than usual, all the way to the house of his former mistress. There he 'blew out' her eye.[17] The abbot of Byland ordered that Tankerlay's corpse be dug up. He then commissioned a local man, Roger Wayneman, to take the remains in his cart to Gormire and to throw them into the lake. This he duly did but not before the draught oxen had sensed something about the body that they did not care for. They approached the lake unwillingly and 'nearly drowned for fear' as they came to the shore. Somehow Wayneman got the body into the lake. It sank, the waters closed over it and the hauntings ceased.

Of James Tankerlay there is now no trace. There is no record to prove that he was ever the incumbent of Cold Kirby; no one has yet uncovered his name in church records. But the story told about him still speaks eloquently; it reveals the uncertain shape of medieval fears about the returning dead. For this tale has no easy theology. This was no soul pleading for help; it was a malignant corpse spreading destruction and deserving, ultimately, unchristian burial away from the living rather than in their midst in a graveyard. It was a true winter's tale to make the hairs stand on end as it was told around the fire. The darkness and ambiguity made the Byland monk anxious. He pledged that he had told the story exactly as he had heard it from trustworthy men but he was still troubled that he had defamed Tankerlay's bones. His watery end suggested he was a lost soul; if such a story spread few would pray for James Tankerlay. 'God have mercy on him', the monk concluded, 'if he was indeed among the saved.'

People had told stories like the tale of James Tankerlay before. Some two centuries before the Byland monk collected his tales, another churchman, William of Newburgh, wrote about the dangerous dead. He was an Augustinian canon living a few miles

from Byland at Newburgh Priory. There he wrote a chronicle of
English affairs but at some point in the 1190s, just after he had
reported terrible famine and disease, he broke from his story of
kings, battles and politics to describe stranger happenings closer
to home. There had, he intimated, been a string of terrible hauntings – more of them than he had time to record – in which the
dead did violence to the living. Like the Byland monk, the truth-
fulness of the stories worried him. He went through ancient
books, searched the writings of Greek and Roman authorities,
but found nothing quite like them. The stories beggared belief
but trustworthy men had told them and so he could only think
that they were true.[18]

The longest was about anger and adultery. A man, whose identity William did not know or chose to conceal, had become
convinced that his wife was cheating on him. Determined to
discover the truth, he hid in the rafters of his house and waited
for her next liaison. His suspicions were swiftly confirmed; he
caught wife and lover in flagrante. In his rage he fell from his
hiding place, banged his head on the floor and was left delirious.
His wife explained that he had imagined it all but he would have
none of it. Injured but still enraged, his life began to ebb away
and yet he refused to believe it and rejected the ministrations of
a priest fetched to administer the last rites. Sure enough, the man
succumbed to his wounds; he died during the night full of spite
and without the rites of the Church. He was buried in the churchyard in the customary way. But soon after burial he rose again,
'by the handiwork of Satan', and began to stalk the village.
Followed by barking dogs, he wandered the streets after dark
beating 'black and blue' any who got in his way. He corrupted
the air and spread disease with his rotting flesh and the villagers
began to die one by one. The ineffectual local priest did little to
stop the hauntings but two young men took matters into their
own hands. They dug up the corpse and dragged it away from
the village. They tore out the heart and burned the body to ashes.
Only then, when all trace of the 'hell-hound' had been eradicated,

did the trouble and pestilence among the villagers come to an end. When they told their story, the young men claimed that gore gushed out when they opened up the bloated corpse with a spade. It was, said William of Newburgh, a *sanguisuga,* a leech, a blood-sucker. Bottled up in its body was the blood of many poor men and women, not only killed but also consumed.

In the twelfth century, from western Scotland to southern England and from the midlands to the Welsh marches, the bodies of the wicked dead had been known to wander. Full of anger, full of spite, with faces set against God and their fellow men, they resumed their own dead flesh and harried the living. The devil, perhaps, raised them up to do his work or they were able to re-enter the flesh of their own volition. An ecclesiastical manual, a penitential, from the twelfth century warned that the dead should be properly buried 'lest they take vengeance'.[19] For a time dead people still had power and the wicked dead might use it to do harm. They disturbed the peace, startled dogs which chased them about barking madly, leaked miasma and spread disease and battered and murdered the living. These were not fluttering diaph-anous things but wandering corpses. The bloated bodies of the culprits were hauled from their graves, their supernatural corrup-tion, their failure to dissolve naturally in churchyard earth, but rather to survive and swell, demonstrating their ongoing vitality and capacity for harm.[20] They were dismembered, burned or drowned; hearts, which were thought to be the seat of the spirit, were ripped out and holy water was cast on the remains to keep demons from the corpse.

These stories sprang from the way in which twelfth-century men and women located the dead in the visible and invisible world. By 1190, many generations had laid their dead in church-yards attached to churches which stood at the heart of their communities. But not all of the dead were loved: some were hated and some were feared. Deeper in the past, in the Anglo-Saxon past, ways of handling the corpses of these men and women had been devised that did justice to the emotions they stirred up.

Bones, artefacts and archaeology are almost the only clues. Some of the dead – executed criminals perhaps – were consigned then to mounds and barrows, ancient pagan places. The wicked dead were not reverently laid in consecrated ground, they were buried profanely, like carrion. Decapitated, torsos tossed into the grave, severed heads stowed in another place or between their feet, they were banished to places far from home and church. Others were staked so that they could not rise or were buried prone, face down in the earth, so that if the spirit resumed the flesh it would dig itself deeper rather than out of the grave. A few were even buried with myriad seeds, to distract them, perhaps, with the task of counting the grains. Such rites kept the dead buried and away from the living. But they also hinted at a desire to intensify their suffering. Burial in hallowed ground set a seal promising resurrection to eternal life on a life lived tolerably well. Laying a body in a deep watery place, hacking it to pieces and burying the remains in a plain field or burning the corpse so that its residue was lost in the breeze suggested the opposite. Trapped forever in faraway fields, barrows or pits or imprisoned in the winds that carried away their ashes, they would never rise. These ideas had no place in the strict theology of the Church; God was sovereign in the matter of souls and could resurrect a body as well from disarticulated fragments or ashes as from a skeleton. But the instinct that human beings could play a part in determining the fate of the dead through the rituals they chose for them was itself congruent with much that medieval Christianity taught about death, even if here it found expression in unorthodox guise. Only in 1312 did the Church forbid the practice of denying the last rites to felons who were about to be hanged, a practice which powerfully suggested that a punishment determined in this world would extend into the next.[21]

James Tankerlay had behaved rather like earlier generations of dangerous ghosts and suffered the sort of rough justice decreed by the old lore. But he was almost the last of his line. Leafing through the Byland book, few of its ghosts are very much like him. Sinful souls were still prisoners on the moors but few were thought to be eternally lost. For in the two centuries separating the Byland monk from the twelfth-century storytellers for whom ghosts were usually malevolent, assumptions about the dead had altered in subtle but important ways. The little churches and chapels of moor, vale and wold had filled down the generations with memorials soliciting prayers for souls. Ordinary men and women formed guilds dedicated to aid the souls of members when they were dead. Chantries proliferated in which priests sang masses daily for the soul of the founder. Bede rolls recorded the names of the dead of each parish, ensuring they would be remembered. Behind all this activity loomed purgatory. Purgatory, more sharply defined and more clearly understood, was, by the early fifteenth century, held to be the destination of most of the dead. A soul detained there suffered for its sins but could and should be helped through prayer and masses undertaken in its name. To write it off, to forget it, was a terrible thing. It was a sin. It was to rob the soul of the prayers that were its right. When a ghost walked, the living must harken to it. They must conjure it, let it speak, discover what it wanted, for it was likely to be suffering and in need of aid and deserved the benefit of the doubt. Theology had moved on, leaving James Tankerlay marooned in his lake. He was an old-fashioned reanimated corpse, a lost soul imprisoned in a dangerous body, an anomaly too. This is why, once the Byland monk had told his winter's tale of super-natural vengeance and black ritual, he was so troubled by the things he had written.

Gormire

Looking roughly westward from the top of Sutton Bank, an outer rampart of the North York Moors, the land falls away steeply to the vales of York and Mowbray with their good agricultural land, tight-knit villages and the market town of Thirsk in the middle distance. To the east is higher, wilder, thinly populated country. A modern Ordnance Survey map shows this as terrain littered with barrows and mounds. On foot they are still to be seen: unnatural undulations in the contours of the moor. These places of the ancient dead are far older than any of the stories in this chapter. The Byland book hints that in spite, or perhaps because, of their antiquity they were still touched by the numinous in the Middle Ages. Byland ghosts haunted roads fringed by tumuli; one cried out with a 'terrible voice as if from the hills' and then appeared suddenly before a traveller, a man called William de Bradeforth, who had, unwisely, called back.[22] They were, perhaps, thought to be exiled on the moors or imprisoned underground in ancient mounds, as they were sometimes thought to be in other parts of England and in other periods. There are echoes in these tales of a time when such places were reused to bury the unwanted dead, confining them forever in the earth.

Immediately at the foot of Sutton Bank is Gormire lake, that other resting place for a dangerous corpse. Seen from the high land of Whitestone Cliff, the lake appears out of place. It is the only major stretch of water for miles and it lies on the boundary between moor and vale. Counter-sunk in the landscape, its steep banks are shrouded by Garbutt Wood, which reaches right down to the shore, shading its surface and turning it grey-black. It is a place between worlds. Whether this commended Gormire to the abbot of Byland as James Tankerlay's watery grave or whether he knew old tales identifying the lake as the right place to get rid of a dangerous body is unknowable. Its lore may well have supplied him with a script as he wondered what to do with the ghost's malevolent remains. The lake, in a similar fashion to other uncanny features in the landscape, certainly had a power to attract and hold stories to itself.

In the nineteenth century, when there was a passion for collecting folklore, North Yorkshire was not insulated from such antiquarian searches and the collectors came and questioned the people. Some of them asked about Gormire. What they learned was not about ghosts as such but they did hear about a lake that was treacherous. Its edges were places where cattle feared to tread. It had no bottom. It was, some said, an entry-way to hell itself.[23] The Byland book could not have been the source of these tales. It languished in the British Museum, little-regarded until M. R. James, the ghost-story writer and antiquary of the early twentieth century, found and transcribed the matter from the endpapers in the early 1920s. The stories the folklorists heard were half believed, or not believed at all, but still remembered. Their endurance reminds us that some stories and ideas can be tenacious; they survive even if they have ceased to make intellectual sense because they still have an emotional resonance. So it was with so much in the Byland stories. Their ghosts had come to be construed in terms of Christian teaching about the fate of the soul, but the hauntings and human reactions to them rested on more primitive sensations and instincts about the dead.

3

THE END OF THE IRON WORLD

War Upon the Dead

On a summer night in 1549 a group of men approached the lodgings of a sleeping man, a royal commissioner named Matthew White.[1] He was staying in Seamer, a small Tudor town at the eastern end of the Yorkshire Wolds set against gentle hills and within sight of the sea. For Matthew White, the evening must have seemed unremarkable. He had been travelling through the county on the king's business for many months and Seamer was just another place to lay his head. But trouble was coming. Four local men – William Ombler, Thomas Dale, Henry Barton and Robert Dale – and unknown numbers of accomplices burst into the house where White was staying. There they found him in company with Sir Walter Mildmay, a man surnamed Clopton who was White's brother-in-law, William Savage, a merchant of York, and a servant of Mildmay's named Bury.[2] Ombler and his confederates rounded the men up. White tried to get away but despite having a horse was still caught. He, along with the others, was taken for a mile or so from the town along the highway running south towards the wold. Then, stripped of their purses and their clothes, they were butchered at the roadside, their corpses being left naked 'in the plain fields for the crows to feed on'. It was for the wives of White and Savage, both then at Seamer, to come later to the scene and give their menfolk a Christian burial.

This was no random act of violence; nor was it a simple robbery.

It was brutal theatre. Matthew White and his colleague Walter Mildmay were royal officers with a very particular brief. They were chantry commissioners. Sent out by Protector Somerset, who headed the government of the boy-king Edward VI, they were tasked with dismantling things that had long meant much to the women and men of the wolds. Chantries where masses were offered for souls in purgatory were to be dissolved; lights burning in memory of the dead were to be quenched. All monies paid for anniversary rites were to be seized in the name of the Crown. The reform-minded, cash-hungry government had, in other words, sent Matthew White to Yorkshire to take, in the Crown's name, all the property and paraphenalia that sustained prayers for souls trapped in purgatory fire. Adding insult to injury, suspicious quantities of the land and silver that accumulated in these confiscations were, local people rightly surmised, finding their way into the pockets of White, Mildmay and their friends. For these loyal officers were also men on the make; men who saw in the implementation of religious reform a chance to get very rich very quickly. They were, in their way, robbing the dead, or so William Ombler and his friends would have seen it. Snatching the purses from their corpses and stripping the clothes from their backs was more than the work of thieves; it was a move by rebels keen to make a point.

And rebellion this was: a small, localised, complex but violent rebellion, which had been plotted for days, perhaps weeks, and burst into life on St James' Day, 25 July. John Foxe, historian, martyrologist and staunch Protestant, offered the only full account of the plot.[3] Writing during the reign of Elizabeth I and unstinting in his support of religious reform, he was unremittingly hostile to the rebels. They were base-born men with 'traiterous hearts' ready to challenge the king and rend the fabric of society for the sake of religious practices he considered superstitious and idola-trous. They planned, he said, 'at the first rush' to murder 'such gentlemen and men of substance about them as were favourers of the king's proceedings, or [any] which would resist them'.[4] To rally forces, Ombler and his confederates would use the government's own early warning systems. Running along the high ground of the wolds was a line of beacons designed to warn of invasion and allow the local levies to be roused. The Seamer rebels would put the beacons to the torch, 'and thereby bring the people together, as though it were to defend the sea coasts'. Then they could persuade them to take up arms in their own cause, rousing the 'ignorant multitude' to violence by pouring the 'poison' of treason into their ears. Foxe thought he knew how this might work. The shiftless and the poor – 'the rudest and poorest sort' – would be most easily whipped up. These were, Foxe thought, nature's rebels. 'Pricked with poverty, and unwilling to labour', they would be the more ready to 'follow the spoil of rich men's goods'. And the ringleaders could soon convince them that this was justified by 'blowing into their heads' notions that divine service had been set aside and sundry malign innovations in religion introduced. Once men were under arms, the rebels would spread fear, giving 'the more terror to the gentlemen at their first rising' by devising 'that some should be murdered in churches, some in their houses, [and] some in serving the king in Commission'.

This, according to Foxe, was the plan. And, initially, all went well. Ombler and Dale and others 'so laboured the matter in the parish of Seamer, Wintringham and the towns about that they were infected with the poison of this confederacy'. But then things started to unravel. Archbishop Holgate, Lord President of the Council of the North, said he 'smelled' sedition in Yorkshire. The scent, mixed with alcohol fumes, came from a 'drunken fellow' named Calverd who, in his cups at the alehouse in Wintringham, began to talk rather too freely about what was intended. The rebels, aware that the government was stirring, revised their plans. They now 'drew to another place at Seamer by the sea coast' and there, by night, they launched the rising. Riding to the beacon at Staxton, they set it alight. Men gathered as they had intended. Thousands would eventually rise but a smaller number must have gathered round the burning beacon to hear what William Ombler had to say. Whatever he said – it is not known – enough were convinced to allow the work of resistance to begin. Soon a 'rude rout of rascals out of the towns near about' were heading back to Seamer and to the house where Matthew White lay sleeping away the last moments of his life.

What had brought things to this bloody pitch? At the heart of the rebel agenda was the religious policy of King Edward's government in faraway London.[5] That government, and the precocious young king himself, was set on religious reform of a radical kind. As firm Protestants they mocked the idea that the souls of the dead suffered in purgatory after death; rather they travelled directly to heaven or hell. It followed, then, that prayers were of no use to them. For what need did a soul in heaven have of men's prayers and what value could prayer have for a soul consigned to hell? Masses for the dead failed not only on this ground but also because they were a nonsense. There was no 'power' in the mass to be applied to the needs of men, whether living or dead, for the breaking of bread and pouring of wine at the communion table was no more than the Lord's Supper. There was no miracle or magic about it, only a memory of what Christ had done so that men might live.

That Edward's regime meant business had already been made plain in London. The capital had a great house of the dead, the 'Pardon Churchyard' of St Paul's Cathedral. Here bodies of the citizens were laid to rest, bones piled on bones in charnel houses. Prayers and masses were said for their souls and the dance of death, with explanatory verses by John Lydgate, was painted on the churchyard walls.[6] But on 10 April 1549 the charnel, chapel, cloister and dance, along with the tombs and monuments, were pulled down on Protector Somerset's command. 'Nothing was left', so it was said, 'but the bare plot of ground.' Not even the bones of the dead were safe. Borne away to Finsbury Fields by the cartload, they were unceremoniously dumped in 'moorish ground and in short space after raised by soilage of the city upon

them'. Windmills came to be built on Finsbury Field, catching
the breeze by dint of the bonehills on which they stood. Dwellings,
sheds for the stationers, were set up in place of the charnel and
chapel. Rubble from the Pardon Churchyard itself was used to
build Somerset's new house in the Strand.[7] If news of any of this
had come to the people of Seamer, small wonder they feared
what Matthew White would do when he arrived in their town.

The View from Staxton Beacon

Staxton Hill long ago lost the beacon that summoned the
woldsmen to war in 1549; reused in 1938 for radar masts, it is now
the site of an RAF station arrayed with the aerials and domes and
warning technologies of the modern age. But gazing north from
this changed place we can still see something of the landscape
over which the rebels marched. The North York Moors and Wolds
flatten as they approach the coast, and the land between them
forms a broad, gently undulating vale where the farmsteads and
villages implicated in the Seamer Rising lie. Remade in the nineteenth century, as land was enclosed and new farms staked out,
the vale is now a patchwork of bright cornfields and stands of
trees; then it would have been open space, given more to pasture.
Seamer was 'a great uplandish town', to the eye of the Tudor
antiquary John Leland, but little that he saw survives. The church
at Seamer, already old in 1549, and the occasional outlying farmhouse are all that he would recognise. Road and rail now tie the
town to Scarborough, York and beyond. But in the sixteenth
century this would have been a bleak and in some ways remote
land. Stephen Glynne, touring the region's churches by coach and
horses in the nineteenth century, still spoke of 'bare wretched
country' between Flamborough and Hunmanby; Elizabethan petitioners complained of 'evil and miry' winter roads, which made
travel difficult.[8] Hedged in by moor and wold, readily accessible
only by sea, left usually to its own devices, this would have been

a hard-to-control place for a government based in London. All this can be seen from Staxton Hill. What is harder to discern is the way by which men had come to fight and die over faith and why the dead themselves were at the heart of that battle. The answer to that question lies in the south. For in the south, in London, changes had been set in motion by Tudor kings, by Edward VI and his father, Henry VIII, which would change forever the ways in which the English thought of their dead.

As late as 1520, the Reformation was but a small cloud in the sky of Catholic England, a cloud across the sea, no bigger than a man's hand. Yet it was growing. During the next decade the words of the renegade German monk, Martin Luther, were floating to England on ships from the Continent which carried his incendiary works in their holds alongside their more prosaic cargoes. Luther's words were explosive because they threatened the whole edifice of Christianity as the Church had constituted it. Shaken by the mercinariness of Catholicism on a visit to Rome, Luther had sunk initially into despair but out of his anguish he crafted a radical attack on the Church's claims about salvation. Convinced of his own wretched unworthiness, he began to see that only through Christ could a man be saved; for Christ had already paid his debt of sin through his sacrifice on the cross.[9] Salvation was not a gift that could be earned: good works were surely good things, but men could not build their own bridges to heaven. Still less was this a gift to be bought; purchased pardons and arranged masses could not speed a soul through purgatory. They could not do this, Luther thought, because they did not work. But they also failed because purgatory, so Luther came to believe, was itself the Church's invention, its fires stoked by mercenariness and desire for donations. Some, especially in the cosmopolitan metropolis of Tudor London, were coming to share these views, often because their own emotions described the same curve as Luther's, from despairing unworthiness to elated discovery that faith alone might be enough to save souls.[10]

That elation at a new truth encouraged some Englishmen to

attack the old ways openly and triggered argument about the fate of the dead where once there had been agreement. In 1529, even before Luther's new theology was fully formed, the Protestant reformer Simon Fish was offering up for public consumption a tract called *Supplication for the Beggars*, which attacked masses, pardons and purgatory. By these means, he said, the dead drove out the living; money was wasted on useless intercession that might more profitably be used to help the poor. Thomas More replied with a *Supplication of Souls*, in which he conjured up the images of needy souls forgotten in purgatory-fire suffering. Men like Fish were guilty of uncharity; for so consumed were they by hatred of the clergy that they would sooner see their own fathers burn in purgatory fire 'until the day of Doom' than give a penny to a priest to pray for them.[11] John Frith, an innkeeper's son from Kent, replied in turn to More, pouring scorn on unscriptural purgatory, the fantasy that souls of the dead were detained there and the words of priests who mulcted a fearful laity by conjuring with this 'vain imagination'.[12] But in the 1520s, to attack purgatory in this way was to play a dangerous game. For these words were still heresy. They kept Simon Fish in exile for most of the decade; they ensured John Frith was shunted from the Tower to Newgate prison before being burned at the stake at Smithfield in 1533.

Yet the embers of John Frith's pyre had scarcely cooled before his words began to be turned from heresy into orthodoxy. Within days of his execution, Henry VIII was cast out of the Church by the Pope, solemnly excommunicated in Rome. Henry's quarrel with the Pope had been gestating since 1527 when the king began his quest for an annulment of his marriage to Catherine of Aragon so that he might marry Anne Boleyn. The king, 'terrible in his lust for women and in his wrath against men', was not to be thwarted in this ambition but nor was the Pope ready to yield.[13] There was now the most powerful of new motives for religious reform in England. Protestant ideas once branded as heresy were to be cautiously welcomed, not least because Anne Boleyn herself was a noted Protestant sympathiser who was uniquely placed to pour the merits of the new theology into the king's ear. Vaunted as a new, true way to salvation, these ideas allowed Henry and his Protestant counsellors to gild with intellectual justifications the political necessity of breaking with Rome and the king to crown himself head of a new Church in England. The hunters now found themselves hunted. The antagonists of Fish and Frith, including the king's chancellor Thomas More and Bishop Fisher of Rochester, went to the block as neither could stomach Henry's sweeping new claims to supremacy in matters of religion.

During the 1530s, slowly accumulated verities of the old faith were called into question in the span of a few years. In many ways Henry proved a reluctant Protestant, formed as he was since childhood in a world of Catholic rites. Although eager to be rid of the Pope, he let the old ways go falteringly. Henry's pious mood might change with his queens and advisers but the slow disintegration of the old consensus about the fate of the dead could not be stopped once debate had been set in motion. In 1536 the so-called *Ten Articles* were issued to give England's emerging Protestantism firmer scaffolding.[14] The old religious calendar was one casualty. Once filled with celebrations of saints who were celestial helpers in this world and the next, it was now reduced to bare bones. Purgatory survived in the 1536 blueprint but it was a pale imitation of its old self. The Church could no longer bind or loose souls detained there through its solemn ministrations. Purgatory's inextinguishable fires were quenched. Its ceaseless torments were stilled. Purgatory became a shadow world in which the soul travelled a dark way unknown; a journey on which scripture shed little light and which 'superstitious' medieval visions were no longer allowed to illuminate. Prayer for the dead survived too – for it was a charitable thing and long centuries had hallowed the practice – but the *Articles* reduced its value to vague proportions.[15] Henry's doctrinal clarification was blurring purgatory out of existence.

Even as Henry restrained religious reform after 1539, purgatory continued to fade away. By 1543 not only was purgatory stripped of its essential medieval characteristics of fierce fire and torment but utterance of its very name was forbidden.[16] Where were the dead in King Henry's other world? How did prayers help them? The ageing king's theology had no answers. The king also allowed that masses be said for the dead to ease them in their pains, but now the benefits of such masses accrued to the souls of *all* of the dead. There could be no special benefit for named individuals as they navigated the Henrician afterlife.[17] Here then was a move which struck at the heart of private salvific enterprise. For requiem masses, obits, chantries, guild masses – things so central in the medieval cult of the dead – no longer possessed the power to help a specified beneficiary. Intercession was democratised; but its benefits were spread thin for the souls of all the faithful dead.

Early in 1547, it became clear that the old king would not see the winter out. He lived his last days caught, as England was, between two tales about the fate of the dead. Although he had set his face against the Catholic story of purgatory fire, saving masses, pleading saints and the power of good works to save, Henry had never fully accepted the Protestant counter-claims that the dead passed immediately to heaven or to hell, faith alone securing their destiny.[18] So when Death came for the king on 28 January 1547, his will still provided a thousand marks for the prayers of the poor and established obits and daily masses for his soul.[19] Across England the parish priests sang requiems for him in the old style. But it was easier to know what to do than what to think. Where Henry thought he was going as his life ebbed away, and where ordinary men and women thought he had gone once he was dead, was a good deal more uncertain in the midst of that hard Tudor winter than it had been when he was born, at the height of summer, in 1491.

Certainty, at a price, came with Edward VI. His tutors were Protestant men; so too was the Lord Protector, the king's uncle, Edward Seymour, Duke of Somerset. By 1549, when he was only eleven, the king himself was penning a polemic which proved the Pope in Rome to be the Antichrist. Under Edward, steered by his uncle, reform went ahead with a new zeal. Much changed quickly as religion was made more austerely Protestant. Lights burning before the Rood were snuffed out; processions were stopped; candles at Candlemas, ash on Ash Wednesday and palms on Palm Sunday were all no longer to be used. So too the things of the dead were transformed by the new regime. In place of Henry's equivocation came a firm conviction that faith justified the repentant sinner, that eternal life came through trust in Christ alone. To believe that works could speed a soul to heaven was like a sailor thinking that by breathing into the sails of his ship he could get it under way. The soul's transit at death was swift; its destination final. No amount of prayer on the part of the living, however heartfelt, could help the soul since its course, whether for hell or to heaven (there was no other destination), was inexorably fixed from the moment it left the body. Such a theology finally spelt death for the mortuary institutions of the medieval world. Chantries where priests were still singing for the dead, guilds whose brethren kept alive the memory of deceased fellows through prayer, humble funds – sustained by bequests of meadow or hives of bees – to keep lights burning before a saint who might help a soul in purgatory, all were vulnerable.

At the very end of 1547 a bill was enacted to sweep all these things away.[20] It opened with the idea that faith in Christ was wholly necessary, and entirely sufficient, to save one's soul but the bill acknowledged, nonetheless, that many laboured in 'ignorance of their very true and perfect salvation through the death of Jesus Christ'.[21] Instead, trapped by 'blindness and ignorance', they were still busy 'devising and fantasising vain opinions of purgatory and masses'. So the new legislation embarked upon a comprehensive Reformation of the things of the dead. Chantries, guilds, light-funds and obits were all suppressed; even the bede rolls, listing the parish dead so that they could be prayed for, were to be removed from churches. The surface logic was that all such monies might now be turned to the good of the living: charitable giving to the poor must replace solicitude for departed souls.

Great iron-bound poor boxes appeared in parish churches to receive the bounty. Schools for the quick, not masses for the dead, should be endowed by pious benefactors. These things did not save the soul – faith alone did that – but they were emblems of godliness, good things that should be done for their own sake rather than narrow salvific ends.

By 1549, this legislation was being implemented and the Royal Commissioners were moving steadily through Yorkshire. People probably had more than an inkling of what was coming. The crumbling remains of the monasteries bore silent witness to earlier dissolutions during Henry VIII's reign. In York, St Mary's, once one of the greatest religious houses in northern England, now served as offices for the king's Council of the North; St Leonard's, the huge medieval hospital, was now a royal mint. Holy Trinity survived as a glorified parish church but the city's friaries and nunnery were all in ruins. Out on the moors, Rievaulx, Fountains and Byland were wrecks. Around Seamer, Whitby, Bridlington, St Mary's Yedingham and the Cistercian nunnery at Wykeham had all been swept away.[22] Henry had shown that no cowled monks, mitred abbots nor even the Pope in Rome would frustrate his ambitions. Even miracle-working saints could not stay his hand; for their shrines were shattered and plundered for their gold and jewels. At York, St William's statue, in the Minster itself, had been taken down and broken up in 1541, its disarticulated silver parts fetching the princely sum of £65.[23]

In 1549, the chantries, guilds, masses and lights of the Minster and the parish churches of York were going the same way as St William; Matthew White swept through the city in July. Before his death he had seized funds which sustained obits and lights and silenced chantries further east, at Seamer and nearby Ayton. Others, as yet unvisited, must have been waiting for the blow to fall, for the eastern end of the Vale of Pickering and the Yorkshire coast were lands full of chantries. There were two in the castle at Seamer itself, three in the busy port of Scarborough, and manifold scattered through the villages of Osgodby, Kilham, Burton

Agnes, Harpham, Lowthorpe and further afield at Pickering, Wykeham, Brompton, Appleton-le-Street, Kirby Misperton, Malton, New Malton, Towthorpe and Wharram Percy.[24]

Dry words of the Commissioners' accounts and certificates say something of these institutions and their fate, reducing them to money values and commercial stuff to be sold on in due course. But statistics hide the shock these changes must have wrought. The familiar cadences of chantry and guild masses, the guttering commemorative lights, the annual rhythm of anniversaries and regular readings of the bede roll kept the dead of the parish alive in human memory. Now those bonds were being broken and the dead left to their own devices.[25] And the living too were often robbed of things they held dear. For chantry priests with their rounds of masses offered them more chances to hear divine service. Something of the value attached to this is revealed in the church at Wintringham, one of the epicentres of the Seamer Rising. For here someone had cut little holes in the baseboards of a chapel screen standing in the north aisle. One was in the shape of an arched church window, the other a tiny hand, as if pressed flat against the wood and traced around. This was not vandalism, it was medieval devotion. Kneeling down and peering through these holes, there is a clear view of the altar. And this was what the amateur wood-workers wanted. Kneeling in adoration, they wanted to gaze at the wafer and wine as the priest celebrated mass and these things turned into the body and blood of Christ. So they made windows in the wood. They would probably have liked to touch these things of power too and this, perhaps, is why they fashioned the second hole in the form of a hand.

To the Wintringham carver the mass was miraculous. It fed the souls of the living and helped the souls of the dead. But in 1549, mass and chantry were to be swept away. And that blow was the more cruel in places like Seamer and the hamlets round about because this landscape of wolds and moors had large parishes not easily navigated by a single parish priest. Many people, living far from their church, depended on chantry priests, often lodged in isolated chapels, in order to hear divine service at all. They also needed them to baptise their children, a vital consideration since an infant who died without proper baptism because a priest was not to hand might be trapped forever in limbo; its unquiet spirit might even be thought to walk the moors. And the parishioners of these scattered communities also relied on these priests on their last day, for shrift and housel were still vital things to dying men and women brought up in the old religion. Inaccessibilty of a priest might leave salvation itself at stake.[26] During Mary's reign, when vestiges of the old religion were briefly restored, eminences further south in Pontefract, John Hamerton and Purston Jaglin, explained a similar problem to the queen's minister, Cardinal Pole. Memories of the Edwardine Reformation were still raw there, wounds still fresh. The petitioners lamented that before the Reformation 'we had in that town one abbey, one anchoress, one hermit, four chantry priests, one guild priest'. But all were now gone save for a single unlearned vicar and, as a result, the good people of 'Pomfret' were 'neither relieved bodily nor ghostly'.[27] This was the kind of transformation that the people of Seamer feared, for the wolds around them were well populated with priests because the dead had funded them. But the government in London was disinclined to hear pleas about such things from the faraway north, not least because many of the fears which excited the pleas were bound up with 'superstitous' beliefs that the Reformers sought to banish.

The Seamer rebels nursed hopes that their enterprise would spread. And for a time it did. The ringleaders went from town to town 'in their raging madness', gathering men for the cause. The juggernaut of Reform might yet be stopped. Foxe thought ultimately three thousand men across the north-east of Yorkshire had taken up arms; Archbishop Holgate later puffed the numbers up to between ten and twelve thousand. William Ombler and his confederates knew that there were other 'commotions' elsewhere in England. Kett's Rebellion had ignited (literally) in East Anglia, where barrels of gunpowder were used to blow up rabbit warrens belonging to hated landholders. More seriously, rebels in south-west England had rallied to the colours of the old religion, their 'Prayer Book Rebellion' encouraged by the Edwardine regime's bid to impose a communion service in English in place of the traditional Latin mass.[28] If the rebel hosts could unite, then the Edwardine government, and its project of Reformation, would be in grave danger.

But the rebellions did not spread; the insurgent hosts did not unite and Edward's ministers had their Reform. With a mixture of pardons and menaces, the government moved to quash disorder during August 1549.[29] Perhaps seeing offers of pardon as a sign of weakness, perhaps buoyed by early success, perhaps aware that government promises of clemency in the wake of rebellion had in the past counted for little, the Seamer rebels spurned the olive branch. William Ombler, claimed Foxe, 'contemptuously' refused it. Contemptuous or not, Ombler's decision proved unwise as the government's power in the wolds, checked by the rebellion, was waxing again. Soon after, while riding the Hunmanby road, he was 'espied by the circumspect diligence' of a group of gentlemen who were in the king's service. Chased and quickly caught, Ombler escaped the kind of summary justice meted out to Matthew White but he could have had few doubts about what would happen to him when he came to trial. He was 'brought in the night in sure custody into the city of York to answer to his demerits'. Other 'first chieftains and ringleaders' Thomas Dale and Henry Barton were captured and taken to York as well. Meanwhile further 'busy stirrers' of sedition and commotion – John Dale, Robert Wright and Edmund Buttrye – were rounded up as they travelled about trying to breathe life back into the embers of their dying insurgency. In satisfied fashion, John Foxe noted that all were 'committed to ward' but he gives little detail of what happened next. The captives probably had to wait in York Castle for a special commission to come up from the south to hear their case. When it came, they were 'lawfully convicted, and lastly executed at York the xxi of September 1549'. Archbishop Holgate agreed that this was the denouement, noting shortly that the 'commotion at Seamer [was] stayed with executing of eight persons'. The Seamer Rising had ended with a whimper rather than a bang. The would-be allies of the northern rebels met similar fates. Kett was taken and executed; the peasant army of the Prayer Book rebels was destroyed near Exeter and the leaders put to death. Examples were made. Robert Welshe, the outspoken vicar of Exe Bridge, was hanged in chains, dressed in Catholic vestments, from the steeple of his church where he was left slowly to die.[30]

The truth for the Seamer rebels was that their hopes were probably always little more than pipe dreams. Seamer and its 'uplandish' hinterland of moors and wolds, with its especially heavy dependence of the living on the dead, felt the burden of Edwardine Reform more acutely than most places. Rebels in other parts of England had different agendas; the East Anglians, in particular, were moved in large part by economic grievances and far fewer of them marched under the colours of the old religion. The Prayer Book rebels did rally to those colours but they soon found to their cost what the Tudor war machine could do in a pitched battle. And, though many in the north surely sympathised with the Seamer rebels, strikingly few took up arms to help them. Most of Yorkshire was brooding, but still, in 1549. For here memories of an earlier Henrician rebellion, the Pilgrimage of Grace, and its bloody suppression by the old king were fresh. In 1537 Yorkshire had indeed risen, to defend the monasteries from dissolution and traditional rites from change.[31] But outmanoeuvred by the wily Henry, almost a hundred and fifty were executed, ringleaders being hanged in chains from the city walls as 'goodly experiments' in Tudor justice.[32] Small wonder that when Matthew White was busy liquidating chantry property in York on 7 July 1549, there might be anger but little action from the people of the city.

4

FIRE AND FLEET AND CANDLELIGHT

Instability and Newfangledness

Some seventy-five miles south-west of Seamer and Staxton Hill, where Yorkshire fades into the midland plains, is the village of Adwick-le-Street. The 'street' of its name is Ermine Street, an ancient road lying a little to the west of the settlement which was first built by the Romans for troops and for trade and with a view to tying north to south in the furthest-flung province of empire. The road long outlived the Roman administration that built it. Still an essential artery of sixteeth-century England, it was relied upon by travellers, traders, messengers and royal forces as they marched north to crush resistance to the Crown. Nearer to the centres of power than Seamer, Adwick responded more typically to the changes wrought by the Reformation; it was an altogether quieter place to pass the turbulent mid Tudor years.[1] In one way it was singular. It had a curate, a man named Robert Parkyn, who was an unusually voluble commentator on religious change for a man of his lowly estate. Born of yeoman stock in nearby Owston, he was in holy orders by 1541 and served the people of Adwick right through the tumultuous Reformation years until his death in 1569. He witnessed the changes wrought by two kings and two queens, the 'grevus matters' as he called them.[2] He watched the monasteries vanish and the reform of parish religion begin under Henry VIII. He saw the pace quicken under Edward as everything 'tending to idolatry' in the Reformers' eyes – all images, crucifixes,

tabernacles and the like – was 'utterly abolished and taken away'.[3]
He testified to the appropriation of the things of the dead that
had caused such anger in Seamer as 'hospitals, chantries and free
chapels within Yorkshire and other [of] the King's dominions was
given up by compulsion into His Majesty's hands'. And he
observed too the furnishings and fittings of those holy places –
'all manner of jewels, chalices, books, bells, vestments, with all
other ornaments pertaining thereto' – being turned into cash
which wended its way into royal coffers.

There is no trace now of Robert Parkyn's resting place, though
his bones lie somewhere near the choir door of the church he
served down those long and turbulent years. The monuments of
his friends – Leonard Wray and James Washington – are still to
be seen in the north chapel. The latter lies fixed forever in stone
beside his wife and children. He sports a distinctive Tudor ruff
and his high standing is proclaimed by the armorial bearings of
the tomb chest. But while the monuments of Wray and
Washington are mute, Parkyn speaks from the grave.[4] Writing
around the year 1555, during Mary's reign when Catholicism was
briefly restored, he chronicled the Henrician Reformation
sketchily and its Edwardine successor in detail. He knew the
outlines of the politics which he personalised. Thomas Cromwell,
architect of Henrician Reform, was bad, a 'wretch and heretic';
Protector Somerset – 'very heretic and traitor to God' – was
worse. But as he wrote, Parkyn revealed not only his enmities
but also his loves; for he held firmly to the view that eternal life
was to be found, for himself and his parishioners, through the
traditional rites he saw being abrogated. The very first words of
his chronicle are powerfully suggestive in this regard, for he opens
with an invocation: 'Pray for the soul of Sir Robert Parkyn.'
Parkyn was born into a world where the dead needed prayers
and so it remained quite natural for him to beseech all who
picked up his little book to be his bedesmen, hoping that they
might be moved to pray for the suffering of its author when he
was gone. Robert's other writings, assembled in commonplace

books, are of a piece with that sentiment. They suggest a man steeped in Catholic theology, formed intellectually by monastic devotions still alive in Yorkshire when he was young, absorbed in the seemingly timeless Catholic rituals he had grown up with and latterly administered himself.[5]

Parkyn knew about sin and death and hell and his beliefs were the durable ones of the medieval Church. Death, for the body, 'is a long sleep'; it was 'a fear to rich men, a desirous thing to poor men, a change incurable, a thief to man'. Such words could have been plucked straight from sermons preached in the days of John Baret in Bury St Edmunds. Parkyn knew too the Christian remedies for these terrors, long-hallowed by holy Church and long-used in the parish. People, he pointed out, needed to live in constant remembrance of death so that they died well when their time came. For, Parkyn warned, 'the soul goeth to everlasting pain' if it left the body in mortal sin. These words may have echoed in his preaching to the people of Adwick. They would certainly have underpinned the expectation that the parishioners must come regularly, at least once yearly, confess their sins to him, receive a penance and hear the absolving words of their priest, through whom Christ himself spoke. By these means sins were melted and men and women restored, able to live ready to die. At the last, the dying parishioner needed a priest again and still more urgently. He would hear confession for a final time – a vital chance to seek forgiveness while still in the body; perhaps a last opportunity to save the soul from hellfire if it were stained by a grievous sin – and administer the last rites. So that he might know the better when this shrift and housel were needed, Parkyn had among his writings a list of diagnostic signs which revealed when death was imminent. If he had not learned it from long experience, the text told him to watch for misting eyes, the nose turned cold, the skin of the face sinking, the mouth falling open and spittle running, hand and heart trembling and breaths turning shallow.[6] When the dead were gone, they needed masses and prayers and Parkyn was equipped for that too. He surely sang more often for the dead than he cared to count during his long years of service and he, with others, certainly sang a trental for the souls of Nicholas and Agnes, parents of his fellow priest William Watson. Humphrey Gascoyne, a rich local churchman, left Parkyn a featherbed in the hope that he would say a mass for his soul in return.[7]

When change came, Parkyn hated it. 'It was a marvel', he wondered, 'that the earth did not open and swallow up such villainous persons.' But the earth did not open. And although admiring of a martyr like Thomas More, Parkyn was not himself made of martyrs' stuff; nor, though hailing from yeoman stock, was he to be a rebel like William Ombler. Perhaps Parkyn was simply too comfortable in his Adwick living to risk it all; his will hints at this with its long list of creature comforts ranging from featherbeds and silver spoons to fur-trimmed gowns and coal enough for several hearths. More certainly, Parkyn was fearful of royal power, for dissident priests had gone to scaffolds if treason was detected in their religious conservatism. So he soldiered on through Edward's reign, perhaps trying to make the best of it and hoping for better things to come. But before they did, things got worse. Again Robert Parkyn watched. Protector Somerset fell but his place was taken by the Duke of Northumberland. Having spent his superlatives on Somerset, a word-weary Parkyn seems to have struggled for new ones to characterise the wickedness of his successor. But he clearly saw him as a reformer cut from not dissimilar cloth, another stirrer of 'great instability and newfangle-ness'.[8] During his years of dominance yet another new prayer book was brought out in 1552. Unlike the one that made the West Country boil in 1549, it entered circulation without major incident 'at All Hallows' Day' (1 November 1552). Yet it was still more radical and it broke more of the bonds that had for so long connected the living to the dead. According to the 1549 funerary rites, the priest would address the corpse, as medieval priests did; the dead person was still there, watching, almost, their own funeral. But in the new prayer book ritual of 1552, the priest spoke of the deceased in the third person, as though they were far away. And that was firmly the message. The dead were gone. The corpse was a shell, deserving of decent burial but needing no more than that; the minister's words were for the living only. It followed that all traces of intercession were utterly extirpated from the contours of the funeral service too; the living, so the Church now emphatically taught, could not reach out to the dead through prayer and could no longer help them.[9] As for the dead, so too for the dying. The rites by which men were prepared to die were transformed: confession, mass, unction were all to be swept away leaving scripture reading, strengthening prayers and perhaps a final communion as, one might think, a colder comfort for many who had grown up in a different world. This was certainly Robert Parkyn's view. He observed mournfully that 'extreme unction was utterly abolished and none to be used . . . And no diriges or other devout prayers to be sung or said for such as was departed this transitory world for they needed none [said the book].' Parkyn also noted the reason for this. It was 'because . . . souls were immediately in bliss and joy after the departing from the bodies, and therefore they needed no prayer'.

The last great act of Reform followed the curve of early changes to their logical end. The clarified theology and stripped-down ritual of Edwardine Protestantism meant that the ecclesiastical clutter of the parishes might with profit – in every sense of that word – be cleared out. By the end of the Middle Ages, England's churches were filled with patens, chalices, vestments, bells, books, candlesticks and the like, gifted by parishioners. Short of ready cash, as Tudor administrations perennially seemed to be, it would have been foolish for Reform-minded men to neglect so tempting a source of revenue. And so they set to work. After several false starts, the regime finally launched a comprehensive survey of parish churches. And so in 1552 and 1553, purges were launched in earnest. 'The Church,' observed one later commentator, 'once the richest House in the Parish, is become the poorest.'[10] But in doing their work of spring-cleaning, Reformers did something very profound. They broke up fields of memory long in the making by generations of donors; for the paraphenalia they cleared from the churches had been given down the ages by men and women who hoped that, during its use, they would be remembered, their names rehearsed, their souls eased with grateful prayers.[11] But such false hopes counted for little in the reformed order. Indeed, the transformation of the churches even extended in some places to memorial brasses which solicited forbidden prayers and offensively Catholic tombs and grave slabs. All were on occasion broken up or melted down and the remnants sold on. In York, an alderman buried as recently as 1535 had his tomb smashed; an effigy of a knight on another ended up as a way-marker on Hob Moor. The antiquary Henry Keepe looked back on it all a hundred years or more later as he burrowed into the history of the city and lamented how 'stone coffins and other monuments of the dead [were] made the receptacles for rain water, mangers for horses, hog troughs to feed swine; and the lintel of many a noted senator or other deserving person [was] laid on the coping of some old wall'.[12] The pattern in these parts of Yorkshire was replicated in the other counties of England as tombs and brasses were scraped clean of their precatory formulae or plucked from their beds.

Not all of this destruction was wrought by zealous reformers; some was the work of committed Protestants within the parish, for Reform was slowly changing the religious chemistry of England and the numbers adhering to the new ways were growing. Once, such far-reaching appropriations of the things of the dead would have surely been resisted. The Pilgrimage of Grace was nourished, in part, by rumours that parish churches might go the way of the monasteries and be spoiled of their plate and other valuables.[13] None resisted now in such open ways, although in some parishes churchwardens, noticing the way the winds were blowing, began selling the things of the dead back to parishioners so as to thwart the coming seizures.[14] Other responses to the confiscations, more base, mingled with favour and fear. Everywhere some were to be found who, with an eye to the main chance, 'plucked up the Brass of Tombs and Gravestones' contrary to the words of the Edwardine Statute but very much to their own financial benefit.[15] Material gain might blunt the sense of spiritual loss. Michael Sherbrook, an Elizabethan churchman from Yorkshire who wrote in the 1590s about an earlier conversation with his father, a man who had been there at the beginnings of the Reformation, was sensitive to this.[16] Sherbrook's father had held firmly to the old ways, yet he had still plundered what he could from the wreck of Roche Abbey when the monasteries were dissolved by King Henry. How, Sherbrook had wondered, could that be? His father's answer was plain: 'What should I do? . . . Might I not, as well as others, have some Profit of the Spoil of the Abbey? For I did see all would away anyway; and therefore I did as others did.'[17] In many places, these words might explain something of the fate of monasteries, chantries, memorials and monuments across the span of England's Reformations.

Given the fine survivals of Tudor tombs at Adwick, it seems likely that with or without the active intervention of its conservative-minded priest, the little village survived the worst of these excesses. But in other ways, Robert Parkyn and his parishioners were forced to bend. Robert himself had to follow at least the letter of the new prayer books of 1549 and 1552; to do otherwise would have been highly dangerous. The central, saving rite of his youth was now utterly transformed. The mass, with all its ancient power to help the souls of the dead, had gone. When Robert sang the trental masses for William Watson's parents, wafers turned into Christ's body in Robert's fingers and wine changed to blood in the chalice. By remaking Christ's sacrifice on earth, Robert helped the souls of those named sufferers in purgatory fire. But now in place of the Latin mass was the Lord's Supper, a service said in English, a remembrance of Christ's sacrifice not its renewal; in place of the holy wafers was a good 'loaf of white bread such as men use in their houses with meat'.

And that this new rite had no power to fetch souls out of purgatory did not matter. There were no souls to fetch. There was no purgatory. And so the house of prayer and memory made by medieval men and women could be, and was, dismantled by the Edwardine Reformers. When Edward died, still little more than a boy, in 1553 the times were, in Robert Parkyn's eyes, out of joint. It was for the dead boy's sister, Mary, to set things right; for she was of pious Catholic conviction and determined to restore the old religion. Parkyn thought her accession popular in London but doubly so in the north where 'the whole commonality in all places of the north parts greatly rejoice, making great fires, drinking wine and ale, and praising God'.[18] The old ways slowly, falteringly, were resumed. Hidden chalices and vestments were brought out anew and dusted off. Prayers and masses for the dead began again; some even countenanced new chantries. And, of course, Parkyn let out his pent-up anger about the Protestant past in his chronicle. But Mary did not live long enough to see her plans through. When she died in 1558 her Protestant sister Elizabeth, daughter of Anne Boleyn who, one might say, started it all, ascended the throne. Protestantism, albeit Protestantism with blunted zeal, was back. This time for good.

Robert Parkyn lived long enough to see all this. The times had changed and he, unwilling, had changed with them. His handwriting is almost a metaphor of his 'modernisation'; for through his long life it slowly transforms from a formal bookhand redolent of the monastic scriptorium into a freer cursive.[19] But these were changes of outer forms and shapes. We know far less about his later thoughts; his chronicle stops early in Elizabeth's reign. And we know nothing of his meditations about what waited for him as he neared his end in 1569: in Elizabethan England, discretion was the better part of valour in such matters, not least because the year saw one last gasp of Catholic rebellion in the north with seditious masses sung in Durham Cathedral.[20] Robert, as we have seen, was not a valorous man. Even the hard words of his chronicle had been carefully framed. For Parkyn had glossed

Henry's reign quickly and made Reformation the work of a treacherous Thomas Cromwell; the worse enormities of Edward's rule, this time rendered in detail, were easily ascribed to evil counsellors who had dominated the child-king. Northumberland, so Parkyn surmised, had even brought about the boy's death with poison. By these means, Parkyn edged around the dangerous claim that kings were to blame for the religious traumas. But that narrative strategy fell to pieces as Elizabeth embarked upon a new Protestant settlement. And it became redundant, too, for Parkyn had to make shift as best he could in a world he probably did not like. Even his will, which still survives, has little to tell us.[21] For all his heartfelt anguish about the loss of the old ways, he was at the last willing to conform to the new ones. This document, which was of course a public one, is most eloquent in its silences. It betrays few hints of his Catholic sensibilities. His Catholic books, shared out among friends and family, point back to his old beliefs. But there was nothing in the will about the Blessed Virgin or the saints; rather there were simple bequests to those attending his funeral and charity for the poor. Parkyn's is, on the surface at least, a perfectly Protestant testament.[22]

It is not easy to breach the silence Robert Parkyn spun around himself as England turned slowly but decisively Protestant under Queen Elizabeth. And it is not easy to see what survived of the old world of the dead in the years after he laid up his pen and the blood of the Seamer Rising had run into the earth of the wolds.[23] But while public rites might be transformed, thought and private utterance could not be so easily policed even by the mighty Tudor state. In York the old ways lingered for a time. Medieval mystery plays were still being performed in the city far into Elizabeth's reign, including a judgement play with its old-fashioned intimations that through good works one could build a bridge to heaven.[24] Unreformed messages endured in images in many Yorkshire churches. In York these were still full of stories of the saints and the drama of the Doom. Even as parishioners followed new rites which pivoted round prayer book and communion table, the old narratives hovered on the edges of their fields of vision. The same was true out on the wolds. At Wintringham the masses for the dead were gone but saints were still blazoned in some of the windows.[25] Some, perhaps many, still recalled the old ways. In York a man asked to be buried close to the place where St William's shrine once stood in the Minster, holding on, perhaps, to the conviction that the power of saints in their shrines trickled down to the bones of the ordinary dead laid to rest around them.[26] As late as 1585, one witness recalled that Agnes Maners, a woman cold in the grave for eighty-five years, had left city tenements in her will to the church of St Margaret so that her name might be remembered on the bede roll and her soul prayed for in its extremity.[27] Small wonder that Edmund Grindal, the Elizabethan Archbishop of York, was worried that people in his diocese, in papistical fashion, were still praying for the dead.[28] In rural parts this was being done as late as 1612, some sixty years after the practice was first forbidden.[29] And in remote Holderness in 1567 the authorities discovered parishioners and a priest who, true to reformed religion, celebrated the new communion service. But they also offered it, like the old mass, as a sacrifice for suffering souls.[30]

The dead continued for a time to claim a collective place in the ritual year too, much to the irritation of the authorities. When darkness fell on 2 November 1578, people stole into the church at Gilling on the southern flank of the North York Moors and broke the silence by ringing the bells deep into the night; it was the feast of All Souls and medieval custom dictated that parishes should ring peels for the dead, perhaps to comfort those in purgatory fire or else to keep the dead at bay, for ghosts might creep more easily over the threshold between worlds at that time of the year. The practice was still alive some miles away in 1587 and elsewhere in England it lingered too, forming a minor battleground between Protestant bishops and some communities determined to cling to the old ways.[31] So for a time, at least, there were people who carried round in their heads an old religion of purgatory fire and prayers for the dead even if they followed the rites of a new Church.

If public prayer for the dead lingered in many places visibly enough for Reformers to castigate it, it was still more likely to be abundant in private. Family and friends had always prayed for their dead in the Middle Ages, a loving obligation that seldom needed mentioning. Robert Parkyn may have expected as much when he left bequests for fellow priests in his will; silent assumptions could be there in giving and receiving. His books, many of them Catholic books, might carry with them hope for prayers. And someone, of course, inherited the book with his little chronicle in it, a work prefaced by that explicit plea for help when he was dead and gone. Gifts in wills, especially rings with mourning messages, might carry with them unspoken assumptions that went beyond mere remembrance.[32] Uttered at home or quietly, inwardly, during the silences of funeral rites or communion services, prayer for the dead might remain in some quarters long after the Reformation. Beliefs formed in childhood about the saints and prayers were not quickly or easily to be erased. They lingered in memory during the reign of Elizabeth until the turn of the generations caused them to fade.[33] And by the early seventeenth century, some leading divines were even trying once more to find a place for prayer for the dead in the theology of the Church of England.[34] The urge to reach out to the dead, to help them in their extremity, was powerful indeed.

As for prayer, so for charity. Pennies, food and drink were still doled out at many funerals, though the old contract in which these things were given in expectation of prayers was abandoned down the decades.[35] Some also left money for an annual dole in their memory, dispensed on the day of their death or funeral. Often this was in the form of bread for the good of the poor; it might even be dealt out from the flat slab of the donor's tomb lest anyone forget their benefactor's generosity.[36] Many still left money in their wills for the help of the poor or the benefit of the parish. The rich endowed almshouses for the deserving poor or they built schools. Neat almshouses, set beside a chapel, still stand at Thornton-le-Dale in Seamer. All these things could be done by men and women who were impeccably Protestant. The Reformation had made charity a mere sign of godliness rather than a means to salvation. Those of the new religion provided it for this reason and for simple remembrance.[37] But when Robert Parkyn left money in his will for the poor, he surely hoped it would smooth the way in the next life. For these things were deep in his soul.

Fire and Fleet and Candlelight

Blakey Ridge runs roughly north–south through the heart of the North York Moors. Often bleak in summer when heather turns the landscape purple, it is desolate in winter. The main road that runs along it is frequently closed by snow and the tracks that run off its flanks are choked by drifts as high as the stone walls that enclose them. The Red Lion pub, on the crest, is a refuge. From it views of the moors, higher and harder than those above Byland Abbey, unroll in all directions. The Red Lion is also near the midpoint of a curious long-distance walking route. It runs roughly from Osmotherley in the west to Ravenscar in the east, crossing almost forty miles of moor but without any defined path. It is known at the Lyke Wake Walk. Those hardy enough to complete it within a time limit of twenty-four hours are entitled to join the New Lyke Wake Club and to sport its coffin-shaped badge. The origins of the walk are modern: in the 1950s a moorland farmer called Bill Cowley invented it as a walkers' challenge. But he made use of an old tradition with roots reaching into the pre-Reformation past. For the Lyke Wake was originally not a walk but a vigil, which was kept through the night beside the body before burial.[38] A song, a dirge, was associated with this business of watching in parts of Yorkshire. Recorded only in the seventeenth century, it was said to have been sung by women of 'vulgar' families over the bodies of their dead. It described the journey the soul would make and spoke of an other-world landscape strangely similar to that of the wild moors.[39] This began in 'fire and fleet and candle-light'. The body rested in the warmth and light of the cottage as it was watched and waked by friends and kin who kept it company in its last hours among the living. The women sang to the corpse of the journey that the soul must make. It would stand in the middle of the spiny furze of Whinny Moor and would have to make its way, a passage made easier or harder depending on how the person had lived. Those who had given shoes and stockings to the poor would find shoes waiting for them in the next world as protection against the sharp whins but the uncharitable would have to cross unshod; 'pricked to the bare bane', their feet would be shredded by the thorns. The soul then traversed the 'Brig O' Dread', a bridge 'no broader than a thread'. Some, the wicked, would slip as they tried to cross, falling into the chasm beneath. For those who passed over safely there was a final trial. Near the end of their journey was purgatory fire. Those who had fed the hungry and given drink to the thirsty would be spared the flames but the mean-spirited would be 'burned to the bare bone', cleansed of their sins before they entered heaven.

The song was written down by a seventeenth-century scholar called John Aubrey. No native of Yorkshire, he was a son of the south-west, born and bred in Wiltshire. But in 1687 he had made a journey up to Ripon and then onwards to Durham.[40] This is probably when he found out about the dirge. An enthusiast for all things antique, he had a keen eye for customs and 'superstitions' of the people. Unusually in his day, he thought there might be 'truth and usefulness' in some of these things even if they seemed 'gross' to the learned. So stories about ghosts, fairies, charms, omens, divinations, witchcraft and spells were all subjects of his works. In this spirit he set out the verses of the dirge, explaining that the song was once widely sung but had now fallen into disuse. What Aubrey had found was a medieval world in miniature, alive still in the songs of Yorkshire. For here, over

Whinny Moor and beyond the Bridge of Dread, the Reformation had not taken hold. Souls wandered after death in a middle place between heaven and hell, good deeds smoothed their way and purgatory fire still burned bright. The dirge was dying out in Yorkshire funerals when Aubrey wrote it down but it was no flight of fancy. Others had heard about Whinny Moor too. A wondering letter from Cleveland in 1600 mentioned singing at funerals about 'a great land full of thorns and furze', which souls must cross barefoot after death; folklore collectors discovered traces of the dirge in different parts of the north-east a century after Aubrey recorded it.[41] Other stories also told of landscapes of punishment and the dead suffered not only amidst moors and cataracts but also in the depths of the earth. On the way to Darlington, the Tudor chronicler William Harrison noticed that there were pits, the Hell Kettles, in which the souls of the dead were still said to be seethed for their sins. Long reputed to be bottomless, a bid to banish the belief was made in the 1690s by Jabez Kay who success-fully plumbed the depths.[42]

Memories of the old religion – its purgatory, its pains and prayers, which gave the song its sense – dulled with the passing genera-tions.[43] Rhyme, rhythm and custom helped the old song to stick in memories. But something deeper kept the dirge alive in funeral rites of the 'vulgar' moorlanders down to the 1620s and perhaps beyond – something deeper than the old religion, deeper than the new. For just as the song began with 'fire and fleet and candlelight' so it ended in the final verse. In the in-between time that ran from death to burial, a newly deceased person still had a place in the land of the living. The body altered little, the face still familiar, he or she had a right to hearthside warmth and candlelight for a few final hours. But soon these must be forsaken. The dead loved one would be eased out of the world, the body into cold earth and the soul into the afterlife. The dirge marked this departure but it also smoothed the way; it told the dead that they must go.

When an old lady in the village of Fryup in Cleveland, in the heart of the North York Moors, was dying she was very particular

ouses of those soon to die. Others feared 'Jenny-wi't lantern', a
ill-o'-the-wisp that bobbed about on the moors and was
angerous if the traveller did not immediately turn jacket or apron
nside out on seeing it.[45] There was even an elderly lady who was
ure that, when it came to laying spirits, the Catholic priests of
ld were better conjurors – 'vast mair powerful' – than Anglican
Church-Priests', a notion scattered through the folklore of many
ounties of England.[46] Such considerations were still material for
ome in this part of Yorkshire. For, as the old lady from Fryup
ndicated, the dead had to be eased out of the world in the old-
ashioned way and they might walk if proper rites were not
espected. Just for a moment, something of the world of John
aret or the Byland monk glints in this nineteenth-century lore
om Danby: there was still a sense among some that the dead,
s a manual for medieval priests had once put it, might 'take
engeance' if denied their rights.

Strange customs hinting at early origins were not the preserve
f wild northern uplands alone. Bookish clergymen and itinerant
olklorists mentioned them in many parts of England. Some
ories are tantalising fragments. John Aubrey, in his further
anderings, heard about a 'long lean, ugly rascal' who lived in a
ottage on the Ross road in Herefordshire. He made a crust as a
in-eater', turning up at funerals where he would take a six-penny
oaf and sup a 'mazar bowl' of beer passed to him over the coffin
d. 'In consideration whereof', Aubrey explained, 'he took upon
im . . . all the sins of the defunct, and freed him or her from
alking after they were dead.' The custom, Aubrey said, was rare
ven then but the folklorist Ella Leather discovered a trace in the
nd of the nineteenth century. A man of Hay-on-Wye went to a
neral at a farm near Crasswall and found the dead woman's
offin draped with a white cloth set with six glasses and a bottle
f port. The old farmer said he must take a glass and drink, for
was a 'sacrament' that would 'kill' the sins of his dead sister.[47]
ch things were mysteries to most, rituals followed by few; the
isitor told Mrs Leather the tale precisely because it was so strange.

about how she should be buried. She told those a
she must be carried to the grave by the 'church v
tional route by which coffins were conveyed to the
at Danby. Although the season was snowy and th
wound up a steep bank, the bearers obeyed. Carry
local fashion, at waist height, cloths wound unde
form handles, they slipped and slithered in the sr
church. That they did so was bound up with mor
respect for her wishes. The old lady had warned the
took a short cut she would be angry. She would '

The story was no medieval relic, not even a frag
seventeenth century. It was recalled by Reverend J
a Victorian clergyman who served the people of D
than forty years in the second half of the ninet
Baptising, marrying and preaching to them down t
buried them too. In winter, bodies might be com
frozen ground, amidst blizzards that blew away l
the burial service might be read over the grave i
guttering candles because the funeral party had be
the moors. Sprawling over the hills and taking in
farms, Atkinson knew his wild and remote paris
where customs that had vanished elsewhere wer
He did not believe the stories himself and wonder
the practices he encountered, but he treated tho
who held onto these things with sympathy. In the v
stone-made, book-filled, sitting between Danby a
– he wrote them down, describing a way of life z
through with things that were probably ancient. H
a landscape that still had numinous places that son
feared – crossroads where suicides were buried, barı
bones of the ancient dead, tracks, field boundar
places attached in some way to tales of an untimely
still talked of the newly dead appearing as 'fetcl
relatives to tell of their passing. Some told tales
Ratchets, phantom dogs baying in the night and g

But nineteenth-century England was full of more commonplace customs that hinted failure to do right by the dead might be a mistake. When someone died certain things should be done. Windows were opened to let the soul loose. Clocks were stopped. Mirrors were covered or turned to the wall.[48] Once the body was 'chested' a plate of salt might be laid on the coffin lid.[49] The front door of the house where the dead person lived might be kept open for the duration of the funeral and then closed when the mourners returned.[50] The living must do the right things, 'see off' the dead in the right way, and if they did not then there might be peril. The soul might be glimpsed in a mirror. Spirits, kept from the corpse by salt, might trouble it or else it might swell ominously inside the coffin. The signs of life – ticking clocks and hearthside warmth – must be put into suspension lest they draw the dead back to the world. They must, like the soul poised on the edge of Whinny Moor, go out into the cold and onward on their way.[51]

And yet this panoply of nineteenth-century custom was no strange Catholic survival: Protestant England had long since gone its own way. When Irishmen came to Slaithwaite in West Yorkshire in the 1860s to find work during the harvest, they brought their Catholicism with them. When one of their number died, they watched and waked the corpse with songs and prayers and candles burning, a simulacrum, almost, of the medieval rites, as they waited for the Huddersfield priest to come down and perform the funeral. The Protestant natives of the village looked on at it all in bewilderment. They were gazing into another world, the world of their ancestors, but it was long forgotten.[52] For if not completely erased, most of the medieval world was long gone. Even the things that seemed to survive were transformed, a work of transformation in which the long and slow processes of Reformation were deeply implicated.

Travelling over the moors to Whitby on the coast on 2 November in the early nineteenth century, the visitor would be able to acquire special little cakes at the bakers. These were soulmas loaves, baked for the season. This bit of confectionary had a long history. For 2 November was All Souls' Day, a feast established in the Middle Ages. The cakes, given in charity, solicited prayers for needy souls in purgatory. Old already in the fifteenth century, when 'good people would on All Halloween Day bake bread and deal it for Christian souls', the custom ran like a thread down the centuries to the edge of the modern age.[53] In many parts of England children, sometimes adults, still went souling in the nineteenth century. Moving from house to house, they sought the special cakes or apples or beer and sang at the door a song full of promises in return. Songs, recipes and customs had gone different ways in different places; even the cakes had different names. There were soul cakes, soul mass cakes, 'soamas' cakes or loaves, and psalm cakes, many names shedding all connotations of helping the dead. Occasionally the songs had echoes of older ideas. St Peter or the Virgin Mary might appear; a cake might be given 'for a soul's sake'. But more often than not the soulers' song promised things like prosperity, rich crops or simple good luck in the coming year. Souling had once been about the dead but the Victorian cakes no longer nourished their needy souls. Souling was now about the living; it was a means for the poor to claim charity, a chance for children to enjoy fruit, festivity and cake.[54]

Medieval eyes might also have seen something familiar in Victorian funeral processions as they wound along the church ways. Before the Reformation these would have stopped from time to time, often at wayside crosses, where prayers would be offered for the soul of the deceased. In Atkinson's day, the bearers still needed to rest but now there were no prayers for the dead. There were only hymns and psalms as they tried to catch their breath. Reverend Atkinson was wary even of these. A good son of the Protestant Church, he made sure to put a stop to any singing at the church gate.

When the dead were buried, they were still often remembered in formal ways. In many parts in the nineteenth century their names were called to mind a month or a year after their funeral, a little as they might have been in the Middle Ages.[55] In the southwest the annual commemoration, folded into a Sunday service, was the 'deathzear'. In parts of the north it was 'minnyng' day. Some still spoke of 'minds', on the month's anniversary or the year-day of the funeral, occasions which sound a little like the 'minds' of the Middle Ages. But they were long since shorn of the requiem masses, prayers and charity that were the heart of the old rite; in the nineteenth century there might be a reprise of the funeral hymns or a special sermon. Anniversary days were about keeping the name of a loved one alive in this world; there was no call to pray for the soul in the next. Often, even when there was an appearance of continuity, the Reformation had brought revolution to the realm of the dead.

5

SURE AND CERTAIN HOPE

Forgetting the Dead?

On 28 June 1651 Ralph Josselin, minister of the little town of Earls
Colne in Essex, climbed into the pulpit. His sermons were seldom
brief – once he began at eleven o'clock in the morning and only
stopped when the light faded, and that when suffering from a
heavy cold.[1] Now hale and hearty, he would certainly not skimp
on this of all days. For it saw the burial of one his most august
parishioners, Mrs Smythee Harlakenden. It fell to Ralph to preach
her funeral sermon. He was forty-four years old and had been
minister of Earls Colne since 1641.[2] It was a quietly prosperous
place, fringed by fields yielding grain, fruit, hops and vegetables.
Ralph himself was of yeoman stock, a man of business from a
farming family as well as a man of the Church, with stakes still
in agriculture and shipping. Piety abutted enterprise unproblem-
atically in seventeenth-century sensibility and there was no tension
between these interests and his religious calling. His marriage to
Jane and his growing family, while it set him apart from the priests
of old, was also no impediment to his vocation, as to be married
was the natural lot of a minister in the wake of the Reformation.
In the delicate local hierarchy he was almost the equal of the
wealthier sort of the parish and he was friends too with the
Harlakendens. As lords of the manor they outstripped him in rank
but they shared his vision of Protestant religion and this drew
them together. For this was a place of reformed faith in which

the things of the Middle Ages had been left far behind. Indeed, with Ralph as minister, a Protestant of the hotter kind, reformation had been carried further forward than in some parts. Ralph was, for want of a better label, a Puritan, although not a radical one. He had gladly purged the last traces of art and stained glass from the church when Parliament required it and had set Bible reading and preaching firmly at the heart of worship. Communion, for him, was simply a meal commemorating Christ's sacrifice rather than a mystical renewal of it. The pulpit, not the communion table, dominated amidst the whitewashed walls and bleached light of his church. The 'godly' of the town met to read and to pray and strengthen their faith among those whose religion was lukewarm and grumbled at restrictions imposed by Josselin, his bids to curtail sport on the Sabbath and festivity at Christmas.[3]

Smythee Harlakenden, whose body lay encoffined beneath the pulpit, had lived at Colne Priory, once a Benedictine monastery, which had long since gone the way of the church art and glass. Dissolved at the behest of Henry VIII, it had been turned into a comfortable home by her ancestors who had bought up the buildings and land. She had long been one of the parish's inner circle and Ralph's knowledge that she had shone with godliness allowed him to speak now with confidence of her salvation. Unusually, what he said from the pulpit is known. For where the words of most of his thousands of sermons floated away on the air and faded in the memories of the congregation, this one was printed in 1652 and so preserved. A small pamphlet, it runs nonetheless to some forty-three pages.

Launching into his sermon, Ralph explained to the bereaved family arrayed before him in the pews how to go about making sense of death. Mrs Harlakenden had, he said, been 'gathered to Jesus'. 'Ripened in faith by many afflictions', she was 'like a rick of corn brought in'. This was the language of harvest-home; rooted in the Bible it still resonated with farming people. Smythee Harlakenden had gone to God 'in her due season', living a long life and a good one, and so made ready for heaven. Then he spoke more generally about the dead. All deaths meant loss and pain.

The house was empty. The wife who once came to the door when her husband came home might never come again. The child in whose hugs a mother or father delighted might never be held again. But the pain must be borne because to fail to bear it was to be selfish: 'Did God not make thy wife and thy daughter whom thou bemoanest more for himself than for thee?'[4] The dead were surely happier there than they had been here, in this shadow world. The bereaved must grasp this, he said, and must get 'above' grief by recalling that the dead had exchanged earthly cottages for heavenly mansions, the company of kin for the friendship of Jesus, ordinary human loves for the love of their heavenly Father. And, horrible but true, the bereaved would struggle after a time to remember the voice, even the face, of the one they had lost. Soon 'we scarce retain their image in our mind' as a terrible amnesia set in. But how, Josselin intimated, could it be otherwise when the frailty of the human mind meant that 'we forget our own face even before the glass is set aside'?[5] To forget was natural in this broken world and it was almost as if God had ordained it. For the dead were happy and the living must gather their lives and move on in their own journey Godward. They must not stew in self-pity, torment themselves by dwelling overmuch on frail remembrances or grieve too much. To sink deep in grief was, as it had been in the Middle Ages, to distrust the providence of God; he in his justice and mercy chose the time when each human being would die and those left behind must acquiesce before his election. God, he said, 'would have us forget the dead'. Confident that loved ones were summoned to life everlasting, the tears of the bereaved must become 'not brinish but pleasant'.

Not all of the comforts Ralph Josselin offered the Harlakendens were quite as cold as these. He imagined, too, the new life that the dead would enjoy. Turning to his congregation, 'your Wives, your Husbands, your Sons and Daughters', he explained, 'are but stepped aside into their retiring rooms, their cool summer parlours, the shady cool grove of the grave to take a little rest by sleep'.[6] The dead had entered another room. For the time being, the living must let go of them but they would come again, waking in heaven, resurrected to eternal life. Then he looked again to Mr Harlakenden. Time would blunt the raw edge of grief; memories of Smythee would one day bring comfort rather than anguish. 'This,' he added, 'I have found and find an experienced truth, and not a notion.'

Ralph and Jane Josselin had lived in an age of trauma and he was qualified to speak about death. He had watched a civil war break out between Charles I and Parliament. It was a bitter, bloody war, which split neighbourhoods and families and was stoked not only by the king's exercise of arbitrary power and different notions of monarchy but also by religious controversy, the unfinished business of reformation. Things that seem like a small detail to the modern eye assumed political and even cosmic significance. Some wanted to turn back the clock, restoring altars and getting rid of communion tables; some edged again towards praying for the dead. Others, Puritans, wanted less ritual not more; some even thought of burying the dead without need of a minister and a few were ready to have their bones laid in the fields.

Ralph had seen the Civil War out, hearing stories of the king gone to the block and watching Oliver Cromwell rise to become surrogate ruler in his place. Unusually, what Ralph thought of all this can be recounted because he kept a diary, running to over six hundred pages in a modern edition, which tells more, much more, about his inner life than can ever be known about most people of his day. For all the political commotion around him, what shines out from the diary is that family and parish, rather than the doings of kings, parliamentarians and generals, filled his waking thoughts and troubled his dreams. He lived his life in the small worlds of home and parish. When the Civil War broke out in 1642, perhaps unsurprisingly the joyous birth of his first child, Mary, weighed far more with him than the fighting. But even when, some years later, Archbishop Laud – a man whose religious policies he hated – was executed, Ralph passed over it quickly. The 'grand enemy of the power of godliness' was dead and his head graced a spike on Tower Hill but Ralph spent more ink on the weather at Earls Colne. For these were days of 'the greatest snow in my memory and all ways made impassable . . . [and] at night it frize bitterly'.[7] His life comes alive in the close observation of daily experience. The weather obsessed him – balmy summers, bitter winters, miry roads; the days when the pump and even his inkwell froze solid. He worried neurotically about his health – his rheumy eyes, streams of colds and then aching bones as he aged. He bought land, ploughed fields, planted apple and pear trees, took pleasure in his 'apricocke' bush set against a garden wall.[8] He described the turning seasons, bursting buds, ripening fruits; the late summer delight of a 'full, ripe-blown, damask rose'. He mentioned witchcraft in passing and as naturally as the harvest and wondered what it might mean when his wife came to him saying that she had seen a phantom army marching across the sky. He worried when barns caught fire one night, filling the darkness with an orange candescence, and trembled when a local man, Guy Penhacke, was thrown into a pond by 'one in the shape of a bull', which he mused might, perhaps, be the devil himself.[9] In the decade after 1650 so disordered did the world around him seem to be, Ralph even began to work out the timing of the apocalypse, thinking in 1650 that it might come in between three and five years.[10] The thought did not trouble him. His heart was, he said, quite settled.

Death intruded into Ralph's life with a frequency that was not shocking at the time; he was sensitised to the fragility of existence thanks to the vagaries of disease, the mortal danger to his wife every time she fell pregnant and terrifying child mortality. Life was 'a bubble', beautiful and yet apt at any moment to burst.[11] But when death came, however terrible or painful, it was, as he had told the Harlakendens, always for a reason. In season or out of season, God gathered people in for his own unsearchable ends. The whole of creation testified to this truth of divine ordination. For all things – the everyday and the extraordinary, the national and the parochial – were held together in Ralph Josselin's head by one idea: that nothing happened without a purpose. Defeats in battle, deaths of kings, fire and pestilence, mild winters, late frosts blighting the fruit trees, balmy summers, floods that threatened the harvest, armies in the skies, the devil in the next village – they all meant something. Through them God signalled his favour or anger, warned and chastised, tested the faithful and called sinners to repentance. That philosophy, which discerned God's provident hand everywhere in the textures of human experience, was Ralph's guide as he preached before the Harlakendens and it was his comfort as he faced the deaths of his own children.

On 19 May 1650 came the first signs that Ralph's daughter Mary and his little son Ralph were ill. In the diary he traced the course of their illnesses, asking God to reveal why he 'contended' with him so by making his children sick. Mary slowly deteriorated over the following days, falling into deep sweats and talking 'idly' in her sleep. On 22 May, for all his inclination to put his trust in providence, he went up to the priory nonetheless and fetched medicine. Then he immersed himself in prayer and meditation on the psalms and thought she was perhaps a little better. Terror at losing her, pleas to God for succour and affirmations of the Lord's goodness lie in even balance in the diary entries down to 26 May when Ralph finally knew that Mary was dying. He struggled then to resign himself to it, taking comfort from the knowledge that God would soon hold the child in 'his everlasting arms'. On 27 May he noted the moment: 'This day at quarter past two in the afternoon my Mary fell asleep in the Lord.' She was, he computed, only eight years and forty-five days old. Her birth had been a blessing; he 'had abundant cause to bless God for her, who was our first fruits, and those God would have offered to him'. 'God is her life', he said, and 'she shall enjoy it in heaven not here'.[12] And so he relinquished Mary to him who made her. But the giving-up was terrible. The child had been 'a bundle of myrrh, a bundle of sweetness'. She was 'a child of ten thousand, full of wisdom, woman-like gravity, knowledge, sweet expressions . . . tender-hearted and loving, an obedient child . . . [she] was to us a box of sweet ointment'.[13] The town came to the funeral. Tradition dictated that women bear the body and Mrs Margaret

Harlakenden, two other worthies of the town, Mrs Elliston and Mrs Clench, and Ralph's own sister carried her to the church. After Ralph had read the service she was taken to her burial place in a prominent spot – 'near the uppermost seats' – a measure of how much the child had meant to Ralph and Jane. He 'kissed her lips last' and committed her to the grave.

Divine providence was not yet done with Jane and Ralph Josselin. With 2 June there dawned another day of tragedy. Mrs Mary Church, an old friend, had been ill for some days. Early in the morning she finally slipped away. The loss was the less sharp as the death was a good one. She was a woman full of years. Her goodliness marked her out as one of the godly, and free from pain, pure of sin, she was now in Christ's care; Ralph and Jane, as he noted, had another friend in heaven against their going thence themselves. The same could not be said of the death that came to them in the dark hours that night. Little Ralph, the Josselins' infant son, who had been sickly for months, finally succumbed to his illness a little before midnight. His father tried to wring from the death some drop of comfort. The little boy's life had been one of 'sorrow and trouble' because he lacked a strong constitution. Now the tribulation was over and his broken body would rest in Christ's arms until wakened to a new and better life. But Jane was near despair. She had lost two children in the space of days and was so ill Ralph feared that she too would die of grief. He tried to master himself, to resign himself to the loss, to think of Mary in heaven folded in the arms of the Lord who had made her. He 'eyed her glory and gain and set that against her life and my loss'. Seeing the balance was much in the little girl's favour, the Lord gave him strength 'and quietness of heart to submit to him'.[14]

By the end of the year, something of the tranquillity he had striven for had come to him. He could write of his dead children that 'they were not mine but the Lord's'. Time was transforming grief. The sharpest memories lost their edge and the dead slipped more frequently out of his thoughts. Recollection of the voice disappeared, even a clear memory of the face was lost. In a world with no photographs, in which there were only a few portraits and these for the rich, it was hard to remember the dead. Forgetting was a natural, sometimes painful part of grief. And Ralph thought it proper and pious, too. It was part of the business of entrusting them to God. This was what Ralph had told the living at Smythee Harlakenden's funeral and this was what he tried to do. Rarely mentioned in subsequent pages of the diary, Mary and Ralph joined the ranks of the dead family about whom he also seldom wrote. There were no hints in his writing of grave-visiting, no remembered anniversaries. He recalled once, briefly, that his mother and sisters lay in Stortford churchyard on a visit to the town but otherwise said little of his dead kin. All of this was of a piece with the hotter Protestantism Ralph espoused, which had little time for monuments and treated the body, once dead, as a thing deserving only respectful burial. Deeper reverencing smacked of the magic that reform had sought to banish.

All this might make him seem hard and cold and his portrait does not help his case. He has collar-length hair, a priest's bands, and wears a black gown. He is the very image of a Puritan minister. The gaze is firm; the expression stern. There are hints of a double chin, more than a suspicion of creeping middle age suggesting this might be how he looked when he preached the Harlakenden sermon. But behind the public face was a more complex figure, betrayed in a diary that speaks, sometimes reticently, of pain, anguish and struggle, of a man using his faith to work out his grief and navigate tragedy.[15] However composed he seemed, fear of more calamity lingered. When yet another of his children fell sick 'as if he would have died', Ralph 'cried to my God with tears for him'.[16] And, for all his efforts of pious forgetting, he did remember his children. Mary, lying close by as he preached Smythee Harlakenden's sermon, came to mind and informed an intimate moment in his address. Speaking to the dead woman's family he explained that 'I have thoughts of my sweetest Daughter',

but 'now with comfort' when once 'I had thoughts of her like
the bitterness of death'.[17]

The Everlasting Sabbath

Ralph lived long enough to see Oliver Cromwell die. His death,
in 1658, was attended by the portentous appearance of a whale in
the Thames and a great storm, which swept in from the west.
Soon the Protector's experiment in government without a king
was blown away too and Ralph watched apprehensively from rural
Essex as a new king, Charles II, returned. He observed from a
distance as London was struck first by plague in 1665 and then
burned to the ground in the Great Fire the following year.
Sometimes great matters impinged on the parish but more usually
Earls Colne was tranquil, even if its minister was troubled by the
restoration of a lukewarm kind of Protestantism that obliged him
to use a new version of the old Anglican prayer book for his
services.

In these later years Ralph worked out in the pages of his diary
something of what heaven might be like. In the Middle Ages heaven
had been figured in art as a celestial city or a luxuriant but ordered
garden.[18] Protestant iconoclasm had banished visual images but
Ralph and his fellow divines often painted similar ones in words.
He thought of heaven, as many did, as the 'everlasting sabbath'.[19]
In it there would be 'no sickness, no childhood but all perfection'.
Heaven was up far above, for 'the body goes downward and the
soul [goes] upward'. It was a place of many mansions 'shining like
oyster shells', according to one of Ralph's children who had a dream
about it.[20] Sleep, rest, glory, joy, many mansions, a shining place, a
wondrous city, a sweet and ordered garden: the images with which
preachers like Ralph conjured were those of scripture itself.
Protestant and Catholic divines quibbled on certain points about
the place. Catholics envisaged a hierarchy there: the saints would
be seated closest to Christ. For Protestants, the social structure of

heaven was flat; there were no grades of glory and everyone who was saved could be named a saint. But Catholics and Protestants did tend to agree on what heaven might be like because both drew from a common stock of biblical metaphors. They also grappled with a conundrum that was still not settled: neither were sure how much of the earthly self survived after death.[21]

Most hoped for some kind of reunion with those they had loved. In old age Ralph recalled happily a gathering of his children, now grown up: 'I saw my six children together on earth, blessed be God, and let us all be together in heaven.'[22] Ralph's more august contemporary, the politician and diplomat Bulstrode Whitelocke, confronted the question of reunion more starkly in 1654. For as Ralph was going about his business in Earls Colne, Bulstrode stood, along with his sons, on the deck of a ship that was foundering in a storm. Driven hard against the Dutch coast, Bulstrode thought the ship would surely be wrecked and so put a small gold tablet in his pocket bearing his wife's picture, an earnest that he was a gentleman and a token that might ensure a decent burial when his body was washed ashore, and then set about prayer for deliverance. Lamenting the premature deaths of his boys, but facing his own with equanimity, he comforted them with the thought that 'they should shortly meet together in heaven'.[23] His notion of heaven and meeting again were learned not only from the pulpit but at his mother's knee. Sensing that death would soon come to her, she had walked with Bulstrode when he was still a young man in 1630, visiting for a final time a spot that she held dear and consoling him that death was 'but a passage to a better life' and that one day 'they should meet again in heaven, and there partake of everlasting joys'.[24] Like Ralph, Bulstrode went on to face family tragedy and the premature deaths of children; he would look for solace to the reunion that his mother had elaborated. All these things framed his thoughts as he knelt on the deck of the stricken ship. In the event, his fears were misplaced. The boatswain had a premonition that God would save them from danger and so he did. The ship did not sink but floated free;

Bulstrode would not die for another twenty years, and not in the ocean but in his bed.

Isaac Archer grew up not far from Earls Colne, across the county boundary in Suffolk. The tribulations of his life were worse than any that engulfed Ralph and Bulstrode Whitelocke; he and his wife would watch eight of their nine children die in infancy. He listed their names at the end of a diary filled with their short lives.[25] He took comfort where he could and found it faltering, in the same place as his contemporaries. 'Oh that my confidence were more in God,' he said, worrying about his own salvation, for then, 'I may so live to meet my little babes, sent to heaven before me, in the joyful resurrection.'[26]

In his struggles to make sense of heaven, Isaac Archer, and many like him, turned to a book called *The Saints' Everlasting Rest*. Running through many editions, it was widely read in seventeenth-century England and was still reprinted and perused at the beginning of Queen Victoria's reign. It was one of the most popular evocations of what heaven might be like. It was written by Richard Baxter, the minister of Kidderminster and a contemporary of Ralph, Bulstrode and Isaac. A scholar, Puritan, prolific writer and hypochondriac, Baxter wrote the book while he thought, wrongly, that he was dying after catching a chill in the February snows of 1647. He knew that describing heaven, even if observing it from the higher vantage point of the deathbed, was an impossible task. An earthbound man attempting to tell of heaven's joys was like a blind man trying to make sense of the sun and its light but this did not stop him trying, exhaustively, in a book of many hundreds of pages.

In it he reached for all the commonplaces of scripture to capture the idea of rest and glory that were heaven's main motifs. Then he moved on to more complicated questions of the senses and which of them might be retained in heaven. Sight, he thought, would certainly be needed. The Bible said so. Job had meditated, 'I shall see him with these eyes.'[27] Speech would be needed too since the mouths of the saints 'shall be filled with his praise'. Taste, however, might be a casualty of transfiguration. There would be no need of eating and heaven would be no place for gluttons, for even in the unlikely event that a glutton was saved, a celestial existence would be a trial since heaven was not 'a place of good fellowship, of wine and wantonness'. Likewise, there would be no sex and no marriage. The saved would not know each other as husbands and wives and lovers but only as saints; the grubbier pleasures of the sublunary world would be sloughed off with the earthly body.[28] Instead there would be 'knowledge of God and His Christ, of a delightful complacency in that mutual love, an everlasting rejoicing in the fruition of our God, a perpetual singing of his praises'. He would no longer be seen as if through a glass darkly but face to face. This was 'a heaven for a saint, a spiritual rest suitable to a spiritual nature'.[29] Memories of earthly life would follow the saved to heaven but all terrestrial 'doubts and fears are but terrible dreams which . . . do all vanish as they awake in joyful glory'.[30] With a head full of sights he never again wanted to see – of fields of the slain and churches full of mourning blacks for men who had died too young in the Civil Wars – Baxter's heaven was, above all, a place where the turbulent motion of a world torn apart would cease. It was a comforting vision for many who read the book but for some, perhaps, the straitened joys of the spirit that he promised fell short of hopes founded on a fuller reunion in the flesh.

Quite how many were to see such sights was a vexed question. Strict divines prognosticated that one in a thousand, one in ten thousand or even one in a million would be saved.[31] The rest would be turned over to the devil and cast into the eternal fire. Ralph Josselin made no estimates but he seems not to have been quite so gloomy. He was sure that little Ralph, his daughter Mary and his friend, Mrs Mary Church, were among those in heaven. Their fate, he reasoned, was legible in the goodness of their lives. So too Mrs Harlakenden, for 'her life and death was evidence she was a real saint'.[32] Protestants could not earn a passage to heaven through action; they were chosen, elected, by God to eternal life. But that election could be visible in the godliness of a person's life and it could be announced by the drama of a 'conversion' experience, a dramatic illumination in which the chance of salvation was grasped. It followed, of course, that if signs of election could be inscribed on the lives of the saved, the destiny of lost souls might be marked on their lives too. Ralph was coyer in the diary on this point, as unwilling to admit them to its pages as God would be to let them into his kingdom. Once he ministered at the deathbed of a man of mean temper, unconfident that he had any chance of salvation. There were parishioners who came infrequently to church, some who hardly came at all. He saw packed pews only once, and that was in a dream.[33] In the waking world, congregations were sometimes thin. Some absentees quibbled with his theology. Others lacked the stamina for his sermons. Those who did not frequent Ralph's church separated themselves from the godly. The optimism in Mrs Harlakenden's funeral sermon was not for them and Ralph said so. His bright account of heaven was 'no map of their condition'.[34]

How troubled the 'ungodly' were by their ungodliness is hard to tell. But there were enough complacent people about in seventeenth-century England for other churchmen to criticise a cheery hope-for-the-best approach to salvation. A divine called Arthur Dent painted the sorts of people who did not bother over much with church services. They thought it enough to observe the commandments, say prayers, 'say nobody no harm nor do anybody harm' and 'have a good faith God-ward'. They would be saved 'without all this running to sermons and prattling of the Scriptures'.[35] For if sabbath-breakers and swearers were damned, who could be saved? Behind this cartoon-like image were real people, or kinds of people, who needed to be warned that God was not 'all mercy'.[36] Another divine, Robert Bolton, also thought that too many people subscribed to a 'country divinity' full of lazy assumptions about future joy. It was, he suggested, 'as if one should busy himself much and boast what he will do in New England when he comes thither and yet . . . he hath neither ship, nor money, nor means, nor knowledge of the way, nor provision

for his comfortable planting there'. But wills and epitaphs told a
different tale – a tale of men and women commending their souls
into God's hands and confident in their hope of heaven.[37] So too
does the diary of Samuel Pepys. When Tom, the brother of
Samuel, lay dying in March 1664 and was asked 'whither he thought
he should go?' he knew there were 'but two ways'. He was not
sure which would be his but he thought his modest piety might
be enough to save him, for 'I hope I have not been undutiful and
unthankful in my life but hope I shall go that way'.[38] Samuel could
not bear to watch Tom die but once he was dead, he stayed with
his brother as he grew cold; he went home and went up to bed
and lying 'close by my wife, being full of disorder and grief for
my brother'.

There was comfort for Pepys too in the Prayer Book. Put in
place by Elizabeth, its service for the burial of the dead saw the
bodies of the dead committed to the earth 'in sure and certain
hope of resurrection to eternal life'. The words had stuck in the
throats of some ministers and a number of Puritan stripe had
even refused to read the service over obviously unregenerate
parishioners. The book was swept away during the years after the
Civil War but it was restored again during the reign of King
Charles II. Even then, anger at the promiscuousness of its promise
of eternal life obliged the editors to amend the new version.[39] The
change was subtle. The dead were committed to await sure and
certain hope of *the* resurrection to eternal life; the event was
assured but not the individual's fate. The nuance was likely lost
on many and it was open to Samuel Pepys to place a positive
construction on the words as he stood at his brother's grave. In
that way, the Prayer Book's words, uttered at countless gravesides
down the decades, gave succour to the cheerful hope of heaven
that Arthur Dent and his fellow divines condemned as complacent.

Ralph Josselin was made of different stuff to Samuel and Tom
Pepys, of very different stuff to those who subscribed to 'country
divinity', and he faced death differently. As he aged, his diary

entries grew more sparse. His handwriting turned spidery. At sixty he 'grew an old man' and began to look beyond the span of his own life. His surviving children, in whom he and Jane had invested so much love and – he was not shy of saying it – money, now cheered the couple 'in their grey hairs'. They promised a future for the family in a condition of modest prosperity won by Ralph's business enterprises.[40] But of his own fate in eternity he was less sure. Through his life, fear of death had welled up from time to time. It sometimes struck as he tended a deathbed or as he presided over a funeral; on other occasions there was no obvious cause. When it struck, he begged the Lord to help him beat it down. It came back to him, again, more naturally, in old age. Judgement, not annihilation, was the cause of his anxiety; there is no trace in the diary that he ever doubted the existence of a world beyond the grave. But while he was confident that Smythee Harlakenden was one of the chosen and that his children were in heaven, he wondered about himself. Forever examining his soul's condition, reading his life like the book he had made of it, he searched for signs of his own election. In the darker moments he saw only imperfection, faithlessness and sin. In the hard world he had helped to make, in which Protestant theology taught that souls were bound either for heaven or for hell at the moment of death, and most for the latter place, he could never be so sure of his own fate. This was a dark undertone of zeal. A deep, old and durable fear, haunted the austere minister gazing out from his portrait until the very end of his days.

Strange Resurrection

In the Dulwich Picture Gallery hangs a painting of a beautiful young woman who appears to be sound asleep in bed. She lies, propped up on pillows, her head resting on her hand. She wears pearls round her neck and pearl earrings. The image is not what it seems. When the artist set brush to canvas, he knew that his subject would never wake: he had been commissioned to paint a mortuary portrait. A fallen rose, its pink petals scattered across the silk sheets and rich, gold-embroidered blue coverlet, is a sign that this is a picture of death not sleep. The woman in the painting is Venetia, the wife of Sir Kenelm Digby. She had died suddenly, in the prime of life.[41] What happened after her death reveals that there were other ways to grieve and other ways to think about the dead in Ralph Josselin's England.

Sir Kenelm and Venetia had married covertly in 1624 or 1625, in defiance of Kenelm's mother. The Digbys had almost come to grief when his father, Sir Everard, took part in the Gunpowder Plot against King James. Everard had gone to the block but Kenelm came into his own and redeemed the family, rising high in the court of Charles I. An adventurer, amateur scientist, ultimately a councillor of the fledgling Royal Society, he was so handsome, graceful, noble and clever that 'had he dropped out of the clouds in any part of the world he would have made himself respected'. Venetia was a rare beauty, or at least this was the quality the men who wrote about her isolated. John Aubrey waxed lyrical about her lovely face, her delicate dark brown hair, good skin and 'dark-brown eyebrows about which much sweetness as also in the opening of her eyelids'. Her cheeks, he said, had a colour 'just that of a damask rose, which is neither too hot nor too pale'.[42] When the two married they became the starry couple of their age.

On the night of 30 April 1633 Venetia went to bed in the house that she shared with Kenelm at Charterhouse Yard in London. Although nothing had been amiss during the day, in the small hours of the night something happened. In the morning Venetia could not be roused; she had died in her sleep. Kenelm was fetched. Tears, panic and gossip ensued. Talk of poisoning circulated at court; some fingers even pointed at her husband, claiming he had made Venetia drink 'viper wine' in a bid to preserve her beauty. Charles I ordered an autopsy. It found horrible decay of the brain but no indications of foul play: Venetia had died naturally but young, a curse, it seemed, on the women of the family since her mother had died prematurely too. The gossips assimilated these details. Venetia had, they said, known of her likely fate. There had been premonitions of death and she had even donned a hair shirt to mortify the flesh and make ready. Whatever the truth, the expected exequies followed their course. Night burial was the aristocratic fashion and so, with mourning blacks and a procession by torchlight, Venetia's body was carried to Christchurch Newgate. The great beauty was laid in the grave; in time, Kenelm raised up a tomb of black marble and placed a bust of Venetia upon it.

Kenelm followed the custom, having casts made of Venetia's hands and face before she was buried: the aristocracy of Stuart England were not afraid to look on death and he was no exception. His decision to have a portrait of the dead Venetia painted was more unusual.[43] He knew that no painter could ever capture her beauty – 'she lay dead as she was alive, like an Angel' – but he had commissioned the best there was, asking Van Dyck to aim at the impossible. When the painting was done Kenelm retreated with it for company to Gresham College in London. Dressing in 'a long mourning cloak' and a high-crowned black hat and leaving his beard uncut he turned himself into a hermit.[44] He spent his time in stricken contemplation, penning letters about his desolation and Venetia's virtues, unable to accept the idea that her death was God's will.[45] All his happiness, 'as great as any man ever had', had vanished 'like a shadow that leaveth no sign behind it'. He tried immersing himself in books but there was 'no balsamic or healing quality' in philosophy or divinity and even time did not seem to 'abate the edge' of grief. It bit ever deeper and she began to haunt him. 'I can sometimes fancy to myself', he wrote, 'particular passages between my wife and me so strongly that me thinks they are even present with me; I see her and I talk with her.' The painting became a sinister object.[46] In its presence there could be no forgetting. The image sharpened horrible presentiments of her body mouldering in the ground and it recalled the moment when Kenelm had first seen Venetia dead, thinking she might simply be asleep. At night, he noted, when he went to his chamber, he set the painting close by the bed, watching it by candlelight, and for a moment she was with him, for 'lying in such a position as requireth neither speech nor motion, it had the advantage to deceive one in judging whither it were a picture or no'. Then he looked again at the image. The shadows moved and the illusion failed; the terrible moments after her body's discovery flooded back and he saw her once again 'dead indeed'.[47]

Kenelm's mother, alarmed by her son's behaviour, warned him delicately that people must never set their hearts 'over much upon any fading object'.[48] His was the kind of grief that worried clergymen.[49] Ralph Josselin, some years later, would warn that those who mourned too deeply should wet their eyes by all means but must not drown in weeping.[50] This suggested distrust of God, doubt about the future life; it was to grieve almost like the heathen for whom there was no hope.[51] That criticism was close to the mark in Kenelm's case. He wondered openly in one letter, written soon after Venetia's death, whether it was wise to hang much on hopes of an other world 'where we know not in what estate we shall be'. But whatever doubts and fears plunged Kenelm into melancholy, he did not live his life as a sceptic or a heathen. Scripture suggested, and the Church taught, that a deep solace was to be found in the ambiguity of the painting – that perhaps Venetia did indeed simply sleep. For to die was to fall asleep in the Lord and the dead would waken. These beliefs offered cold comfort at first, but Kenelm warmed to them slowly. Consolation came from the idea that Venetia's spirit was already enjoying new life as 'an intellectual substance infinitely more perfect, more active, more beautiful than she was in her body'.[52] Heavenly grace and glory would perfect their human affections, 'making them permanent and eternal which upon earth were subject to distempers and change'.

In time, Kenelm's fears crystallised not so much in scepticism about a life beyond death but in apprehension that heaven might be a place of dissociated souls, rapt in pious contemplation of the Creator and with little time for each other, the very heaven that Richard Baxter imagined. He knew, as theology taught, that the vision of God in heaven would surely 'fill us over the brim' but he dismissed the idea that 'it drowneth all joys arising from other grounds'. There would still be a place for deep, companionable and perhaps passionate love in heaven.[53] He might even hold Venetia again. For although 'we part at diverse days, and by diverse ways, yet we shall all meet at one place, and at one day . . . the day of glorious Resurrection'. So preached Kenelm's near contemporary, poet and churchman John Donne.[54] The afterlife promised more than a mingling of ethers and spirits. Kenelm spent much ink in his letters on the idea of resurrection. He even calculated that there would be space for all of the resurrected dead on a renewed earth because after the Last Judgement the elect would have no need of food and so fields and orchards could be given over to dwellings. All the earth could then be a glorious city. But here there was, perhaps, niggling doubt on a crucial point. During his time at Gresham he began experiments on crayfish that he had killed. Squinting over the corpses of the little creatures, searching for some specks of life, he looked for signs that regeneration might come about through principles woven by God into the fabric of creation. The crayfish might, he hoped, quite naturally, begin to come back to life. They remained quite dead. But Kenelm still wanted an explanation of resurrection that did not require a special intervention by the Creator. 'I cannot place,' he admitted, 'the resurrection of our bodies among miracles but do reckon it the last great work and period of nature.'[55] The scientist in him wanted to prove a thing that Donne knew through faith alone.

Kenelm was an unusual man shaped by many contradictions. He loved Venetia deeply, perhaps more deeply when she was dead than when she had been alive. For all the depth of that love, he knew that he had not always been faithful to her. After she died he said that he would never love again, but he did, although he never remarried. The intensity of these emotions made him place uncommon stress on the idea of full and fleshly union in the afterlife and his eagerness for that consolation made him fearful that it might be illusory. He was also caught in the contradictions of his age. The son of a Catholic conspirator who would have blown the Anglican England of James I sky high in the 1605 Powder

Plot, he had risen in court as a loyal servant of the new king, Charles. He was a good Anglican by his own affirmation but he flirted with his father's Catholicism, even quietly having prayers said for Venetia's soul. He moved in an elite world in which there was a degree of religious choice but he struggled to make sense of death amidst these differing narratives, especially when assailed by doubts born of experience and bleak intuitions about the human condition. Nonetheless, when death came for Kenelm in 1665, thirty-two long years after it had come for Venetia, he was clear about where he must go. He directed that his body be laid 'near unto hers as may be . . . who was my greatest worldly blessing while she lived'.[56] He had struggled with the idea of resurrection but now his dust would mingle with hers; he would be with her again to sleep and to wait. That is not quite the end of their story or their tragedy; their rest was not long undisturbed. In 1666 the city church in which Kenelm and Venetia lay and the elaborate tomb he had commissioned were reduced to ashes by the Great Fire. A few years later, in 1675 or 1676, John Aubrey remembered stumbling across a remnant of their monument in Newgate Street. 'I saw Dame Venetia's bust', he said, 'standing at a stall in the Golden Cross.' The fire had burned away the gilding. He looked on it for a while and remembered her, then went on his way and never saw it again. He heard that the shopmen had melted down the cast of Venetia for money. These people, he observed, 'would be quite forgotten did not such idle fellows as me put them down'.[57]

Towards Heaven's Plains

Not so very far from the Dulwich Picture Gallery, in the heart of London rather than its suburbs, a little to the north of the City and a short walk from Old Street tube station, are Bunhill Fields, a small oasis of trees and ancient stones surrounded by glass and concrete towers, the corporate and commercial sprawl of the capital. An inscription at the gate tells visitors that they are entering a churchyard 'inclosed with a brick wall at the sole charges of the City of London, in the mayoralty of Sir John Lawrence, Knt., Anno Domini 1665' and that the gates were put up during the term of office of his successor, Thomas Bloudworth, in 1666. In these years of pestilence and fire, it was the plague outbreak of 1665 that led to the churchyard being laid out. Fearful that there would be no space to bury the dead as disease raged, Bunhill Fields were commissioned as a cemetery, which then lay near the edge of the metropolis. That is not quite the beginning of Bunhill's mortuary connection. This place had earlier been a dumping ground for remains of the dead when the pardon churchyard of St Paul's was pulled down during the Reformation and its charnel house was cleared out. It was, then, a dubious place of sepulture and it was never consecrated. But that, oddly, was the very thing that made it attractive to growing numbers in the wake of its enclosure.

England had undergone an inner transformation in the turbulent middle decades of the seventeenth century. Censorship of religious writing had crumbled during the Civil War and unorthodox religious ideas had run riot in print. New cults had sprung up; some violent, radical and short-lived, others more moderate and enduring. When Charles II came to the throne in 1660, the genii could not be got back into the bottle. During the war years and in the decades beyond, there steadily began to emerge a varied religious landscape of modernity, populated not only by Protestants and Catholics but also by Quakers and Baptists – and eventually Methodists too in the later eighteenth century – as well as many smaller and often stranger sects.[58] These were all Dissenters, men and women who would not 'conform' to the demands of ritual and belief made by the Church of England. They worshipped separately in their own ways. They opted out in life, and also, often, in death. These men and women became the clientele of Bunhill Fields long after the plague burials were done. By the time the cemetery was closed by the Victorians in the 1850s, well over a hundred thousand people were thought to have been laid to rest there, among them the writer of *Pilgrim's*

Progress, John Bunyan; Daniel Defoe; Richard Cromwell, son of Oliver; and the poet and maker of apocalyptic art, William Blake. But of the masses, only a tiny proportion have known graves.

Somewhere among the anonymous dead is a man called Thomas Rowe. Almost forgotten by history, he was a West Countryman born in 1687, the son of a Nonconformist minister. He had moved to London when he married an older woman, the writer Elizabeth Singer. Born in 1674, she was also from dissenting stock – her father had even gone to prison during the reign of Charles II for his unorthodox religious convictions – but she was to emerge as an author of modest fame. Elizabeth and Thomas lived in Hampstead. The marriage was happy but it was brief, cut short after just five years by Thomas's untimely death from consumption on 13 May 1715. He was only twenty-eight years old. Her head full of remembrances of her pale, gasping lover on his deathbed, Elizabeth withdrew from society, going back whence she came to Frome in Somerset.[59] Thoughts of her London life were infinitely painful. 'I look back', she said in a letter, 'and recall nothing but tormenting scenes of pleasures that have taken their everlasting flight', while looking forward, 'every prospect is wild and gloomy'. In Frome, she began to write in earnest to exorcise the grief, imagining Thomas's spirit wandering in blessed vales and verdant groves, which she came to think might characterise the world beyond the grave. She ventriloquised his final thoughts and words in a poem. He bid her 'haste to meet on the happy plains, where mighty love in endless triumph reigns'. That idea, of charmed vales and groves, of reunion again in heaven, formed a clue that drew her out of grief and led her to write a book.

In *Friendship in Death* she imagined a collection of the correspondence that the dead might have sent to the living if only a celestial postal service permitted interchange between heaven and earth. Death, in this vision, was conceived in all the traditional ways. It was a release from the mortal prison, a waking from the dream of life, a way to a better place. But, above all, it was a journey. If for Ralph Josselin the dead were in another room, for

Elizabeth Rowe they had migrated to another country. Burgeoning trade and global empire – a world filling with English travellers – made new sense of the ancient figuring of death as a passage. Just as some plied the seas to and fro on mundane business, so others, whose time was up, were called to navigate 'the trackless ether'. One of her imaginary correspondents informed his loved ones in his letter that instead of arriving on the coast of India, as planned, he was safely landed on the celestial shores. The writer, a sailor, had drowned at sea.[60] At times, Elizabeth longed to take ship too; she feared the voyage but longed for her promised land. 'I could wish myself got safe beyond the thick darkness,' she told her friend Lady Hertford, for, 'a thousand fantastic horrors guard the gloomy passage, and yet 'tis inevitable and must be passed'.[61] Released by the journey from the 'tempestuous regions' of this world, she would alight among 'soft and peaceful habitations' and the 'summits of everlasting hills'.[62]

Elizabeth Rowe's heaven was formed of old images too. It was almost beyond words. But not quite. 'How shall I describe', she wondered, 'this fair, this fragrant, this enchanting land of love? The delectable vales, and flowing lawns, the myrtle shades and rosy bowers, the bright cascades and crystal rivulets rolling over orient pearls and sands of gold . . . the broad transparent lakes.' The 'cold regions' of the material world offered foretastes of heaven's happiness in the virtues of living men and women but these sparks of goodness quickened into flame in heaven, burning with eternal splendour.

Many sublunary things lost their importance in the world above and beyond. Elizabeth imagined how the only child of a landed family was able to reassure his grief-stricken mother, telling her that now he was lodged with 'thousands of happy spirits of my own order'. Her grief was misplaced for her child was in 'a place of tranquillity and joy' and the family's distress that there was no heir was of no account. Gently reproving, he reminded them that to build up an earthly estate was to build in straw; in heaven, estates were built in gold. She pictured another soul sending news that a woman's brother was well in the afterlife: 'vital pleasure danced in his eyes, life and celestial bloom sat smiling on his face . . . a golden lute was in his hand'.[63] The elect did not spend their time there in rapt contemplation and endless worship; God was almost an absent superintendent. He had made his celestial kingdom and set things in motion but then left souls to their own devices, each to delight in the company of the others. Nor was Elizabeth Rowe's God vengeful; no harsh arithmetic shadowed her account, suggesting that few would be saved. Even imperfect believers were to be found on heaven's plains. A man with shaky faith who feared to die because this might mean 'to be insensible . . . to be no more . .'. to find his eyes closing in eternal sleep' was happily confounded. He woke from death to see heaven with immortal eyes.[64] If there were lost souls, Elizabeth Rowe was too polite to speak about them.

When *Friendship in Death* was first printed in 1728, Bunhill Fields already held the bones of many kinds of believers who had been allowed to tread their different ways to salvation. In this climate, Elizabeth Rowe was free to publish her cheerful account of heaven and a growing reading public, so long as they had modest resources, was free to buy it. Some critics were worried that she had dwelt too much on the delights of the senses in heaven, on the fleshly delight of meeting loved ones again, and that she had drawn a veil over the fate of the damned. They kept alive austere visions like those of Richard Baxter, and his *Saints' Everlasting Rest* continued to be widely read well into the nineteenth century. But Elizabeth Rowe's book found a large market too. It went through almost sixty editions in the eighteenth century alone.[65] 'Read and believe, believe and be happy' were her watchwords to readers; hers was a mission to lift sepulchral gloom and damp down the fear of hell's flames. The stories she told about the dead resonated with many who trusted in a less vengeful deity, whose epitaphs spoke hopefully about salvation and who had laid loved ones in the grave looking forward to a day when they might meet and hold them again.[66]

6

A NEW AMERICA?

In the year 1587 a Catholic priest named Thomas Pilchard, who had been evangelising for the old religion, was arrested by the Protestant authorities and committed to Dorchester gaol.[1] Sentenced at the Lent Assizes to be hanged, drawn and quartered, he suffered a messy death, 'the executioner being a cook and unskilful or careless'. As a result, Pilchard was still very much alive after the initial hanging. When the business of quartering began (with the drawing forth of the bowels), he was alert enough to hold up his innards with his own hands while 'crying out *miserere mei*' to the watching crowds. The grisly death was a token of stranger things to come, for Thomas Pilchard proved more dangerous and unpredictable in death than in life. The officers presiding at his execution said after the event 'that they were poisoned with the smell of his bowels' and soon died of the effects. A worse shock awaited the warden of the prison. In the wake of the hanging, 'going into his garden somewhat late' he saw Father Pilchard coming towards him. The ghost said that he was on his way to visit another prisoner, a fellow Catholic called Mr Jessoppe, adding ominously that 'presently I will return to you'. Mr Jessoppe duly died after the encounter with his unsolicited guest and soon after that the warden followed him to the grave. Not yet done, Pilchard troubled a pregnant gentlewoman, also a Catholic, who was held in the same gaol. She 'wakened one night suddenly in great fright . . . and affirmed that she had seen Mr Pilchard who told her she must come to him'. After this bidding the woman 'fell that night into labour and died in childbirth'.

Dorchester in 1587 was perhaps still a little too close in time and space to the Western Rebellion that had rocked Edwardine England in the middle of the century and the tale of a Catholic priest's vengeance must have been troubling for the Elizabethan authorities as they struggled to put down popery and round up Catholic agitators. Not only was it being bandied about that a felon had struck back against the forces of law and order from beyond the grave, but the very idea that the dead could return to the world of the living, even if their purposes were not so nefarious, offended against the teaching of England's Protestant Church. By the end of the Middle Ages, ghosts had become entangled in the theology of purgatory. A leading Protestant, Henry Smith, argued that Catholic priests peddled tales of 'sprites that walked in the night' to convince people that the dead needed to be ransomed out of the fire.[2] But the coming of the Reformation saw the abolition of purgatory and with it a concerted bid on the part of Protestant divines to banish ghosts too. Ghosts did not exist. People might well *think* that they saw them but in truth they were deluded by tricks of the light or vain imaginings or too much cheese giving rise to a vivid dream. Or they might indeed see a spirit but this spirit was a demon counterfeiting the appearance of a dead person. Or else – and this was a favourite explanation – hauntings were frauds. Keen to encourage the faithful to pray for the dead, Catholic priests not only peddled tales but faked apparitions. Henry More, a seventeenth-century scholar-divine, mused that the medieval clergy in seaside parishes had even been known to fix candles to the shells of crabs and set them scuttling about at night to give the appearance of unquiet souls in need of priestly prayers and masses.[3]

The reasons for abolishing ghosts were clear in the post-papistical world. The dead were sequestered from the living in heaven or in hell. Those in hell could have no help from the living for they were sundered forever from hope; those in heaven needed nothing of them for they were already in bliss. Naturally, God, if he chose, could cause the dead to walk. Having so ordered the world, the Protestant point was that he had no reason to permit it.[4] 'The gospel', they said, 'hath chased away walking spirits.' But ghosts were not to be driven so easily from the face of the earth. Catholicism fell, the priests disappeared and purgatory faded from memory, but a century after the Reformation, spirits were again the object of learned debate.[5]

Undeceiving the Half-Witted World

Sixty miles further inland from Dorchester and a little to the east is the Wiltshire town of Tidworth. It is a large town now, much altered in the nineteenth century when military garrisons were positioned there and augmented since with many housing estates, which have helped merge once discrete hamlets and villages into a single settlement. In the seventeenth century, when Charles II sat on the throne, much more of this was open country and Tidworth, or Tedworth as it was more usually known, was an obscure spot. Then events which played out there in the early 1660s, probably in a house near the church or Zouch Manor, drew the gaze of many, the king included, to the town. The story began in autumn 1662 with events that were commonplace enough.[6] A man named William Drury, an itinerant musician, was apprehended by a constable in the village of Ludgershall. Drury said he was a soldier, a drummer, in Colonel Aycliffe's employ and presented papers in the colonel's hand to the constable in a bid to claim money. Suspicious about the document's authenticity, the constable alerted Mr John Mompesson, a local gentleman and Justice of the Peace, who lived in Tedworth. Mr Mompesson had William Drury fetched out of the local alehouse so that he might see the papers for himself and, knowing Colonel Aycliffe's handwriting, saw at once that the paper was forged. He had Drury taken into custody and an item of his property, a prized drum, was confiscated. If the colonel vouched for him, said Mompesson, he should have his drum. The constables did not think it worth holding Drury for long but, despite his pleas that he might have it back, the drum was kept in custody. Taken to the house where Mr Mompesson lived with his wife, three children and elderly mother, it was lodged, securely Mompesson must have thought, in his mother's room and there it rested, his children playing with it from time to time.

Then strange things began to happen. While Mompesson was away in London on business, such a noise was got up around the house during the hours of darkness that his wife was convinced that burglars had been trying to break in. Three nights after Mompesson's return, he heard the noises for himself and, taking his pistols, blundered downstairs to investigate. There was no one there. It became plain that human beings were not necessarily the cause of the disturbances. For a month they persisted but no one was detected and no explanation could be found. Then the sounds invaded the house itself, emanating especially from the room where the drum was kept. Bumpings and bangings, scratchings and a noise resembling a panting dog were heard. Household objects flew through the air. Beds floated. The smell of sulphur filled rooms. Candles went out. Lights appeared. Some burned blue, the colour flames were thought to turn in the presence of spirits. And on clear nights, when the air was still, drumming was heard high over the house.

At an early stage, the drummer was suspected as the cause of the Mompessons' woes. But it was soon discovered that his involvement could not be straightforward. For much of the time that the house was beset he was under lock and key in Gloucester gaol having been arrested 'for stealing hogs'. Mompesson soon began to wonder if William Drury might be attacking him by unorthodox means. For the drummer was a man on the edge of society – a petty criminal, a jobbing musician, a man known to make a living with jugglery and 'hocus pocus' acts performed for a crowd. It seemed quite possible that he was capable of magic, of witchcraft too. The surmise was all the stronger because mid seventeenth-century England was alive with anxiety about unnatural forces and strange spirits.[7] This was a place where many women, and some men, had only lately been executed for witchcraft and the old legislation remained on the statute book.

Against a witch there were imperfect defences. Trial and error began. Prayer was tried. Sometimes the sound 'would move a little away' but 'sometimes it would not'. Mompesson conjured what he took to be a malevolent spirit, raised by the witch, asking in God's name what it was and what it wanted. Answer came there none. The local minister, Mr Cragge, was called in and the family joined him in arduous prayer. Unseen hands threw a bedstaff at the churchman, hitting him on the leg and the haunting was not abated. Mr Mompesson took the drum into the fields and burned it but that did no good. He began to worry that the hauntings were a sign, marking him as a sinner, and that his neighbours were gossiping about what the wonders meant about the benighted household. Letters were sent out. One went to William Creed, Regius Professor of Divinity at Oxford and a relative of the Mompessons. Creed and his fellow Oxford divines seem to have been split about what should be done but a second letter, to Mompesson's cousin, Sir Thomas, elicited practical advice. Sir Thomas suggested the family should leave the house and lodge with him so that they might have some peace. When that offer was turned down he took advice himself from one who had encountered a haunting in France. Convinced the case was one of witchcraft, he told his cousin to assemble armed men in the house, close up the doors and windows and stop up the chimneys and then have them slash the air with their swords. Any witch at work in the place might be wounded in the melee and, on blood being drawn, would materialise. Others offered different opinions. A neighbour told Mompesson's mother that the fairies had been known to trouble houses. Mompesson himself began to talk of the 'goblin' that plagued them and there were indications that such beings might be at work. One morning a Bible belonging to his mother was recovered from the cold ashes of the hearth, open, it was later said, at the place in St Mark's gospel describing how Christ cast out the evil spirits.

By early January 1663 the net seemed to be closing on whatever was disturbing the peace. A party of gentlemen interrogated the spirit, having it communicate with them by means of knocking and asking whence it came. It revealed that William Drury had indeed sent it into the house. The news was something of a relief. Now Mompesson could rest easy that the spirit was not active in a quest for hidden treasure or to disclose a murder, causes which might point to the agency of a ghost rather than a witch. There was also now a possible way forward: to seek Drury's prosecution for witchcraft. This, at some point in 1663, he set in motion.

By this time, Mr Mompesson's troubles were not straight-forwardly supernatural ones. His servants were growing uppity, sensing that they would be hard to fire when few would want to replace them in the haunted house. Worse, visitors began to troop in rising numbers to his home. At first local people came. It was hard to keep news of the hauntings quiet; neighbours and labourers out in the fields could sometimes hear the noises and gossips went to town with the stories. In the England of Charles II the uncanny mattered. Acccounts of signs in the skies, lightning strikes on churches, phantom armies marching in the hills, black dogs running amuck in villages were all interrogated to discover what they might mean, to find out what God intended by showing such things to his people. People from further afield and men 'of quality' appeared on Mr Mompesson's doorstep too, intrigued to discover what substance there might be, if any, in these tales of haunting. Anthony Ettrick, a friend of the antiquary John Aubrey travelled all the way to Tedworth and so did other gentlemen, Sir Ralph Bankes and Sir Thomas Chamberlain. Sir Christopher Wren came too, heard some knocking but noted that this devil 'kept no very unseasonable hours' and suspected a maid was contriving the sounds. So many people came that they became as bad a trial to Mompesson as the hauntings; some even threatened violence to the fabric of the house, one party wanting to prise up the floorboards to discover if witchcraft or human ingenuity lay behind the noises. So far and wide did Mr Mompesson's dubious fame spread that, at some point before the end of March 1663, he was taken to London by Lord Robartes. King Charles himself was keen to hear first hand about the Drummer of Tedworth.

In March 1663, the law finally, fitfully, caught up with William Drury. Having languished in Gloucester prison on charges of pig theft, he was brought to trial and convicted. Sentenced to transportation he was on the point of being spirited away when he jumped ship and swam for shore. Unable to make good his escape, he was apprehended again. Mr Mompesson now put into action the plan he had for some time been evolving and brought a prosecution against Drury at Salisbury Assizes for the crime of witchcraft. The eel-like Drury escaped again when the case collapsed. But there was still the business of the stolen hogs so he was sent back to Gloucester. There his sentence of transportation was reaffirmed. Put aboard another ship, this time there would be no escape. Borne off to the New World, he vanished from Tedworth, from the tale and from history. But his story now had a life all of its own; it no longer needed William Drury.

For although the Mompesson house now fell quiet, the gossips did not. After his audience with the king, the earls of Chesterfield and Falmouth had been dispatched to discover the truth of the haunting. Both men 'could neither hear nor see anything extraordinary' and thought fraud a likelier explanation than the work of spirits.[8] That view began to circulate and their sceptical reaction was coming to be shared by many of the learned. A well-informed John Aubrey did not think the house was haunted. He agreed with Christopher Wren. The agency of a maid in confederation with the imprisoned Drury was the most likely explanation of the noises and lights.[9] Meanwhile Samuel Pepys noted in his diary a jolly evening spent at Trinity House in London with his superior at the Navy Board, Lord Sandwich, where 'both at and after dinner we had great discourse on the nature and power of spirits'.[10] Lord Sandwich thought that the best evidence for such things being abroad in the world was the appearance of the phantom drummer in Wiltshire, 'much of late talked of', but noted that while he was rumoured to have the power to play any tune a bystander wished on his magical drum, sometimes he proved quite unable to manage it. His Lordship surmised that surely the powers of the air would not be hampered by a limited repertoire. So even the best evidence for the existence of spirits was not very good. Pepys agreed. 'I think this is a good argument,' he concluded.

Some learned men reacted differently. One of them was called Joseph Glanvill. Made vicar of Frome in 1662 and then rector of Bath Abbey from 1666 to 1680, Glanvill was something of an authority on the spirit world and was tied into a network of clergymen who shared his conviction that spirits really did have commerce with human beings. Unlike Elizabethan divines who blanched at many stories of such things because they were the stuff of Catholic superstition, Glanvill and his friends were open-minded. Their refined philosophy predisposed them to accept the possibility of wandering spirits. And so when news reached Glanvill's ears that there was a haunting afoot in Tedworth, he travelled down to the house to see and hear for himself. He visited the Mompessons in January 1663 and what he saw there convinced him the haunting was genuine. Persuading Mr Mompesson to hand over notes he had taken during its course, he purposed to write an account of the Drummer of Tedworth. He would see the story through to the press, offering a 'scientific' account of the phenomena. He eventually published his findings in 1668.[11]

But even as Glanvill was acquiring the papers and studying the case, Mompesson was sowing seeds of the story's destruction. He had a second meeting with King Charles and, it was later said, admitted to the king that the whole business had been put up. There was no haunting. It was a fake. This Mompesson later flatly denied – he had, he said, wanted to calm interest in the case and so stem the flow of visitors wanting to tramp round his house. But the damage was done. Tales of his retraction invigorated the sceptics. In 1670, Glanvill's friend Richard Baxter told him that many now believed the phenomena at Tedworth were down to the 'juggling' of a fame-hungry Mr Mompesson who was keen to be 'taken notice of'.[12] Baxter seems to have toyed with the idea of writing up the story himself in 1663 but was probably relieved to have left it well alone.[13] John Webster, a professional antagonist of believers in witches and wandering spirits, thought anyone of 'sound understanding' must see that the happenings at Mr Mompesson's house were 'abominable cheats and impostures'.[14] Shadowy people 'of quality' had told him as much. Glanvill now had to contend with many of his learned peers who laughed at the story and ridiculed him for being taken in. He was 'haunted almost as bad as Mr Mompesson's house'. To his greater dismay, rumours began to circulate that he had also come to the conclusion that the lights and sounds and other phenomena had all been faked.[15] The Earl of Chesterfield even speculated that 'frighted and deceived' during his visit to the house he was himself trying to 'deceive posterity' and so retrieve his reputation by proving the truth of the haunting.[16]

But Joseph Glanvill would not give up. In the last years of his life he faced down the 'great party of men in this age especially' who laughed at accounts of spirits and 'resolved to explode and despise them as mere winter's tales and old wives' fables'.[17] He died in the act, leaving his friend Henry More to see his final word on the subject, a book, *Saducismus Triumphatus*, through to the press. In it, he retold the tale of the drummer for a final time with new evidence and fresh authentications. There were lively new ghost stories too, thanks in large part to the publishers. Worried that the Drummer of Tedworth was old news, they wanted to add some spice and had encouraged Glanvill to 'take care how he ventured on a new impression, unless he had some new matter of that kind to add which might make this new edition the more certainly saleable'.[18] He, and his executor Henry More, rose to the challenge, sifting available stories for the sort of thing that was wanted, ruling out one about a 'spectre of Exeter' and choosing another which was better attested if 'not of such a tragical kind as that of Exeter'.

A Not Well Discover'd Region

Why was a man of Glanvill's talents so preoccupied with the tale? And how did such a vortex form, which sucked so many great minds of the age into debate about a phantom drummer? In January 1663 Joseph Glanvill had written a letter to his friend Richard Baxter in which he revealed something of his reasons. After visiting the house he said that he had become 'an eye and ear witness of many things which the infidel world will scarce believe'.[19] Here was the project that animated him. Joseph Glanvill thought that 'infidels' were abroad in the world, that there were growing numbers of them in Restoration England – people who did not believe in spirits, who had even begun to lose faith in the invisible realm that scripture itself delineated. Stories of ghosts and spirits might be ways to shake that unbelief. So where Protestant divines of the Tudor age hurled anathemas at those who told ghost stories, Joseph Glanvill and his friends listened to them. In *Saducismus Triumphatus* he told another story which revealed the shape of his fears and how ghosts could help quiet them.[20]

Two army officers, Major George Sydenham and Captain William Dyke, had wiled away time during their service speculating about whether man was truly immortal.[21] The issue was not settled for either man, it could not be accepted on faith alone. But it might be simply resolved, Major Sydenham said, if, when one of them died, he returned from the hereafter, if there was a hereafter, and brought news to the survivor. Captain Dyke agreed to the plan. The two agreed that whoever died first would appear to his friend on the third night after his burial between the hours of midnight and one o'clock in the morning. The major died and the captain remembered the promise. Servants brought the largest candles in the house to the room where he would watch and he sat out the hours in anticipation of the visitor. But the time passed and nothing and no one came. Thinking the question of man's immortality was now answered in the negative, the captain let the promise fade from his mind and went about his usual business. Some six weeks after his night of watching, he travelled to Eton in the company of a relative, Dr Thomas Dyke. They broke the journey at the Christopher Inn and retired to their rooms. The doctor passed a pleasant night but next morning the captain appeared at his companion's door raving. 'With eyes staring and his whole body shaking', he said that as light broke that morning, Major Sydenham had come again. The major said that the soul did indeed survive when the body died and that each must face the judgement of a terrible God. And lest the captain be under any misapprehension that the apparition were a dream or delusion, the major then drew the captain's sword and brandished it. He then vanished into the air. The doctor who witnessed the aftermath of the haunting told Joseph Glanvill the story and testified to the transformation wrought in the captain by the encounter. For his doubts about Christian teachings on the fate of the dead had been resolved in a terrifying instant and he had been turned into a good son of the Church.

The story Glanvill had heard was an old one, a medieval one. Dressed in Restoration clothes, it was the traditional tale of one who doubted Church teaching about the afterlife only to be confounded by ghosts who knew better. But there were particular reasons for telling the tale in the second half of the seventeenth century. Glanvill and other churchmen feared that growing numbers, whether learned or louche, were coming to think of man as merely a thing of clay, that when the flesh died, so too did the soul. Whether or not there were truly unbelievers of this kind abroad in the England of Charles II is doubtful but there were certainly materialist and deist ideas that reduced the role of God in the world he had made. There was also, to the churchman's eye, a good deal too much loose-living. Crumbling morals and radical thinking about the afterlife might look as bad as atheism and godlessness, for the one was intimately tangled round the other. Glanvill thought that many dissolute people were living lives as if there would be 'no after-reckoning'.[22] With no fear of hell to chasten them, these men and women 'stupidly believe that they shall die like beasts, that they may live like them'.[23] Glanvill seized on ghosts as a way to frighten people out of unbelief. Just one authenticated instance of a ghost or spirit would be enough to 'rub up and awaken lethargic minds'. The unbeliever, the wastrel, the loose-liver would fear these new revelations about the fate of the dead 'as the ape does the whip' and, like Captain Dyke, be shaken out of complacency about the soul's survival and the glory and punishment of the dead. As he set out on this mission, Glanvill did not see himself as one who looked back to a Catholic past of superstitions and sprites. He was on the cutting edge. He was an adventurer on the brink of discovery, a cartographer of unknown continents. For just as explorers were setting sail over the ocean in search of new lands, Glanvill hoped to find the other world through his armchair investigations. For him the spirit world was a 'not well discover'd region'. It was a 'New America' whose contours he might yet help to map.

The raw material he needed for his project was stories. Stories came from far and wide as he scribbled about the spirit world in the vicarage at Frome and, later, in his rectory in Bath. He learned of Thomas Goddard, a Marlborough man, who met his father-in-law's ghost at nine o'clock sharp in broad daylight on 23 November 1674. Dressed in the dead man's clothes, the ghost said he had unfinished business. The worst of it was that he had murdered a man and hidden the body; Thomas was to give the victim a decent burial. Then there was kindly Mrs Bretton, wife of the rector of Pembridge in Herefordshire.[24] Quite dead, she knocked at her old front door and was admitted by the startled maid. Standing in her old morning gown and 'cold as clod', she commissioned the girl to go to her brother and yield up land that she had given him so that it might be used to raise money for the poor of the parish instead. Mrs Bretton's father recoiled from the notion that his daughter's shade was wandering the earth. He said it was not his daughter but the devil in disguise. But her brother was persuaded and the poor of Pembridge still enjoyed her supernatural generosity in Glanvill's day. He treated the story as true.

For all the confidence of some Elizabethan clergymen, the new religion had not banished ghosts. By the time Glanvill wrote, they had accommodated themselves to a Protestant England, fitting in there in a rough and ready sort of way. There was no longer any purgatory from which they might wander. No flames licked around their shrouds. No prayers were offered for them. In these respects, at least, they had been successfully 'Protestantised'. But they still came back – to put wrongs right, to deal out charity, to reveal crocks of money or the identity of a murderer, to show that they were trapped on earth as punishment for a terrible sin. They often wandered in their own ways, obedient to an older lore. This did not trouble Glanvill. The strange patterns in the hauntings suggested that the stories were probably true, each corroborating the others. They also hinted at more: that the wanderings of ghosts were governed by yet undiscovered laws, laws he might uncover and which would, in time, form the lineaments of a natural history of the land of spirits.

Such ambitions put Joseph Glanvill at odds with many scientists of his day. And history would bury his reputation as the case of the sceptics strengthened during the eighteenth century.[25] The ghost was a trick of the light, the work of a fevered brain or even a miasmatic emanation from the grave, a suggestion that explained why spirits seemed to frequent churchyards. Yet in the business of hauntings it was not so easy to distinguish sceptic and believer. Samuel Pepys was an affirmed sceptic about wandering spirits. But he still relished a good story about them. And his scepticism, under the right conditions, might be a fragile thing. Several times he whiled away a dark evening talking with friends about ghosts. Staying at a house in Chatham, he learned from his host that a man 'did die and walk' in the chamber where he was going to sleep. 'This', he said, 'did make me somewhat afeared' and, on waking in the early hours he discerned a sinister shape picked out in the moonlight and some distance from the bed. For a few moments it terrified him. Then he realised it was a pillow he had thrown aside in his sleep.[26] He also made nervous entries in his diary when he thought his own house might be haunted and noted on another occasion that, having spent the night listening to and telling hair-raising tales about the invisible world he 'almost afeared to lie alone' when he took himself off to bed.[27] These confessions were confined to the diary's pages. And this is the key to them. Fears of the spirit world still troubled men like Pepys, especially when their imaginations, fed by tall tales, ran riot at night. But to admit them in public was to risk ridicule from those armed with rational argument. Shame, Pepys observed, made him keep his anxieties about sleeping alone to himself and risk a night trembling in the dark.

7

THE SAMPFORD PEVERELL SENSATION

History, in truth, never repeats itself. But sometimes it gives a strange appearance of doing so when people reach again for story-shapes, which explain things that have happened, or they think have happened, before. To the modern eye, the congeries of knockings, touches, lights and occasional acts of violence that was the Tedworth spirit easily assumes the shape of a poltergeist tale. Neither Glanvill nor Mompesson saw it that way; they thought in terms of witchcraft, ghosts, fairies and evil spirits. The term 'poltergeist' was coined only in 1838 but it was minted for stories of hauntings that were widespread and ancient. Even in the 1180s, a Cambro-Norman clergyman called Gerald of Wales heard about invisible beings, which were said to have 'infested' the house of a man called Nicholas Wirriet in Pembrokeshire.[1] They talked to the inhabitants, threw rubbish over priests fetched to drive them out and cut holes in the family's linen. At the end of the fourteenth century a spirit floated around a Bedford house, disputing with the occupants, saying it was a child and knocking over jugs and pots; so commonplace were its invisible interventions that the woman living in the house ceased to be bothered by it.[2] The Drummer of Tedworth was, then, following in a venerable tradition. Deciding whether the tale's similarity with others suggests anything about the authenticity of supernatural claims is no part of the historian's task. But the script of domestic hauntings by invisible beings in which household things are upset and broken and the living bothered with voices, violence, lights and sounds was a durable one. It was draped by the protagonists over whatever was truly happening in the house of Mr Mompesson and it appeared again, further west, some century and a half later, in a Devon village.

Sampford Peverell huddles on a line of red sandstone that runs from Minehead to the Bristol Channel, stone which, in the light of a spring afternoon, lends a ruby tinge to the church and older houses built from it. The road winds up from the valley to the upper, older reaches of the village, its verges smothered with primroses and aubretia and fading daffodils. On a grassy high spot of Fore Street, a bench looks out from the village to the Blackdown Hills beyond. An information board offers orientation to the visitor, noting prehistoric barrows of the valley and traces of Roman camps on the hills. It marks on the village edge where Peverell Castle once stood. Demolished in 1775, only the motte remains. Nearer its heart, and surviving almost into living memory, it reveals the site of a 'Great Pond', which fed the mill race. Now drained dry, its gentle declivity is grassed over for the sheep that have fed and fattened on the hills for generations. Tantalisingly, the board also shows in dotted outline the location of a 'Ghost House'. The ghost and the house it haunted have disappeared, the latter buried in the foundations of modern developments, but the tale is preserved, for the events that occurred at Sampford Peverell in the early nineteenth century became, thanks in large part to the press, something of a minor sensation.

In August 1810 a local newspaper, the *Taunton Courier*, broke the story. A letter to the *Courier* described how 'the inhabitants of a farmhouse near Tiverton, Devon' had 'lately been very much disturbed and alarmed by noises' that human reason, so it was alleged, could not explain. The house was rented by John Chave, a local grocer, and the haunting was reported by his maids and family as well as by Chave himself. A group of gentlemen of the locality had duly authenticated their claims after staying up in the house at night. They had heard around about midnight tapping against the wainscoting of the outer room which then spread into the inner chamber. An invisible weight seemed to bear down on the bed, a sword hanging nearby began to jangle and 'something is heard to pace the room'. A child sleeping with the maids in the set of rooms was said to have been almost suffocated by the supernatural presence, and when the grocer felt it too in his own room and tried to summon help, the spirit threw a candlestick at him. The room was closely searched by the watchers but nothing was found and they pronounced themselves 'fully satisfied that the singular noises are supernatural'.[3]

The great champion of Chave's claims was the minister of a nearby parish, Reverend Charles Caleb Colton. An angler, a gambler and perhaps not the most assiduous of pastors, he was an enthusiast for this tale about a spirit. He had spent some six nights in the haunted house and was perfectly convinced that he had encountered something supernatural there, though he was not ready to commit himself to the idea that it was a ghost. Quite soon after the first stirrings of the spirit, it was Colton who stood at the centre of gossip about the haunted house as the story took hold of the 'fevered brains' of the folk thereabout. But Colton soon found antagonists, for in the early nineteenth century there was also a great deal of local scepticism about the alleged haunting and mockery of those who believed it. Self-designated chief of the vicar's persecutors was John Marriott, proprietor of the *Taunton Courier*. He quickly took up the cudgels on behalf of the sceptics. The story, he wrote in his paper, was 'knavery, folly, disgusting villainy' and he lamented that he should need 'in the present day' to spill ink refuting such nonsense.[4] But spill ink he did, filling many column inches with an extended exposé of the haunting which ran on for weeks.

Marriott's first article was laced with arguments against ghosts that had been accumulated since the Reformation. Stories of ghosts and witches belonged to a Catholic past from which the Protestant Church had emancipated England. In giving credence to the haunting, Colton freely opened 'the sluices of the darkest and most degrading follies that ever branded with infamy the days of monkish ignorance and systematic priestcraft'. Moreover, true religion in the nineteenth century drew no strength from superstition, which was 'so disagreeable to the character of the age in which we live, and so injurious to society in its probable effects on the minds of ignorant persons and young children'.[5] Modern religion was a thing of reason, learning and beautiful rationality. Ghost stories would merely 'rivet the chains of abject superstition and ignorance'. Marriott populated Colton's circle of believers with shrieking servants, nervous children and gullible professors who were ready to think that whatever went bump in the night must have a supernatural cause. He ended his piece with a final titbit. A letter had recently arrived warning the proprietor that, if he continued with his plan to expose the plot in his newspaper, then the anonymous author would be constrained to shoot him.

Charles Caleb Colton corresponded with Marriott through the *Courier*'s pages, but in tones more measured (initially at least) than those of the author of the threatening letter. Convinced as he claimed to be about the hauntings, the minister wrapped himself in the clothes of a habitual sceptic, saying that 'it is not the purpose of this letter to make converts to a belief in Ghosts'. He was at pains to point out that the usual causes when a haunting was faked – hollow walls, subterranean passages, perforated beams, wires and 'every other method of pantomimic deception' – had all been ruled out in this case.[6] The watchers had even fixed seals over the doors and yet the spirit had still moved around the house in its customary way without breaking any of them. After six nights of observations at the house, he was convinced. So were other trustworthy people, among them two surgeons, a local merchant tailor and the landlord of the White Hart in Tiverton. Unlike Marriott, Colton did not think that belief in ghosts was a danger to morals. Indeed – and there is an echo here of Glanvill's voice – belief in such things 'would be rather favourable to virtue than otherwise'. Nor, he mused, did scripture preclude such things and, if anything, tended in fact to confirm them.

Nonetheless, Marriott would not let matters lie. On 30 August he launched a new attack, this time on John Chave, who he said was a common huckster and whose family were a bunch of disreputable blow-ins attempting to deceive the honest folk of Sampford Peverell.[7] Marriott, by this point, had also acquired an ally in his campaign, the landlord of the haunted house, Mr Talley. Talley became the hero of the hour in Marriott's account. He too had been to the house, armed not with a Bible (as Colton had been) but with 'a reasonable degree of scepticism and a considerable share of common sense'. The outcome of his visitation duly appeared in the *Courier* on 20 September. The landlord had observed suspicious conversations among the Chaves and the presence of another man, a Mr Dodge, who seemed to be loitering in the house for no particular reason. The haunted set of rooms were, to Talley's eye, furnished with ample exits to allow a counterfeiter to make good entrances and escapes and he also found a mopstick, painted white, which he thought might be the source of the supernatural knockings. Talley even found that he could replicate the sounds himself and that the building's structure helped the sound to spread in strange ways. All of this was lovingly laid out by John Marriott, who noted with relish that any mason's apprentice, 'however stupid', would have been able to deduce how a haunting could be faked in a building of that type. It was a pity, he said, that 'Mr Colton had not been brought up to some useful exertion . . . instead of being designed to flourish as a Greek scholar and . . . encumbrance to the Church'. But the juiciest detail of the investigation was a revelation about the people rather than the place. For Marriott had discovered that one Mr Tayler, brother-in-law of Chave, had also been lodging in the haunted house. Tayler had lately been at Honiton where he had received an education at the hands of a man called Mr Moon. And this Mr Moon, it transpired, was 'a celebrated conjuror'.[8]

Confident that he had uncovered the means, Marriott also thought he had a motive for the imposture. Chave had recently argued with the landlord, and Talley had told him to turn out of the house. Ghost stories had long been weapons. They could be used to blacken a name, to turn a servant into his master's master by making sure no one else would work in his house. They could also be hawked around to drive down a house's rental value. Haunted houses fetched cheap rents or lay empty and, if Talley's property had a ghostly resident, he would have to let Chave stay on or risk a loss of revenue. The trick was an old one. John Aubrey knew it in the seventeenth century, observing that although 'it is certain that there are houses that are haunted' there were 'not as many as reported for there are a great many cheats used by tenants'.[9] Marriott rested his case.

Colton did not immediately give up. He published a pamphlet-long defence, reiterating that he was a diehard sceptic who had been convinced of the haunting by the evidence of his eyes and ears. For him, the age of miracles was not yet passed. 'Is there mirth', he averred, 'because a clergyman of the nineteenth century has seen and heard things he cannot account for?' The clergy, he said, daily saw things they could not explain.[10] But many of Marriott's charges had stuck. Not least was the claim about the involvement of the magician, Mr Moon. For although Colton complained that Chave's brother-in-law had never been apprenticed to Moon as Marriott had suggested, he was obliged to admit that he had 'attended performances' and on occasion 'been seen in his company'. Colton remained bitter, nonetheless. He thought Chave's reputation had been dragged through the mud and he had been made to look a fool. 'That man deserves to starve and shiver,' said the minister, 'who burns down his neighbour's house to warm his fingers at the blaze.'[11] In a tale of stereotypes, if Colton was a credulous priest then Marriott was a venal pressman. There was more than a grain of truth in that claim. Knowing that ghost 'sensations' made good copy, Marriott had dribbled out the story across August and September issues of his newspaper, trailing Talley's revelation of the conspiracy a week before he published the report and releasing news of the letter in which the threat had been made against his own life so as to whet appetites for further instalments.[12] Eventually the sensation died down, although not before it acquired certain national notoriety, even being reported in *The Times*; the reading and chattering public only lost interest once there were no new revelations to keep the story going.

Charles Caleb Colton left England. A wandering soul, and ultimately a troubled one, he spent his time writing and gambling, taking ship for France and America; he died in 1832, by his own hand. Chave and Talley slipped back into provincial obscurity. So too did John Marriott. Whatever the ulterior motives for his writings about the haunting, he had, on the face of it, confronted what he took to be superstition and had won his battle with it. In so doing, he stood on what was common ground, the idea that religion should be consonant with reason. His was a notion that made nature solid and orderly, 'disenchanted' because reasoned explanations had reduced ghosts to delusions, tricks or vaporous emanations from graves. But he acknowledged too that many round about did not think this way. The haunting had 'kindled poetic fires on the banks of the Exe' and far beyond as people spun stories about spirits. These men and women whom Marriott thought so credulous when a modern world was dawning around them are the kinds of people who are usually silent about their beliefs in the historical record. But something of their thoughts and beliefs, some sense of why they were ready to believe Reverend Colton and Mr Chave, can be traced by looking west. For in the west of England, a man who turned into an articulate commentator on such things lived out his formative years.

Making Chains and Breaking Chains

Almost at the tip of Cornwall, a county thickly encrusted with legends and ghost stories, is the port of Newlyn. It lies a little to the south-west of Penzance, a town which it has now, effectively, joined as a suburb. Granite cottages form much of Newlyn, looking out to sea from roads that follow the arc of the bay.

a woman in Mousehole who had smuggled supplies. After setting
out on the empty road, he soon found himself closing on a solitary figure, white in the moonlight, walking ahead of him. Full
of 'strange fears and curious imaginings' about what this being
might be, he closed the distance between them, reflecting that he
had gone out in search of spirits but 'not of this complexion'.
The figure stopped and waited. Lovett continued towards it, forti-
fying himself with the conviction that good spirits were clad in
white and wicked spirits in black. Then, as he drew close, he
realised that this was not a ghost at all but a flesh and blood
woman. Indeed, she was 'of the earth most earthly', the secret
lover of a Penzance lawyer, and this accounted for her wandering
the highway alone in the dead of night. For she was using the
moonlight to make good an escape before the gossips set in motion
a story every bit as juicy as a haunting.

Not only the Mousehole road but other places around Newlyn
were invested with dread, often because of terrible events reputed
to have happened there. On another night Lovett was walking
with a friend down a lane notorious for a murder. The site of the
crime was marked by a flat stone. As they approached it with
'subdued tongues and quickened pulses', the ghost loomed up,
white-faced, a monster, more than three feet high and horned.
Only very slowly did the pair realise that they were looking not
at a ghost but a pale-coloured heffer which had strayed near the
highway and duly decided to lie down near the murder-stone.[17]
William Lovett was ready to see these ghosts because he had been
told so many stories about them. He had set out on his commission to fetch brandy on the Mousehole road 'with a sorrowful
heart' because 'it was a solitary way along the edge of the cliff
and many were the ghosts and goblins that had been seen on the
road'. His head had been filled with 'numerous stories of nocturnal
visitants' since infancy and not as idle tales for entertainment's
sake but as gospel truths, authenticated by neighbours who, they
said, had glimpsed the ghosts for themselves. The stories coloured
experience and many a traveller, less sharp-eyed than Lovett, did

not appreciate that the distant figure in the moonlight was only a woman in white or the horned monster on the road a heffer. Rather than telling a tale of false fears exploded by a closer inspection of a haunting, he or she came back home full of news about spirits on the Mousehole highway or the murder victim abroad again near the site of the crime. A vicious circle of fearfulness was in operation. Nor did it break when adulthood began. Lovett's master, the tippling rope-maker, was not a shrinking violet but a hard man and one-time womaniser who regaled his younger charges with stories of his conquests. But if business beckoned after dark he always required one of the apprentices to join him since he feared ghosts himself. A clergyman, Henry Bourne, diagnosed these propensities. 'Nothing is commoner in country places,' he said, than 'for a whole family on a winter's evening to sit around the fire and to tell tales of apparitions and ghosts.'[18] All this storytelling 'adds to the natural fearfulness of men, and makes them many times imagine they see things which really are but their own fancy'.

When folklore scholars rewrote these stories in the decades after William Lovett's birth, they made them seem picturesque.[19] People told them tales about Mrs Baines. Catching her servant asleep in the orchard he was supposed to be guarding, she shook apples from the tree to wake him but, startled, he took her for a thief and shot her dead. The unquiet soul had been laid under the sandbanks of the Western Green until she could weave a rope from sand that stretched from St Michael's Mount to St Clement's Isle. Later tradition claimed that her spinning wheel was to be heard at night turning out on the strand.[20] There was a spirit banished to a hilltop from which it could not depart until it had counted every blade of grass and another constrained to card black wool into white. Others had been set under river gravels or stoppered up in bottles sunk in ponds. The most widespread stories were of John Tregeagle. A wicked steward of the seventeenth century, he was doomed to walk the earth as a punishment. His name was tied to places across the Cornish west. He had been banished by a parson to the seashore at St Minver where he was spinning ropes of sand. He walked the Goss Moor chased by dogs. He was sweeping the beach from Nanjizal cove to Tol Pedn or carrying it by the sackload over the estuary at Bareppa to Porthleven.[21] But, in their operation, the stories were often far from pretty. An eighteenth-century tract for the instruction of servants warned against terrifying children with tales of spirits, ghosts and goblins since young minds were like wax; the early impression would be deep and once formed it would be 'almost impossible to root it out of their minds'.[22] John Marriott had pointed out too the 'childish trumpery by which Mr Colton has rendered himself the Bugbear of our nurseries' and lambasted him for adding fuel to the fires of superstition among 'ignorant country people and children'.

The young did not hear only about the legendary dead whose fates were remote and unaffecting. They heard too about men recently entombed in the tin mines after collapses; their bodies lost in the workings, they haunted the tunnels and mineshafts where they had died. There were many more who had passed over the sea, pressed into the navy's service or settled in an expanding empire and were lost forever to their families. Sometimes they came back fleetingly as wraiths or fetches, a vision that offered the faint solace of knowing for sure that someone once loved was now dead.[23] And then there was the terrible harvest of the sea itself. Corpses, sometimes mangled by the rocks, were washed ashore regularly from shipwrecks. The beach could be a place of trauma after a storm. There were worse things too. An old man of Porthleven pointed out to William Lovett not only the graves of many sailors he had buried but also the anonymous resting places of those lost on Loe Bar. When a ship was wrecked there, the youngest and strongest would think that they could run to safety on the exposed sands as a wave receded. But they plunged down into quicksand and sank fast, their cries mingling with the storm wind.[24] Remote, impoverished Cornwall was filled with the ghosts of those who had died trying to win what riches there were out to sea or under the earth. The young, dead before their time, perhaps lying outside consecrated ground or lost at sea, all with business undone and lives unlived, made this a propitious place for visions.

Religion did little to chase away these ideas. Cornwall was no godless place; many of its people were zealous. But the kind of religion that flourished there among the poor in the early nineteenth century worked with the grain of belief in spirits rather than against it. Most looked to Methodism for comfort and meaning in the face of adversity and the Lovett family was no exception. John Wesley, the movement's founder, had preached in Newlyn some fourteen times between 1747 and 1789 and part of his message was that the age of wonders was not passed.[25] God visited rewards on the good, punishments on the wicked and made signs in the heavens and on earth to which all should attend. For the Methodist preachers who succeeded him, many drawn from ordinary families round and about, the air was still hectic with spirits, the devil and his ministers still a presence.

To the eye of the educated clergyman Richard Polwhele, religion seemed so closely twined round magic in western Cornwall that when superstition died religion, too, he worried, might itself 'soon expire'.[26] Lovett was brought up inside this tradition by a mother strong for chapel. He heard preaching thrice a day on Sundays with no book but the Bible for reading and no recreation, not even a walk along the seashore, between the services. If he sneaked off to play on a Sunday and suffered misfortune, this was a divine judgement on him for sabbath-breaking. When smallpox struck his school, his mother eschewed innoculation because, like many, she saw this as distrusting providence. William duly caught the disease from a girl whose skin he remembered being 'beset with dark-scabbed pustules' but, left in God's hands, he survived. He was doubly blessed because he was not disfigured by the terrible disease. All this made young Lovett's religion radically unlike John Marriott's. His world was not a mechanism made by God and left to work in ordered ways. Nature for him was full of sympathy and antipathy; it was populated by signs and spirits and God-sent providences. His kind of Methodism did not for one moment dent William Lovett's belief in ghosts.

Nor did anything that he read. Taught at his great-grandmother's knee when he lived with her in Sancreed, he became a devourer of books. Having quickly learned the *Divine Songs* of Dr Watts by heart, his mother promised him his very own Bible. He remembered sitting on a rock on the day she fetched it, holding up his prize as she walked towards him. It was sometimes said that the printing press and spreading literacy was doing much to banish belief in spirits but this was not its effect on William. Reading did not shrink the spirit world; it expanded it. For he gobbled up not only the Bible and prayer books but also, when he could, wonder stories from borrowed pamphlets and magazine fragments. For generations, profit-minded publishers had fed the public appetite for a good ghost story with 'true' tales of hauntings and such material, much of it vintage stuff, was still in circulation. When William was a boy, the bookshop in Penzance had shelves loaded with 'story books and romances filled with absurdities about giants, spirits, goblins and supernatural horrors'. And because the readers of these books had been brought up on the Bible, the literal truth of whose stories was not to be gainsaid, they treated print with rare reverence. Books became repositories of gospel truths, whether they told Bible tales or retailed wondrous news about the invisible world.[27]

Many years after William Lovett left Newlyn for London, he travelled back to the village. It had altered very little but he had been transformed by 'wise education' and he looked back on his old self, and people who were still like that old self, as slaves to ignorance, superstition and fear.[28] A headless ghost walking by night in the vicinity was causing something of a stir in the town. He mocked the reports but an old acquaintance, a baker, reproved him. Not to believe in ghosts was to doubt the Bible itself, for in its pages was the story of the Witch of Endor, who raised up the dead prophet Samuel, and sundry other passages 'in favour of spirits' that he went on to cite. Lovett concluded that despite 'the progress of knowledge among our people by means of the press, the school and the rail', beliefs about an invisible world were still flourishing.

Others agreed. Robert Lowery, another political agitator, an outsider who toured Cornwall in 1839, found many people ready to point out the sites of apparitions. Tom Oliver and John Harris of Camborne remembered the region still full of ghosts in the mid nineteenth century.[29] One, it was said, had carried a man bodily to a grave in Crowan so that the parson might be fetched to still its wanderings; other hauntings required the services of a local man skilled in the art of laying spirits. Even at the other end of the nineteenth century, ghosts were still part of everyday life. A Perran-born boy, Tom Tremewan, recalled ghost hoaxers who, equipped with sheets and lanterns, tried to frighten his father during a night fishing trip. They appeared on the dunes bright in the moonlight, but Tom's father was made of stern stuff and, seeing through the ruse, gave chase, cornered the tricksters and said he would hit them with his bottle of hot tea if they did not reveal themselves. Others with less steady nerves were not always so sanguine when faced by an apparition; counterfeiting hauntings remained a popular pastime of village youths into the twentieth century.[30]

Cornwall was not a uniquely haunted place; many life stories told by working-class men and women from all parts converge on the idea that tales of ghosts and hauntings were commonplace in the nineteenth century. Samuel Bamford, another radical born into an artisan family in Middleton, Lancashire, in 1788, told similar tales of a landscape as full of ghosts as the Cornish one. Owler Bridge, near his home, was 'thronged by spirits' and his father, a firm Methodist, would always say a psalm as he crossed it; School Lane had a ghost and in another place a *fyerrin* – a dialect name for a boggart – was known to lurk.[31] Bamford said, like Lovett, that these beliefs had dwindled since his youth; unlike Lovett he was nostalgic for them, for a 'lost world'. He mourned 'simple inerradicable rusticity', which had disappeared with a generation of old men who sat by the winter fire and told tales of wonders and spirits and believed, or half believed, they were true. Burgeoning towns, industrial sprawl and a revolution in agriculture helped, he thought, to explain the change. Now streams were 'poisoned by dye vats', valleys 'studded with smoke funnels' and an ancient imaginative world had been obliterated as fields were enclosed, farms created and new roads made. For as places vanished so the stories tied up with them vanished too, especially when mass migration scattered to the winds the remaining people who remembered them. As the landscape people inhabited trans-formed around them, so, suggested Samuel Bamford, the land-scape they carried round in their heads was altered irrevocably too.[32]

Flora Thompson watched the change and recalled it in her trilogy *Lark Rise to Candleford*, set in an imagined village but based on her own experience. Stories were still told when she was young in the 1870s round the winter fire and she heard about ghosts leading travellers astray with bobbing lanterns, spirits taking the shape of dogs, hauntings at places where a suicide had been buried or a felon once swung on a gibbet.[33] No one, she thought, believed such things by that time; the stories had turned into the stuff of entertainment, treated a little as the modern reader might read a novel or mystery tale.[34] But under the right conditions, they still had power over the audience. In a place reputed to be haunted, alone in the darkness when the imagination patched gaps left by the impoverished senses, apprehensions could still take hold. The stories, she said, were still 'half believed'.[35] Especially the young might be marked by them. John Sykes of Slaithwaite in Yorkshire remembered 'terror tales of disembodied spirits' appearing in solitary spots to avenge untimely deaths or haunting houses until a clergyman could be persuaded to exorcise them.[36] Henry Snell, a future Labour politician, walked at the tender age of ten 'through the dark lanes on winter mornings' and thought this 'the greatest horror of my life' because they were pregnant with supernatural dangers. He was born, he said harshly, 'in an ignorant and super-stitious age and the minds of children were systematically terrified by crude and wicked stories concerning troubled ghosts and malig-nant spirits'. Sounds of beasts and birds in the twilight made him sense the presence of a ghost; 'quiet and beautiful lanes' became places of deep anxiety.[37]

Ghosts were losing some of their potency in the nineteenth century; fewer believed in them, or admitted to believing in them, but they still had many young people in their power. For adults, the old stories were often old-fashioned things, primitive and superstitious, bound up with an age that had passed. But for others, those more like Samuel Bamford than William Lovett, this loss was a cause of ambivalence for it was bound up with the passing of the world of their youth, of people and places and fireside stories. It is no coincidence that in the decades that writers like William Lovett and Samuel Bamford traced the fading away of supernatural beliefs they were reborn again in print as Victorian ghost stories and terror tales. Scattered through novels or as stand-alone pieces, penned by the greatest writers of the age and by jobbing authors, they found substantial markets.[38] For the readers of such tales were well acquainted with the invisible world and its workings, were aware of the lore that governed how ghosts haunted, even if they no longer believed it. They could be encour-aged to suspend their disbelief and be carried, in their heads, back to a cottage hearth as a winter's tale was spun or to a lonely spot where a suicide lay or a felon had swung; readers could, for a time, choose to be vulnerable to irrational apprehensions once more.

8

AMONG THE TOMBS

On the north Cornish coast, a short distance from St Ives, lies Worvas Hill. On its summit is a weathered granite steeple, some fifty feet high. Two of the monument's faces are cut with the mottoes '*Nil Desperandum*' ('Never Despair') and 'I know that my redeemer liveth'. The third bears a Latinised name, 'Johannes Knill', and the date 1782. An unremarkable monument, perhaps, replicated in many towns, villages and parks by similar memorials to local worthies of the eighteenth and nineteenth centuries. But today, 25 July 2011, this memorial to the St Ives-man John Knill is a little less ordinary.

Townspeople and tourists thread their way up paths through scrub onto the upper slopes of Worvas and, from their ranks, a party emerges, including the mayor, the vicar, an officer of HM Revenue and Customs, a troop of schoolgirls in white dresses, two older ladies of the town in mourning blacks, a fiddler in early nineteenth-century dress and a master of ceremonies in similar period costume. The party forms up on the monument's plinth and the children dance for some minutes around the pyramid's base to the accompaniment of the fiddle. The company and the crowd hear a short address and sing the Hundredth Psalm. Then the master of ceremonies, children, ladies, fiddler and dignitaries withdraw and return whence they came and the crowd of spectators thins. Worvas Hill and its monument are left again to the wind and the salt spray and to the occasional visitor who might wonder, briefly, who John Knill was and why he is remembered here.

The Knill commemoration has been held quinquennially since its inception in 1801. Through prosperity and adversity, through peace and war, the dancers, singers, fiddler and onlookers from the town have gathered on Worvas Hill on the festival day. Yellowing clippings and faded black-and-white photographs in the St Ives Museum testify to the ceremony's reiteration; it has been absorbed into the town's traditions, guided by a fiddler and master of ceremonies who have officiated many times, involving children whose families often have long connections with the event, drawing townspeople back to watch, themselves changed by the passage of years, to observe once again the changeless ritual. All this owes its existence to one man: John Knill. He wanted, he said, to be remembered by the people of St Ives when he was dead and he gave extraordinary form to that ambition, designing the rites played out at the steeple. If the form was strange, the ambition of remembrance was not. Knill's story is not singular in all respects, it is a clue to a strange and deep, perhaps timeless, desire among human beings not to be forgotten when they are gone.

The Immortal Mr Knill

Many tales were told about John Knill. He had held a most responsible position in St Ives, being appointed Collector of Customs in St Ives in 1762, but some said that he had dabbled in the contraband that he was supposed to seize. There were rumoured to be deep wells under the house he had owned in Fore Street just behind the harbour wall, a place where loot could be stored. Others thought the steeple high on Worvas had been intended as a shore-mark for smugglers with whom he was in league. Then there was a tale that he and some friends had searched for treasure buried on the Lizard by a famous pirate called Captain Avery. In the late seventeenth century this man had been a terror to shipping off Madagascar before retiring to Barnstaple on the proceeds of crime, some of which he did not manage to recover from the earth before his death.

The truth about John Knill was more prosaic. He lived a life of small-town respectability, attending church regularly, taking notes of the sermons that he heard there and serving as the warden.[1] In the town he rose to be mayor in 1767 and busied himself with works to improve the harbour. Far from being the smugglers' confederate, he was their hammer, arming vessels against them and later working out a plan to end the 'infamous hospitality' of wreckers who murdered the surviving crew of vessels smashed on the coast so that they could plunder whatever remained.[2] A trusted agent of Lord Hobart, 2nd Earl of Buckinghamshire, he was dispatched on missions over the water to Ireland and sent to Jamaica in 1773 to inspect customs arrangements there. In 1782 he finally moved away to London. What brought about the move is uncertain. He may have outgrown the little town or been lured away by better prospects. What is clear is that even after he had settled in a new house in the Strand, he continued to think fondly of faraway St Ives.

This does not make sense of why he is still remembered there today. For although he was moderately successful and modestly prosperous in his metropolitan career, there were hundreds rather like him who posterity has quietly forgotten, marked at most by a tombstone or memorial plaque, dusty, crumbling and unregarded in a parish church or civic space. But this is itself part of the explanation of John Knill's unusual commemoration. He knew that oblivion within a generation or two would be his lot and he did not care for it. So he set about engineering his own remembrance. His own handiwork lies behind the dancing on 25 July and the monument on Worvas Hill that is its centrepiece. His 'real affection' for St Ives, still alive long years after he had moved to London, made him determined that this would be the place of his commemoration. For in the memories of its people he confessed 'an ardent desire to continue a little longer than those of whom there is no ostensible memorial'.

And so he hatched a plan. He had a strong oak box made which was to be lodged in the Customs House. In the box he placed a deed and in the deed, which he composed in 1797, he set out the terms of an intricate bequest. Lands that he had acquired in the parish of Mawgan were to be rented out after his death and the monies paid into the box.³ The cautious collector of duties had this secured under three locks and a key to each went to all of the trustees, Knill's successor as Collector of Customs, as well as the mayor and the vicar. Some of the money would be used to maintain the monument. Although built massively out of granite, south-westerlies would scour its faces with salt and sand and so half the annual revenue was reserved for its upkeep. He ordained that the remainder be accumulated for five years and then, as the quinquennial celebrations beckoned, the money was to be expended according to a strict plan. He wanted ten girls to be engaged for the dancing. These were to be the daughters of fishermen, seamen or tinners of the town. He also set aside a payment for two widows who were to keep the children in order. They were to be at least sixty-four years old and the relicts of fishermen, seamen or tinners. There was money too for the fiddler who was to play for the dancing and the Hundredth Psalm and for all the accoutrements of the ritual, white ribbons for the dancing children, white breast-knots for the widows and a cockade for the fiddler's hat. The princely sum of £10 was also set aside for the trustees and their guests to enjoy a good dinner.

Knill even set out a contingency plan in case there was a surplus of cash. When this reached £100, the trustees were to distribute it to particular causes. The man and woman of the town who had raised the largest family of legitimate children without the assistance of parish relief were to receive £5. The best knitter of fishing nets, deserving boys rowing the boat called *Follower* and the finest packer of pilchards were all to have prizes; so too was a woman chosen by the trustees, the wife of a seaman, fisherman or tinner, who is 'worthy and deserving, particular regard being had to her duty and kindness to her parents'. John Knill's deed makes plain that he would be remembered by a seafaring people and so, in a finishing touch, it was fitting that they would

remember him specially every five years on 25 July, the feast day
of St James the Great, the fisherman.

To a contemporary's eye, Knill's plans must have looked eccentric but in some ways they aligned him with the concerns of
others of his day and rank. His bequests reinforced the values of
a 'respectable' St Ives of which he had been a leading light. He
rewarded the industrious worker, the dutiful daughter and the
virtuous poor too proud to live off the parish. His other plans for
remembrance set out in his will were also not so unusual. He laid
out money for no less than fifty-six mourning rings to be dispensed
to friends and relatives. 'Those intended for the ladies', he
explained, were to be 'mounted with a small plait of hair
surrounded by twelve pearls' and those for gentlemen had a similar
device surrounded by twelve small diamonds. He knew that the
most fragile and personal of tokens, a lock of hair, preserved in
gold, would keep him in mind. And he left keepsakes too. James
Edge, a lawyer and a friend, won the plums, a 'silver stewpan,
cover, and stand, [and] silver smoking candlestick, with Chinese
and Turkish tobacco pipes'. They were fitting mementoes of a
man who had spent so much of his life watching over the comings
and goings of ships filled with foreign luxuries.

Keepsakes were a staple of any will, rich or poor, down the
ages and so commonplace were mourning gifts that Samuel Pepys
became something of a connoisseur of them, noting in his diary
what was to be had from a good funeral. William Shakespeare,
John Evelyn and Pepys himself, among numberless others, left
mourning rings to friends and family when they died.[4] Others
left mourning blacks such as gloves and scarves. One country
vicar in the nineteenth century had a bottom drawer full of such
things in his bedroom.[5] Some even gave away 'mourning spoons'
engraved with a memorial message. Nor was John Knill quite so
odd in wanting to carve a place in collective memory, even if his
strategy was a singular one. Endowing a charity which dispensed
aid to the deserving poor after the benefactor's death was an idea
with medieval roots but it was still common in England during

the eighteenth century. Some associated their gifts with a commemorative sermon, which kept the donor in mind. England bristled too with public projects – schools, colleges, almshouses, hospitals – attached to the name of a benefactor, emblazoned with plaques and often charged with the task of remembering their founder in a church service once a year. Such institutions were as close as one might get to immortality in this world and it was to the things of this world that men and women looked as they founded them. Eighteenth- and nineteenth-century bequests were moved by a very different spirit to the gift-giving and charity of the Middle Ages. There was no hint in them of the kind of bargain that John Baret struck as he lavished money on Bury St Edmunds, no suggestion that the donor wanted or needed prayers. Charity was seldom neatly philanthropic but now simple remembrance would be return enough for an investment.

In one way, John Knill was a little like John Baret. There was no prospect of living on in the world through flesh and blood. Knill was a bachelor and he too would die childless. This bothered Knill as it had Baret, especially so, perhaps, because Knill had a keen interest in his own ancestry. He had mounted genealogical investigations and traced his mother's family to Plympton in Devon and his father's ancestors to Herefordshire; he had even visited the village of Knill from which he thought his family hailed.[6] From modest stock, he had risen a little in the world after his fortuitous landing at St Ives. He had won regard in his adopted town and made a fair amount of money. But there were no children to inherit his wealth; his achievements and his line would die with him. So in the absence of a flesh and blood continuation, he built in granite. The childless Absalom in the Old Testament book of Samuel set up a pillar in his memory and, rather like him, John Knill decided to build the steeple that would be the centrepiece of his commemorations.[7] Who gave him the idea he does not say. But pyramids were fashionable things. Rich young men making the Grand Tour of Europe admired the ancient one that was the burial place of Caius Cestius in Rome. A few had chosen such a design for their own monuments. John Knill never set eyes on Rome – a man of his rank seldom had chance of a grand tour – but he rubbed shoulders with those who did. And it is surely no coincidence that when his great patron, John Hobart, Earl of Buckinghamshire, died and was buried at Blickling Hall in Norfolk a pyramid was erected as his monument.[8] It cost his family £2,270, ten times the cost of Knill's steeple, and it is many times the size of the Worvas monument too. Money, as ever, gave the elite an edge when it came to stamping one's name on the landscape. But history is capricious. Few around Blickling now remember John Hobart, 2nd Earl of Buckinghamshire, Comptroller of the Royal Household, Lord of the Bedchamber, ambassador to Russia and Lord Lieutenant of Ireland. Many in St Ives, meanwhile, recall the name of Knill.

Old St Ives today might be familiar to John Knill. His house still stands in Fore Street. Black and white painted, and decked with flags, it serves as a shop but is known as Knill House. The town still feels as it must have done in his day, a little as if it has been poured into too small a space. The houses are packed in tightly with narrow streets and ginnels dividing them. Many are of eighteenth- or nineteenth-century vintage and some still have deep cellars, conceived for storing fish rather than contraband. Built with thick walls and small windows, they huddle together against winter storms rolling in from the Atlantic. But in almost every other way modern St Ives would scarcely be recognisable. Its social fabric is irrevocably altered. Where once catches were landed, fish packed up and nets mended, tourists now crowd. The fishing boats have given up their places to seal-watching craft. Tin and copper is no longer mined and the workings crumble along the coast and up on the moors. Even the customs post has gone.

The minutely detailed accounts of the Knill festivities lodged in the County Record Office at Truro allow something of this change to be plotted.[9] Unaltered in format since the first celebration in 1801, they note names of participants in the ceremonies and monies defrayed to omnibus companies, haberdashers, hotels and to beneficiaries of the charity. The hands change over the years and names change too, although some of the fiddlers and masters of ceremonies served in their posts for decades and family names recur among the children and widows. What is striking is that much of the social world that John Knill knew vanished only quite recently. Many of his bequests were still being dispensed in 1936. Even then the largest family of legitimate children in the parish was rewarded with a prize dole and the best net-knitters and fish-packers got their shillings. Now these awards are either impossible or unthinkable, so much have the economy and mores shifted over the last half-century. It was the social fabric of St Ives, perdurable for a century and a half, and the eccentric skill with which Knill insinuated himself into it that ensured his plan to carry his name down the years took hold. Yet now, even though the inner life of the town has changed so much, the Knill rituals still flourish. Their changelessness in a changing world has hallowed them. Guarded by willing volunteers, enthusiastically supported by the townfolk, they are embedded in the life of St Ives as a communal festivity. John Knill's scheme to be remembered a little longer than was customary has succeeded in a way he could not conceive and to an extent far beyond his modest expectation.

The Metaphysicks of True Belief

If John Knill's project formed in a particular moment and was informed by values that were contingent, the desire for remembrance was much more general. Evidence for it is inscribed on the landscape around St Ives. It is there in memorial stones from the dawn of Christianity in Cornwall, stones cut with insular Latin which proclaims the ambition of figures from a mysterious past – Rialobran, Tegernomal and Conetoc – that something of them should be recalled by subsequent generations.[10] Remnants from deep time, barrows and megaliths, dot the land beyond the town too. The dolmens of Zennor Quoit and Lanyon Quoit, the menhir at Men Scryfa, the Giant's House at Pennant and the barrow of the Nine

Maidens' Circle hint that some of the ancient dead, the dead of the Neolithic, tried to claim a place in memory even before there was writing to preserve their names. From the late Middle Ages, the people of this place have focused their ambition for remembrance around the church of St Ia. It stands a few paces from the harbour over which John Knill presided, a quiet place on a hazy July morning, deserted, in fact, even though the streets are filling with visitors. Standing proud of the surrounding land, the churchyard is constricted by streets on two sides and by the sea on the third, the spray on stormy days washing the east windows of the church and showering the graves. A striking building and large by Cornish standards, the church was built in the early fifteenth century from the profits of the port. As their town overtook nearby Lelant in size and significance, the inhabitants of St Ives petitioned for their own church and graveyard, since the road to the old church town was 'mountainous and rocky and liable, in winter, to sudden innundation'. Children were going unbaptised, the dying unconfessed and the dead unburied.[11] The new church was completed in 1426 and consecrated in 1434. Thereafter the dead of St Ives were laid there.

Like John Knill, but less eccentrically and ultimately with less success, many of these people hoped to be remembered. A single memorial recalls the medieval men and women who had that aspiration. It is a small brass set into the wall of the current Lady Chapel but once embedded in the floor. Dated 1463, it commemorates a local gentleman, Otto de Trenwith, and his wife, Agnes.[12] Otto died 'on the Sunday next before the feast of the Blessed Virgin Mary in the second year of Edward IV'. He was, the brass announces, 'a good man, well-disposed towards God and the world'. Otto has vanished – a large pockmark in the flagstone marks the place where his image once sat – but there is enough in the outline to see that he was probably dressed as a civilian rather than a knight, a man of business not a warrior. Agnes survives. Wearing an ample gown, girdled and hooded, she appears as an elderly woman kneeling in prayer. This is not her likeness. The brass was made in London by a craftsman who had never met the Trenwiths; a mass-produced article, it was still expensive and so in reach only of the local elite. This did not matter much. Above Agnes floats another figure, a winged angel, St Michael, who pins a dragon to the floor with a lance. Joining Agnes to St Michael is a scroll which unfurls from her mouth. On it are the words 'Sancte archangele ora pro nobis', 'Holy archangel, pray for us'. The point of the brass was devotional. It begged for the help of a saint, Michael, the saint of high places, vanquisher of Lucifer, archangelic guide in the other world. And it solicited help from people of St Ives who would not only remember the Trenwiths but pray for them too and so speed them through purgatory fire to bliss and to rest.

The ambition of Otto and Agnes to be prayed for when they were dead put the little brass in danger. Remembering the dead and praying for the dead were intimately connected in the Middle Ages, but at the Reformation they were disentangled when inter- cession for the dead was forbidden. That prohibition let loose pious vandalism. In churches across Cornwall – across England – brasses were gouged out, sold on and melted down, leaving only ghostly indentations. Other memorials were smashed or scraped clean of precatory formulae. Some of the hottest Protestants wanted to carry their obliterative theology further; tombs themselves were 'sacrilegiously stolen, erased and taken away'.[13] That was a step too far for most of the elite and Elizabeth I put a stop to the excesses in 1560. She concluded that it was only right that pleas for prayers be eradicated but monuments had a value extending beyond the solicitation of prayers. Without monuments 'the memory of sundry good and noble persons' – mighty ancestors whose tombs symbolised a family's power – would be lost.[14] Lying behind the prohibition was also a more general sense that the dead deserved to be remembered in thanks if not with prayers. And so the antiquary John Camden defended memorials too but on slightly different grounds. Through them, he said, 'love was shown to the deceased, memory was continued to posterity, friends were comforted and the reader put in mind of human frailty'.[15]

But not everyone agreed; iconoclasm was let loose again during the Civil War and tombs were smashed and memorials defaced. At Exeter in 1644 parliamentarian soldiers 'tyrannised' the town and attacked the cathedral. They broke up monuments, beheading statues of the bishops, opening one of their graves and taking a silver chalice from it. But, again, once the country was quiet, the iconoclasm subsided; respect for the memorials of the dead was reasserted.

Somehow part at least of the Trenwith brass survived these convulsions. Generations were married, baptised their children, and were seen out of the world as it looked on. Their tramping feet ultimately proved more of a hazard than reforming zeal, wearing it down until St Michael's face resembled 'nothing so much as a Dutch cheese'.[16] Why it survived is imponderable. Perhaps tucked away in the side aisle it was not noticed. Most in and around St Ives were never iconoclasts and, over time, while onlookers lost the skill to decipher its Latin plea for prayers, they retained a sense that the dead should be remembered in the world. The Reformation did not, in the end, diminish this sense. People wanted to be remembered when they were gone, and many wanted to remember the dead; the cult of memory was transformed but it did not die. Without the intercessions, which kept the names of the dead alive in prayer, other kinds of monuments grew in importance as means to preserve them. After the Reformation, monuments continued to multiply in England's parish churches. For many, especially among the elite, writing was their defence against oblivion. Printed funeral sermons, obituaries and even family histories were composed as ways to preserve the doings of the illustrious dead. But tombs and monuments were even more important.[17] Elaborate epitaphs set virtues, achievements and claims to fame in stone; for the richest there might even be an image of them, a great stone body set up in church, which might live, they hoped, forever.

There are no elaborate monuments full of statuary in St Ives Church, a measure perhaps of the town's limited economic means in post-Reformation centuries. But there are many memorials. In the Trenwith aisle is one for the Sises. It is made out of a flat slab of native Cornish slate. The family has died out but their house, built in Puddingbag Lane, long survived them and had a memorial stone set into the wall. They were of some substance. Ephraim Sise Senior was an alderman and mayor in 1645 in the midst of the Civil Wars. Politically he leant towards Parliament and in religion his convictions were Puritan, but the memorial tells something of a story more painful and important for the Sise family. For it reveals that 'near to this bed six Sises late were laid'. Four sons, a grandson and a daughter were all buried in succession. The children 'did but taste of earth and with disdain, hoist up their sails for the elysian plain'. The loss of the daughter, Alice, was especially agonising and the monument bore the date of her burial on 16 August 1642. On that day worlds were colliding. King and Parliament were manoeuvring each other into Civil War. But the Sises were in the grip of a more intimate tragedy, which only their reticent memorial recalls. Alice may have known that she was dying, for someone called Alice Sise gave a silver cup to the church in 1641 inscribed simply with her name and the date. In doing this, she helped to recreate some of the commemorative clutter swept away from churches during the reign of Edward VI.

Others were doing similarly. Grace, widow of a local vintner, gave silver flagons to St Ives Church in 1650. The squire of Pendarves gave a communion cup, which bore his name and indicated his rank in 1713.[18] Another notable, Samuel Stephens of Tregenna, had a hatchment – a board painted with his arms – put up in the south aisle; John Stevens put up a board bearing verses he had composed in memory of his dearly beloved wife. Most worthies trusted, like the Sises, to memorial slabs. There was no hint in any of this of soliciting prayer; a simple desire to keep a name alive in the memory of St Ives was enough.

'The greater part', the seventeenth-century writer Thomas Browne contended, 'must be content to be as though they had not been, to be found in the Register of God, not in the record of man.'[19] Only men of standing could command an enduring memorial. But something in the next parish of Zennor, a few miles away, suggests that the same purpose was at work among

the poor too. A woman annotated the parish register, writing
simply, 'Elizabeth Stevens, 1732, of Zennor, here do write, when
this you see, remember me, when I am out of sight.'[20] In the late
Middle Ages a bede roll – a list of the dead – transmitted memory
so that ordinary parishioners might be remembered in prayer.
The Reformation swept away bede rolls with all the other paraphernalia of intercession but parishes were obliged after 1538 to
keep registers. Avowedly secular in purpose – simple records of
births, marriages and deaths – they were still a place where the
names of ordinary men and women could live on when they were
dead. Elizabeth explicitly made a memorial of the parish record.
She did not bid the reader to pray for her. Again, it was enough
that they simply kept her to mind.

Elizabeth Stevens fought against oblivion with paper. In the
churchyard of St Ives, countless more fought with wood and stone
to keep the memory of the dead alive. The story of this graveyard
is, in large part, the story of that aspiration. Most of the graves
of the ordinary dead, laid down over some six centuries, have
long been anonymous. Some were rendered thus soon after burial.
Only wooden crosses or unmarked stones may ever have been
set upon many of them. In some parts of England wooden rails
or flags marked graves or willow wands were bound over them.
Perhaps no more than a grassy mound indicated a burial place.
Rotting wood, sinking stones and levelling earth consigned the
dead slowly to anonymity. But in the eighteenth and nineteenth
centuries, many memorials of ordinary people became more
enduring and more articulate.[21] Sometimes only initials marked
them. Sometimes there was a name. Sometimes a profession was
added. The earliest stones were locally made and inscriptions were
peppered with dialect and more than one corpse in the south-west
slept in hope of eventual 'rezurrection'.[22]

In the nineteenth century, mass production, standard designs
and correct English took hold. The poor were obliged to be less
loquacious in grief; they could afford to have fewer words cut in
the stone, if they could afford a stone at all. But as money allowed,

more detail was added and a little more of the identity of the deceased was preserved. The stone of Thomas Clark in St Ia's churchyard told that he had been a master mariner, who died in 1829 aged eighty-nine. Others had claims to fame that the tombstone kept alive. One recalled Arnold Walters who, in 1744, had circumnavigated the globe with Admiral Anson aboard HMS *Centurion*. He died full of years, but Joseph Hocking, another master mariner, was drowned in 1820 aged only twenty-six. His brother died young, too; he was captured by the Americans during the war of 1812 and escaped only to be lost at sea on Christmas Day.

Even in death, many people wanted their rank – or families wanted it for them. Wandering around another Cornish churchyard at Kilkhampton, an eighteenth-century clergyman, James Hervey, meditated on this in a tract dedicated to tombs and their inscriptions. The 'poor indigent', he contended, 'lay as softly and slept as soundly as the most opulent possessor'. The only distinction now 'was a grassy hillock, bound with osiers or a sepulchral stone, ornamented with imagery'.[23] But these distinctions did matter to many people for whom death's power as a leveller was somewhat overstated. This was not only a matter for the elite jockeying for memorial space in the church. The graveyard too had its prime plots, usually those nearest to the churchyard path and seldom on the shadowy north side where the suicides and unbaptised might be consigned. A Devon grave slab commented on the pattern: 'Here I lie by the chancel door, They put me here for I was poor, The further in, the more you pay, But here I lie as snug as they.'[24] But the sentiment was a rare one. John Knill and the people of St Ives inhabited an intensely hierarchical world. Rank as well as profession and good name were bound up with identity, and people tried to hang onto these things, even when they were dead.

They would hang onto them only for a time. However hard the stone, memorials were fragile things. James Hervey mused in the eighteenth century that 'yet a little while and they are all obliterated . . . characters cut with a pen of iron, and committed to solid rock, will ere long cease to be legible'.[25] Thomas Browne was more precise in the seventeenth century, venturing that stones exposed to the elements 'tell the truth scarce forty years'.[26] This was an estimate for climes less hostile than the north Cornish coast. Even with their backs turned against the prevailing winds, gravestones in St Ives were swiftly anonymised by south-westerlies loaded with spray, salt and sand. The churchwardens' accounts suggest the forces of nature ranged against them, with money spent replacing the church's storm-battered pinnacles, weathervanes and even, in 1697, glass in the chancel when waves broke over the churchyard walls and shattered some of the lights.[27]

People knew that monuments were ephemeral; they watched those of earlier generations crumbling. They understood, as the philosopher William Godwin observed in 1809, that 'ordinary tombstones are removed much after the manner the farmer removes the stubble of this year's crop that he make room for the seed of the next'.[28] Death, as John Aubrey recalled, came in time even to names and stones.[29] Nothing in the sublunary world lasted. Monuments themselves made that point. Those of the seventeenth and eighteenth centuries often carried hourglasses, skulls or vases with flowers soon to wither, marking the transitoriness of worldly things.[30]

The Praed tomb in Lelant church has them, and a skeleton armed with an hourglass and dated 1761 also guards the church's west door. The crumbling tombstone was a metaphor of the same essential truth. But the consolation in the face of oblivion was that even as memory was obliterated in this world, the dead were alive in the next. Earthly oblivion meant little when set against what Thomas Browne called the 'metaphysicks' of true belief. Tombstones affirmed this metaphysics too. They told of the virtue, fame and loveliness of the dead. They spoke of terrible grief. But they found consolation in the hope of heavenly bliss and meeting again.[31]

The nineteenth-century stones of St Ia's churchyard carried messages about these things.[32] Mary, wife of James Berriman, who died in 1824 aged sixty-three, was 'lovely, an innocent'. Death 'snatched thee from our arms' but 'heaven shall give thee brighter charms'. Elizabeth Noall died aged twenty-nine in 1827. She was a 'sweet maid' whose bud winter had seared as it broke into bloom; but there would be waking again and joy and 'an eternal home' where the family would be reunited. Many people of St Ives looked to the sea for consoling metaphors. When John Quick died in 1826 aged forty-four, his body was 'prey to wormes' but he had outridden 'the stormy blast' to find safe harbour in death. Although John, son of Francis and Sarah Bamfield, died young at just twenty-eight in 1831, his parents took comfort that 'the roaring wind and foaming seas will batter him no more'. For, 'the anchor cast', he had arrived on 'Canaan's happy shore'. And at Lelant, the mother-church of St Ives half buried amidst the dunes, Elizabeth Cundy also voyaged through wind and waves to find eventual safe haven in heaven, borne there in a stone ship, in full sail, which still tops her memorial.[33]

If the spirit had sailed for heaven, the flesh waited for resurrection. The stone on the grave of Stephen Jose who died in 1788 and his son Timothy who died in 1808 was full of that hope: 'Corruption, earth and worms, Shall but refine this flesh, Till my triumphant spirit comes, To put it on afresh.' Dead family members were buried together in the churchyard earth not only out of fellow feeling but in the hope that one day 'their bones would meet' clothed again in new flesh on the joyful day of judgement.

Standing in the graveyard of St Ia's Church today, many of these fears and hopes seem remote. Fewer people now are so attached to burial in a particular place as they were in the early nineteenth century. Although many still entertain the idea of life after death, few anticipate the body's physical resurrection. But most still want to be remembered. For the majority of the men and women who had gravestones set up in the churchyard of St Ives, that goal was only partially and obliquely fulfilled: very few of the inscriptions from the nineteenth century can still be read *in situ* on the stones. Most of them have been cleared away and those that remain, many laid flat around the church, have been scrubbed clean of words by the elements. That we know anything about these people is thanks to a modest triumph of paper over stone. A nineteenth-century historian of the parish observed the likely fate of the inscriptions and painstakingly wrote them down. One of his records calls to mind John Knill. For the parish historian noted that in 1830 Nathaniel Thoms Senior died at the relatively ripe age of seventy-two. Like John Knill he served as the officer of HM Customs for many years. Somewhere in the churchyard lie his bones but his memorial has long since weathered to nothing and he is remembered, one suspects, by few in the town.

John Knill is the opposite of Nathaniel Thoms. Remembered so well in St Ives, he is not, in fact, buried in the churchyard. Indeed, he is not buried anywhere near the town. How this came to pass is a final twist in his story. For John Knill wanted to be buried in Cornish earth but he did not much care for the idea of being buried at St Ives. He sent a letter on 30 March 1782 saying that he did not approve of the idea of burial in the church itself. He gave no reasons but he could hardly have worried about the ostentation of intramural burial given his exhuberant plans for commemoration. More likely he disliked the idea of church interiors crowded with corpses, from which noisome smells were to waft up the noses of those in the congregation. This was not the kind of remembrance he envisaged. He set his face too against burial in the churchyard. This, he said, was already too crowded and there was not enough space for local people so it should not be used for a prodigal son. There was also another feature of this sort of overcrowding that he disliked. As God's Acre filled up, the grave-space was reused. Burial fees purchased only a lease on churchyard earth, not an eternal freehold. And so when a monument had crumbled and people had forgotten the person who lay beneath, the ground was broken and a new body put in. The problem was not new. During the Middle Ages, new burials forever turned up bones and some churches had charnels where these could wait in peace for reassembly at the resurrection.[34] More frequently, the dead simply accumulated.

Graveyards were sometimes raised up far above the level of the surrounding ground as, down the centuries, the parishioners were inexorably gathered in. Many parishes fixed burial charges for interment in a shroud at lower rates than those for burial in a coffin; the unspoken assumption was that the grave would be free for reuse in the former case much the sooner.[35] At St Ives the burgeoning population intensified this widespread problem. According to nineteenth-century lore, on three occasions when the churchyard was full, trains of mules had traipsed up from the beach bearing loads of sand. With it, fresh layers were created to receive new generations of the dead. The expedient was ended, so it was said, lest the church itself be buried. There was probably at least a grain of truth in the old tales. At St Neots no fewer than 548 bodies were buried between 1608 and 1708.[36] Richard Polwhele, vicar of Kenwyn, annoyed his parishioners by insisting on a new graveyard because the old one was so full 'that the ground was scarcely ever opened without turning up of putrid bodies, or skulls, or skeletons'.[37] At St Ives, modern folklore bears out the tale of re-sanding. Almost within living memory, it is said, works to widen the road required some cutting into the churchyard which rears a good ten feet above it. When the workmen began to dig, they found layer upon layer of skeletons, packed as tight as pilchards in a crate.

Being packed in like a pilchard was not a fate John Knill relished and so the steeple on Worvas Hill was to be his mausoleum, a stone sarcophagus set in the middle of it. When the living John Knill superintended a dry run of his commemorations in 1801 he planned to be present at the heart of subsequent ones too, quite literally, even when he was dead. His body was to be intimately bound up with his remembrance. But this was one bit of his scheme that went awry. For he never managed to get the church to consecrate the ground on which the steeple stood. The sarcophagus is empty, the pyramid is only a cenotaph and John Knill is there only in spirit at his quinquennial festivities. His body is lodged far away, at St Andrew's Church in Holborn.

9

ADDED TERRORS

On 13 April 2011 the bones of an eighteen-year-old called John Horwood were carried to Hanham on the outskirts of Bristol. They were wheeled to the parish church on a bier, a red rose placed on the coffin. A short service followed during which the chief mourner, Mary Halliwell, laid a hand on the coffin and said, 'Well, John, you have finally come home to Hanham, the place of your birth. We have brought you home to lie in rest with your father, Thomas.'[1] Then the coffin was lowered into the earth among the graves of the dead man's ancestors. What made this funeral remarkable was that John Horwood had died one hundred and ninety years ago. He was buried in 2011, according to rituals that belonged to the early nineteenth century, because his distant relative, Mary Halliwell, was keen that he be accorded the rites he had long been denied. The story of John Horwood – his life, his death and his afterlife – leads from Hanham on the city's edge towards the centre of Bristol, to the New Gaol which once stood on Cumberland Road near to the harbour; it also leads back to the Georgian age, to the year 1821.[2]

The Gallows and the Grave

John Horwood's Bristol was, under a sleek and modern surface, a medieval town. Some streets that betrayed the fact were so narrow, pressed in by overhanging houses on either side, so steep, so honeycombed by cellars beneath, that sledges were used to move goods about for fear carts might get stuck or cause collapses. They had rubbed the paving smooth, making it treacherous in rain and snow. It was away from the higgledy-piggledy backstreets, in the heart of the city and especially down by the docks, that Bristol's transformation became clear. Everywhere there were new buildings of eighteenth-century vintage. Near the quays brick warehouses had been developed as the city grew fat on sugar, tobacco, rum, cocoa, fish and slaves traded over the Atlantic. There were sugar refineries, glass works, brass works and chocolate factories, set up as new industries grew on the back of these trades. Horace Walpole thought Bristol the 'dirtiest great shop I ever saw', its people 'running up and down with cloudy looks and busy faces'. But the hectic vulgarity of the business that Walpole disliked brought great wealth too, and domestic squares and terraces with classical proportions, houses for the nouveau riche, had spread through the centre of the city and up onto the heights around it. And although by the early nineteenth century the commercial heyday was in the past, the city was still full of merchants, many with houses in suburbs set apart from the bustle of the harbour. At Clifton, fine villas crested the hills. In Hotwells there was a therapeutic spring where people of quality could take the waters. Dotted around the city were inns and coffee houses where the middling sort could gather and gossip and browse the newspapers, the press being another industry that had flourished in vibrant Georgian Bristol.[3]

The lives lived in the affluent suburbs contrasted sharply with the situation of John Horwood. His parents were poor but respectable. They had led, to begin with at least, itinerant lives, his father on merchant ships plying to and from the Indies, his mother, who hailed originally from Orkney, finding a place in service. When the two met they settled in Hanham, a village outside the city, and there they put down roots. They had ten children. John was their youngest boy. A little before 1.30 p.m. on 13 April 1821, he found himself poised between life and death, waiting on the gallows at the New Gaol in Cumberland Road.[4] The route that brought him there was not straightforward; nor was the denouement of his story.

It all had all begun quite innocently, with an affectionate connection to a young Hanham woman, Eliza Balsum, who lived with her mother in a cottage in the hamlet. For many months John 'teased the girl with proposals', which she had 'uniformly and indignantly rejected'. She began to avoid him and he became increasingly agitated that his love was not returned. His behaviour became more menacing and, it was said, he 'vowed revenge' on her within earshot of neighbours. On one occasion he assaulted Eliza and she fled to local men for protection and then, just after Christmas in 1820, he threw 'oil of vitriol' over her, destroying her clothes.[5] Eliza withdrew to her mother's house, saying that she feared Horwood might be the death of her. Then in the February of 1821, having ventured out to Bristol, she was making her way back home in the company of a man called Joseph Rees. As they crossed a small stream that ran near to the boundary of Bitton and St George's parishes, a stone whistled through the air and struck Eliza on the head. She fell 'senseless' into the water and was taken to a nearby house. Her hair was trimmed away and a plaster applied to the wound; the stone had drawn blood but the wound seemed small, the sort of injury that might be treated readily enough at home.

Horwood was immediately suspected of the assault; he had been sighted on the 'rising ground' above the brook in the company of two other youths. One of them had fled away, 'being exceedingly frightened at the deadly spectacle of the blood on the girl's face and clothes', but the other had gone to give assistance.[6] At first Eliza seemed to be recovering. Having been treated again at her mother's house, this time with plasters of salt butter, she was well enough next day to fetch water from the well. But then there was pain and vomiting so she made her way to the infirmary in Bristol for treatment.[7] There 'all possible care and attention was shown her', according to the surgeons' notes. Poultices were applied, she was bled, calomel was tried. When this did no good, one of the doctors, a man called Estlin, applied leeches to her head. She continued to sink and, after the surgeons had consulted, one of their leading lights, a man called Richard Smith, decided to open up her head to investigate. The surgeon's notes disclose none of the patient's trauma as she experienced this procedure in a world without anaesthesia but in diagnostic terms the operation was a success. Smith discovered 'a quantity of matter had formed on the brain'. The surgery had little therapeutic value, though; after it Eliza only deteriorated and as 'alarming symptoms' took hold, the magistrate was alerted since an offence more serious than common assault seemed now to be in view. The girl's original injuries had, the surgeons concurred, been far worse than first thought and her life was in danger.

The magistrate, Mr Haythorne, issued a warrant for Horwood's arrest. As he was judged to be a 'desperate, ferocious fellow', the sheriff's yeomen dispatched to fetch him made preparations. They went to his parents' house armed and early in the morning, before Horwood was up. Shaken awake by banging at the door he tried to escape, attempting to squeeze his large frame through an upstairs window. But it was too narrow for him so he turned instead to fight. Taking up his quarryman's hammer, he positioned himself at the top of the stairs and drove the sheriff's men back. They debated using their pistols but eventually went to work with their bludgeons instead. For a time he kept them at bay but then, losing his temper, threw the hammer at one of the men. Unable to lay hands on a new weapon they knocked him down and carted him off into custody in a waiting carriage.

Placid and handcuffed, he was taken to Eliza's bedside at the infirmary; she could scarce look at him but, in the presence of the Justice of the Peace, put her mark on a deposition that made plain she believed he had thrown the stone at her. Within hours of Horwood's visit, Eliza's condition had worsened again such that she could manage no more than teaspoons of broth. She slipped in and out of consciousness, barely clinging to life. Dr

Estlin noted in his case papers that the end came on Saturday 17 February at around eight o'clock in the evening, a little before he left the ward. Eliza was moved to the dead room of the hospital for the rest of the weekend and then, when Richard Smith came in on Monday morning, he performed a dissection. He concluded that Eliza had indeed died from the injuries sustained at the stream. The tiny wound, no bigger than a thumbnail, had generated putrefying matter in the brain which had poisoned her. He did not consider the possibility that the cranial surgery, his 'necessary operation', as he called it, had any part to play in her death. The post-mortem was more then than a piece of pathology, it was an act of self-absolution too.

John Horwood was now charged with murder and witness depositions piled up, more of them for the prosecution than the defence. William Fry, one of the men with Horwood around the time of the attack, had, he said, noticed 'something' in his hand a little before Eliza was struck and while he did not see the stone launched, he did see Horwood's arm raised afterwards as if he had thrown something. Joseph Rees had not seen Horwood throw the stone either but he had been crossing the brook with Eliza when it arced towards them from 'rising ground', a phrase used by several witnesses. They had, it seems, been talking over the incident or even rehearsing their evidence. Ann Fry, the sister of William, added damning circumstantial details. She had heard John say he would kill Eliza because she would not marry him and she retold the story of the vitriol attack just after Christmas too. Sarah Balsum, Eliza's mother, fleshed out the context further. Her daughter, she said, had lived in fear of Horwood. There had been exhibitions near to the house, he had threatened to 'dash her bones to pieces' and her daughter had come to think her very life was in danger.[8]

Horwood was held in custody until Robert Gifford, Recorder of Bristol, arrived at the Guildhall to deliver the gaols of their prisoners by hearing the cases. Before him were instances of house-breaking, violence, forging of promissory notes and a welter of thefts: of articles from silver snuffboxes to tobacco, calfskin to coin, quantities of lead to thirteen pigeons. Gifford was, so his friends said, a model of quick apprehension and accurate reasoning when on the bench and a 'mild, friendly and indulgent man' in private but, whatever his qualities, the law he administered remained savage.⁹ Many of the pettier offences before him were still capital ones and, when business was done, there was little chance that he would don the white gloves, which signified that there was no blood on the judge's hands.

Horwood was the star turn of the sessions and, on 11 April 1821, the courtroom was full. Defence counsel did his best. John was, he stressed, from a decent family. His father was 'a careful, industrious man and respectable in his situation'. John had long been attached to Eliza and that he loved her made it unlikely that he would wish her ill; indeed, they had not so long ago been seen happily in company together. On New Year's Day 1821 the pair were 'reclining' in the chimney corner at the house of Mrs Jones, a place where people of the village often mingled, old folk in one room and young in another. Eliza, Martha Jones deposed, had been cold and so John had given her his coat. Would John have wanted to kill a girl he loved? And even if he was so moved, he had been loitering in company near the Ship Inn at the time of the attack and could not, argued the lawyer intricately, have been in the right place at the right moment to launch the missile. And, of course, no one had actually *seen* him throw the stone. Then there was the business of the wound. At this point the lawyer's argument worked by insinuation. The wound was small, no bigger than a thumbnail, and after treatment with plasters Eliza had been well enough next day to carry a pitcher of water home. At no point did he explicitly say that Richard Smith's intervention had killed the patient but he did query the surgeon's emphatic claim that the stone's impact was the cause of death. How, mused the lawyer, could he be so very sure? Then he added a new, darker undertone. Smith had in his evidence insisted that Eliza had been a virgin. This was an issue he had resolved during the dissection since the defendant had, he said, been putting it about that the girl was a 'common prostitute'. Someone, it seems, had indeed been sowing the seeds of doubt about Eliza's virtue, though not necessarily Horwood. The image of her 'reclining' with him beside the chimney breast on New Year's Day hinted at the rumour and now counsel pointed directly to the matter, asking whether Smith's test was truly reliable in determining a girl's virginity. In a final peroration he turned back to his client. Passing silently over the battle with the sheriff's men, he said that Horwood had betrayed no signs of guilt in his behaviour. The day after the attack on Eliza, he had given no indication of agitation of mind. He went about his business as usual, even going into Bristol to fetch a pig. With that the case rested.

The jury began its deliberations and Horwood waited. He was buoyed up before the trial, confident of acquittal. A minister who went to see him, Reverend Roberts, thought him far too sanguine, a boy battened up in blissful ignorance and unaware of just how slender were his chances of escaping the noose. When the jury returned its verdict it was a shattering shock: guilty. Gifford surveyed the defendant, arranged a black cap on his wig and sentenced Horwood to death by hanging. Then he added something more. He directed that when the condemned man was dead his body be cut down and handed over to the city's surgeons. He would, as an added punishment, be anatomised before an assembled crowd.

When Reverend Roberts saw Horwood again he had gone to pieces. He was fearful that the news would kill his aged father and pious Methodist mother and, as he looked to himself, all his sins seemed to 'rush on his recollection'. He sat on the side of his bed and 'presented a scene of horror and agony of mind'. He cried out, 'Oh my soul, my soul, my precious soul. I am not prepared to die. I shall be in hell.' The minister left him to sleep for a time and then came back and attempted to calm him, trying to make him ready for death by coaxing out of him a sense of his sinfulness and explaining the possibility of regeneration in

Christ. He explained that Christ had died for him, just as he had died for the thief crucified beside him on Calvary, and if only he found his way to Christ his soul might yet be saved. This seemed almost new to Horwood. Bemused, he knelt in prayer. This too was awkward – he was not given to prayer – but his expressions were heartfelt and the minister 'saw some light in him'. Next day he was more composed. He knew he was soon to die and, although 'was not certain of going to heaven . . . he hoped to go to the drop with eyes and heart directed towards God'. The day before he was to hang, his father, brother and sister came to the prison. He came to them in the prison cap and in jangling chains; he was heard before he was seen. His father and sister broke down; his brother, Joseph, a devout man, was more the master of his emotions but still distraught. His father gazed into his son's eyes and stroked his hair, wondering aloud, 'My dear son, my dear son, did I ever think that I should be the means of bringing a child into the world to be hanged?' He told him to be 'much in prayer to God' and to place hope in divine mercy. His mother did not come. Night and day she was on her knees at home in prayer.

Gallows tales told by witnesses to executions and circulating in the cheap prints would have given Horwood more than an inkling of what was coming. He could not be sure death would be quick. The 'New Drop', which promised a swifter and more humane end, had been installed at the gaol but had not yet been tried there; in practice, it often extinguished life slowly by strangulation, much as traditional means of hanging always had.[10] His fate once dead was known to him too. The activities of the anatomists were well publicised enough, but, even before he went to trial, Richard Smith had ensured that Horwood made the acquaintance of two women, Mistresses Davis and Bobbet.[11] They were skeletons. Executed in 1802 for the murder of a child, they had been anatomised and their remains kept at the infirmary. The reasons why Smith did this are cloudy. His scheme was, perhaps, to induce a confession through terror but whatever the motive, the spectacle of the skeletons showed Horwood his future. The

In *The Great Day of His Wrath*, John Martin, the Victorian artist and master of the 'apocalyptic sublime', set out to capture in paint the prophecy of the world's end found in the Bible's final book, Revelation.

The figure of Death in medieval glass. A detail from the fifteenth-century 'Apocalypse Window' at All Saints church, North Street, York, which depicts scenes from the end of the world.

John Baret's cadaver tomb, St Mary's church, Bury St Edmunds. A follower of macabre fashion, John Baret chose to be buried in the kind of tomb that would stir viewers to pity and elicit prayers for his soul, suffering in the fires of purgatory.

The end of the world rendered in rough paintwork of the late fifteenth century at Wenhaston church, Suffolk. The image was common in late medieval churches and its message was plain: the dead would rise from their graves and, after judgement, be delivered up to heaven or swallowed in the gaping mouth of hell.

Annie Besant (1847–1933): secularist lecturer, socialist and convert to theosophical mysticism.

Venetia, Lady Digby (1600–1633) on her deathbed, a mortuary portrait in oils by Anthony Van Dyck, painted at the behest of her distraught husband, Sir Kenelm.

THE LATE

Dᴿ PRICE.

JMS

William Price (1800–1893): medical practitioner, self-proclaimed Archdruid of Wales and pioneer cremationist.

John Knill's memorial 'steeple' at Worvas Hill, St Ives, on 25 July 1896. In fulfilment of the terms of the Knill benefaction, the townsfolk of St Ives have gathered quinquennially on this date since 1801 to celebrate his memory.

The Unknown Warrior's coffin rests in Westminster Abbey.

The Tomb of the Unknown Warrior: fashioned from Belgian marble and fringed with verses from scripture, its central message was that the man interred beneath, and the hundreds of thousands who died like him, had laid down their lives for God and King, for country and empire, for loved ones, for justice and for the freedom of the world.

The Plains of Heaven forms part of John Martin's triptych depicting the end of the world. Newspaper reports intimated that it proved the most popular with the viewing public.

inner sensations as he looked at them are irrecoverable and can hardly be guessed.

The condemned man's turmoil did not have long to run on. Expedition was the British way with the death penalty, and just two days after the verdict, he was made ready. At ten o'clock in the morning, he went to the prison chapel and heard Reverend Roberts preach. When the minister was done, Horwood himself addressed his fellow prisoners, standing before them as a (still just) living morality, a warning to turn away from deeper evils lest they suffer his fate. Then he waited in his cell. The sheriff came, rapped on the door and told him, 'The time is come.' Roberts said that he hoped they were now ready. All manner of people would have come to see the spectacle that ensued – the ragged masses, surely, but also people of quality. Some may have sympathised with Horwood but many probably did not: execution crowds invariably had less fellow feeling about them when the condemned man was a murderer. Before mounting the platform, Reverend Roberts prayed with Horwood in the dead room under the drop, a better place for the condemned man to make his peace, he thought, because he would not have the distraction of the crowd. Then, bound, he was taken out onto the scaffold, into the noise. The noose was placed around his neck. Then there was a long pause as he composed himself. He was, perhaps, lost in terror but Roberts said he was lost in prayer. Eventually Horwood gave the signal and the trap fell away. An eyewitness said he died quickly; after a moment's struggle his spirit was gone, 'fled to eternity'. It was a little after half past one in the afternoon.

Some probably thought there was still potency in his remains. The bodies of felons had magic powers; there was often a struggle to touch them to cure warts or cancers. In 1752 after the hanging of highway robbers on St Michael's Hill, some in the crowd battled the executioner as they tried to strip clothes from the corpses. One woman had come fifteen miles in hope of getting one of the nooses.[12] They held such things were charmed.

Horwood had, almost from the moment of his arrest, lost

control over his body and so it remained in death, for, soon after removal from the gallows, his mortal remains were in the hands of the anatomists. His memory too became the plaything of others. John Horwood was, in this respect, the mirror image of John Knill. Knill intimately scripted how he was to be remembered when he was dead but John Horwood's memory would be appropriated by the clergymen who had been with him at the last. It had been, they said, his dying wish to be commemorated at services, out in the open air on Jeffery's Hill, near to where he had grown up. The notion grew out of conversations with the clergy and although they said it was his idea it might well have been theirs. What emerged was an account of his life and death, preached before the crowds and written up for printing, which turned his story into a morality. His was a tale of sinfulness that led to self-destruction, a tale of a man slithering down a slippery slope. He began with petty thefts of apples in childhood. Then there was idling, sabbath-breaking and overindulgence in the 'vice' of tobacco which shaded into larceny and violence, obsession and murder. But this was not a horror story. By way of the gallows there had been regeneration. John Horwood had died in Christ, his gaze set Godward, and so with a genuine hope of going to heaven. On Sunday 21 April 1821 the services were held on Jeffery's Hill, three of them in total – one in the morning, afternoon and evening. Some six thousand came to hear the message and sing specially composed hymns about the hanged man. Still more would have attended, surmised the clergy, if the final service had not been struck by a great storm of hail, which beat upon all who did not have umbrellas and turned the roads to muddy streams.

As the clergy laid hold of Horwood's memory for the sake of piety, others were seizing hold of it for profit. Newspapermen plastered his story of unrequited love, murder and death over their pages. Printers ran off re-scripts of the felon's life, the specially composed hymns. There was even some poetry, supposedly written by the condemned man in his cell, though it seems

that John Horwood could not write, his 'mark' rather than signa-
ture appearing on case papers. He, the poems, claimed, had never
meant to kill Eliza but admitted that, in his anguish at being
thrown over, he had considered murder. He cursed the hand that
had thrown 'the fatal stone' and lamented his sweetheart lying in
the grave: 'Eliza, oh Eliza dear! Thy spirit, oh, is fled, And thy
poor mangled body lies now numbered with the dead.' Mr Collard,
a businessman with a house in the Hotwells district and premises
in Bridewell Lane, near the old prison, printed more verses, which
he claimed were Horwood's work. A specimen couplet is enough
to give a sense of the whole: 'Murder I told her I certainly would
do, And once I burning vitriol o'er her I threw.'

John Horwood's corpse, meanwhile, was the prisoner of strong
imperatives as it waited for delivery to the surgeons. Convinced
that crime was out of control, Parliament in the mid eighteenth
century had broadened the use of capital punishment as the
'Bloody Code' made death the penalty for ever pettier offences.
But lest the hardened criminal conclude that it were indeed as
well to be hanged for a sheep as a lamb, the law's architects sought
in framing the Murder Act of 1752 an 'added terror' to deter the
worst kinds of felony. Unable to hang a man more than once,
they decided that when the dead body was cut down further
punishments should be visited on the corpse. 'In no case what-
soever', warned the act, 'the body of any Murderer shall be suffered
to be buried.' The injunction had precedents.[13] Hanging in chains
had long been an option in 'the most attrocious of cases', the
victim being suspended in a public place to die and then left there
to disintegrate. The judges could continue to prescribe such
punishment if they wished or they could have a felon gibbeted,
his body bound in an iron cage and left twisting in the wind, open
to public gaze in some prominent spot until the metal rusted,
wood rotted and the body fell to pieces. But the toughening of
the law offered another kind of opportunity. Surgeons were clam-
ouring for subjects whom they could dissect to help in their
exploration of the body's workings. Since the reign of Henry VIII,

they had been allowed a small number of corpses each year from the gallows.[14] Now the law expanded the supply. The worst felons 'expiated their crimes upon the scaffold, and contributed to science by yielding their bodies to the scalpel'. Judges could, and in the worst cases should, pass sentence of death and dissection.

John Horwood's parents did everything they could to stop the full rigours of the law being visited on their son. So much of the 'added terror' envisaged by the statute ultimately fell on them. John would be denied the funeral and peaceful rest that were thought the birthright of most. For him there could be no careful washing of the corpse by women of the parish, no shrouding nor 'chesting' ready for the funeral. The family would not kiss the body and say goodbye. The neighbours would not come into the house, one by one or in small groups, to view his body, perhaps to touch the corpse lest they had troubled dreams about it. There would be no watches over a coffin, no bidder doing the rounds telling people to come to the funeral, no funeral and no feast of cakes, biscuits and meats. There would be no solemnities nor prayer book service; no promise of the resurrection to eternal life would be spoken over the grave. The anguished parents engaged solicitors to plead for them. John Horwood's father also went to the surgeons himself and begged them in 'a painful interview' not to carry out the dissection but to let his son's body home. It might yet, he hoped, be laid to rest at Hanham, if only on the north side of the church among the shadows where undesirables were buried. The surgeons were moved by 'the tears of so respectable an old man' but duty was stronger than sentiment and the judge's instructions pellucidly clear. They were bound by the court and by obligation to their fellow citizens: murder must be deterred and anatomisation was a deterrent. So Horwood must be cut up. In a last, desperate throw of the dice, a group of relatives tried to waylay the cart conveying the corpse to the anatomy room but their 'ambuscade' failed; the law then began to take its course.

On the evening of 14 April, John Horwood's body was laid out

on a table in the middle of a theatre in readiness for the first of
two lectures to be delivered by Mr Richard Smith 'upon the body
of the unfortunate malefactor'. This task was far from new to
him. Smith's interests were perhaps more pathological than therapeutic; they ran in the family – his father had even created a
museum of human specimens. It had been natural for him to
take up a post in 1797 which required him to give lectures in
anatomy and he had, in commercial terms at least, made a success
of the venture. So popular were his courses and so lucrative were
the fees that he had been obliged to move into larger premises.
As this was a punitive dissection, and because the case had acquired
notoriety thanks to the press, the demonstration took place not
only before his students but also with gentlemen, non-medical
men, in attendance 'who pleased to honour the surgeons with
their presence'. There were some eighty or more in total crowded
on the benches; indeed, to make sure of a decent crowd of the
quality of Bristol, Smith had, it seems, sent out invitations.

Smith began his exposition with a discourse on the nature of
blood circulation in simple animals. Then he moved on to reptiles,
fish, birds and quadrupeds before turning to the 'human frame'.
At punitive dissections the cutting customarily began with an
incision in the shape of the cross.[15] Smith and his fellow surgeons
then worked inwards, revealing the workings of his subject's body
to the gaze of the audience, transforming the human remains
into so many specimens. He continued on a second night for
some two hours and 'demonstrated the viscera of the abdomen'
to his mixed audience of students and gentlemen. All manner of
drawings and 'beautiful anatomical preparations' were used by
way of illustration and the lecture proved a crowd-pleaser, all
present departing 'highly satisfied' with the experience. Some even
wrote appreciative letters, which Smith kept with his papers. Dr
Estlin, who was engaged in the dissection of Horwood along with
two of Smith's other pupils, took careful notes in neat copperplate.
'He was', he concluded, 'only eighteen years old but extremely
muscular.'

This was not quite the end of the matter. Smith had warned in an earlier communication with Horwood's parents that their son must be formed after dissection into a skeleton and thence would join others to be an object of further study. He paid the princely sum of three guineas to an 'articulator' of Hillgrove Street who set about this task. The man's business card is preserved with Smith's papers. Its motif is a skeleton, standing arms akimbo with one bony hand gesturing faintly towards the articulator's name, which is wreathed in scrolls. In the end Smith seems to have been especially pleased with the outcome. He took Horwood's skeleton home and there it resided in a cabinet, being brought out, on occasion, for visitors to view.

There is a horror about John Horwood's fate that transcends time. But the sentence of death and dissection handed down by Judge Gifford was heavy with implications for the condemned man's destiny which were of their age and of earlier ages. Protestant theology dictated firmly that the fate of the body did not affect the trajectory of the soul but many ordinary men and women stubbornly believed otherwise.[16] Disintegration, profane burial and non-burial all hinted at damnation, perhaps at annihilation, and herein lay the chiefest 'added terror' of the mid eighteenth-century statute. Instinct taught that the funerary rites smoothed the way to salvation and did not merely symbolise it. And did not the Church's own theology say that bodies would be needed again at the day of resurrection? Treated usually with reverence on this basis, to do otherwise suggested a bleak fate. Visceral fears were at work under the surface of this folk theology. Dead bodies were numinous things. For a time they still had life in them, since the spirit separated itself from the living not in the twinkling of an eye but more slowly. Death rituals suggested and formed this idea, speaking of the need to set the spirit in motion, to help it on its journey, to see it safely out of the world. All too lifelike, the dead person seemed merely to sleep. The spirit lingered in dreams or wandered as a ghost. Apprehension that the body itself might return to life, might turn into a vengeful revenant, had evaporated by the nineteenth century but unusual corpses were still thought by some to be charged with special powers. A murder victim's body might bleed if the killer were conducted into its presence or touched it. Myth even had it that a 'hand of glory', a candle made from his remains, was inextinguishable by ordinary means and ensured householders would not wake as a burglar went about his business. Certain kinds of corpse called for special treatment. Infants who died unbaptised were often obliged to lie outside hallowed ground or on its edge. Suicides were interred on the north side of the churchyard or were denied burial there altogether. They were laid in fields or at crossroads or on the shoreline between land and sea where their bodies might forever be washed by the waves.[17] Such rites not only symbolised separation from the saved but, perhaps, helped to bring it about, an intuition that not only gave the living power over individual fates but also, reassuringly, implied human power over death itself.

The worst of fates was to be sentenced to die and disintegrate above the earth's surface, for the flesh and bone to be cleaved apart and scattered, never to find rest in the earth. Events that took place in Bristol in 1735 suggest as much. They befell a ship's captain, a man called James Newton, who was of bad repute in the city. He already lay under suspicion of piracy and of brutal treatment of sailors but somehow he had escaped punishment for his crimes. Then in September that year, he flew into a rage with his wife and trampled her to death. After this outrage, justice finally caught up with him. He was tried in Bristol and sentenced to death. But on being committed to the city's Newgate Prison he cheated the hangman by swallowing poison. A piece of judicial theatre then played itself out. Newton's corpse was hauled to a crossroads. There it was buried and a stake was driven through it, the uppermost part left protruding as a monument and a warning. This was the procedure that custom, though not the law itself, decreed and John Weever explained in the seventeenth century that suicides were buried in this way 'to terrify all passengers' as they glimpsed the tip of the stake from their coaches. Then, by 'so infamous and reproachful a burial', they would be encouraged 'not to make such their final passage out of this world'.[18] The full rigours of the punishment were, in practice, usually remitted when the balance of a suicide's mind was thought disturbed but in this case, as society struggled to punish a man who had evaded its sanctions, the corpse suffered the unhallowing rites in unexpurgated form.[19] And yet in John Newton's case not even burial staked at a crossroads slaked the public thirst for vengeance, or at least that of a section of the public. A crowd returned to the burial place. They plucked up the body and tore it limb from limb, scattering the dead man's remains along the highway.[20] It seems that even before the law made the arrangement commonplace, the mob knew that disintegration of the body was the best way to deal with the worst kind of felon.

In the second half of the eighteenth century, the law had turned the anatomists into the accomplices of the tearing, rending mob. Yet they also stood apart from the crowd, and not only on account of rank and manners. Plying their trade and doing the judge's bidding in a city on the cusp of modernity, they were engaged in a strange double-think. For even as they participated in a piece of terrible theatre predicated on the idea that the corpse had some kind of vitality, they were coming to see it as an insensible thing, a piece of biological machinery the mechanism of which was stilled when a person died. Richard Smith had been at pains to locate his account of the human frame during his dissection of John Horwood in the context of reptilian and mammalian anatomy; he had positioned man's body in a sequence among the animals. He also made the insensible remains the subject of science. He inspected the features of Horwood's cranium in a phrenological study, describing them minutely because he thought that by these means he could describe the man's inner qualities. His tables survive, pre-printed and then filled in by hand with numbers that measured the subject's animal propensities, moral sentiments, knowing faculties, intelligences. It was as if by feeling the bumps on Horwood's head, Smith thought he could catch in his lattice of grids the stuff that made a criminal mind. The case was of such interest that the skull was bodied about among his colleagues for second opinions and learned comparisons. Letters were exchanged about its features. And yet all the time, Richard Smith was an actor in a penal process built on another, entirely different, kind of belief: that the human corpse still possessed a certain kind of sensitivity and that its treatment after death in some way influenced the soul's onward journey.

The search for inner knowledge of the body which left surgeons like Smith thus marooned between different traditions of thought also confronted them with a further problem. By the time John Horwood went to the gallows, even the hanging judges of early nineteenth-century England could not keep up with the insatiable demand of the anatomy schools for corpses. But then if the dead body was truly insensible, if it was simply a shell, a mechanism that had stopped when the soul fled, its fate did not matter in the way that vulgar people thought. Need the surgeons confine themselves to the dissection of felons from the scaffold? Increasingly, they concluded that they need not. Surgeons were ready to furnish their table not only from the gallows but also from the grave.

The Narrow House

In the heart of Bristol on a Sunday afternoon some time in 1822, a woman called Mrs Rice was laid to rest with due ceremony in the graveyard of St Augustine's, the cathedral church. Husband and children bade her farewell, the mourners dispersed and her body was left 'to moulder in parent earth'. But not for long. When darkness fell, a group of men came to the churchyard, opened the grave and spirited the body away. To read the newspapers of the day, this was far from a unique event. Bristol was alive by night, so it seemed, with men digging up the newly buried dead, trying to evade the attentions of watchmen and constables and trading in corpses for cash. Some were 'perfect adepts' in the art of body-snatching. They went about their work with wooden shovels, turnscrews for opening the coffins and an array of sacks, needles and ropes for hauling off the remains.[21] Sometimes surgeons were involved. In the year that Mrs Rice was roused prematurely from her long sleep, a group of medical men entered the nearby church-yard at Bedminster in a bid to seize another body (a 'fine specimen' in their eyes) which had been interred there the previous Sunday. Constables caught the 'depredators' in the act and battle was joined among the tombstones. 'Pistols were snapped and rapiers drawn', noses bloodied and heads broken. Eventually, five members of the medical profession were placed under arrest.[22]

The theft of that corpse was thwarted before any cutting could begin but not so with the unfortunate Mrs Rice. Quite where her body was taken after its theft is not clear as there were a number of different anatomists at work in the city at the time. Some said it was taken to a room above a greengrocer's shop in College Street. Others thought it was conveyed into the cathedral itself. Wherever it ended up, the different stories converged in describing its fate. Mrs Rice's body had fallen into the hands of an infirmary surgeon who purposed to dissect it before an audience of students. By the time he was ready to begin, news of the snatching had reached the woman's poor husband. He went to the place where the dissection was said to be happening but could not get in to see. Eventually some of his friends held him up so that he could gain entrance through a window. Only then did he discover 'the mangled remains of the late partner of his toils'. The dissection was well under way. Mrs Rice's arms were opened from the wrist to the elbow, her legs had been 'cut' and her back broken. With help, the distraught husband seized the body, carried it away and had it restored to the grave, although some said the body was taken up a second time and had to be rescued again.

Whatever the facts of the case – and no one can be quite sure what happened on the streets of Bristol that night – lurid reports filled column inches of the local newspapers. One editor asked readers to consider the unbridled horror of what was afoot in the city's churchyards. Everyone had friends or relatives interred there. 'What would your feelings be,' he enquired, 'to see their remains taken from the mother earth and manacled and cut into pieces' so as to satisfy the curiosity of the anatomists? The horror welled up out of visceral sensations, out of the religious imperative of proper burial denied and from the shame of the body's exposure to public gaze, especially strong in the case of an innocent woman dissected by male surgeons. It was refracted too through stories like that of John Horwood and James Newton. For to be cut in this way on the surgeon's table was to suffer a fate reserved for the worst kind of criminal. So grim was this prospect that branches of mortuary engineering developed to frustrate the resurrectionists. In churchyards in cities vulnerable to their attentions – from Aberdeen and Edinburgh in the north, London in the east and Bristol in the west – the dead were buried in iron coffins with elaborate locking mechanisms to secure them. Massive ledger stones were lowered over the bodies. Graves were dug extra deep and at least once in Bristol grave robbers were defeated because the body was enclosed 'in a strong shell'.[23] Mortsafes locked corpses safely into the earth and grilles were fastened over graves, sometimes giving rise to rumours that they kept a malevolent corpse in rather than the body snatcher out.[24] Some tombs began to resemble minor fortifications. In some cities with medical schools and bodysnatching problems, watch houses were built and men armed with pistols were posted to ensure corpses were given time to moulder to the point when the anatomists had no interest in them.

There was, of course, another side to this story. What lay behind the battles over bodies was the urgent need for cadavers in the medical schools. There was, as the *Bristol Mirror* pointed out, little choice between a surgeon being 'a torturer of the living' for want of anatomical knowledge or becoming entangled in a 'dreadful trade' in bodies needed for training in the theatres. For sure, no one wanted a loved one snatched away to the slab but neither *in extremis* would one want to be at the mercy of a surgeon with a fumbling grasp of anatomy.[25] This was an obvious conundrum; but underneath it was another. The anatomist's findings were, as John Horwood's post-mortem fate suggested, turning the corpse from a sentient and numinous thing into an intricate but senseless cadaver, a notion that had power to dissolve the sentiment, super- stition and magic formed round the corpse. But it was a logic that the surgeons could not quite accept themselves. The shame and fear of one's own body, or that of a loved one, being opened by the scalpel to public gaze was perennial. A mischievous corre- spondent wrote to a Bristol newspaper in the wake of the Mrs Rice scandal asking why, if the practice of anatomy was as bene- ficial as the surgeons claimed, they did not bequeath their own corpses and hand over those of their kin for dissection?[26] Few surgeons were ready to take these steps. The poet Robert Southey made fun of them for it. They would rather be 'buried in lead' when they were dead. They wanted patent coffins of the latest kind, which would be proof against jemmies and hammers. Watchmen must stand over their graves 'with blunderbuss and ball' until their bodies decomposed and they were useless to their colleagues.[27] Even if someone was noble enough to surrender his own body to science, few would be ready to let their loved ones go that way. The novelist Walter Scott saw quite clearly the value of anatomical studies and he was ready, at a pinch, to countenance his own dissection. But he would never let this 'indignity' be visited on friends or family. He would fight to his last breath to prevent it. 'So inconsistent', he observed, 'are we in such matters.'[28]

Mrs Rice, if the newspaper stories had it right, was permanently consigned to the earth in St Augustine's churchyard some time later in 1822 but there is no detail about the later history of her corpse. The final acts in John Horwood's story can be recon- structed with more precision because many of the details were collected by Richard Smith in a little volume now in the posses- sion of a Bristol museum.[29] This little tract is invaluable to any

historian interested in the case; between the covers there are
surgical notes, copies of depositions and trial proceedings, many
newspaper clippings and even a sketch map of the crime scene.
But this is no ordinary book. An inscription on the cover reads
Cutis Vera Johannis Horwood, words which warn readers that the
book they are holding has been bound in John Horwood's skin.
When he was done with the dissection, Richard Smith decided
to have his subject flayed and the skin tanned to make leather.
This had been used to cover the book. Skull and crossbones motifs
were added on each corner by way of decoration.[30] The Horwood
book was at once a source of knowledge and an advertisement
of the murderer's fate. 'It distinctly shows', mused a mid Victorian
reader, 'what dread, what thrilling fear, that sad sequel to an
ignominious death, the dissecting-room, produced upon the lower
manifestations of human character.'

Richard Smith died in 1843 in the affluent suburb of Clifton
where he had made his home. He had risen to be a significant
figure in a town which, for a time, remembered him. But his
standing was no more than provincial: in a lifetime of cutting, he
had made no lasting intellectual impression on his discipline. The
world in which he had made his name had also changed. By the
time of his death, the punitive dissection of felons' corpses had
been abolished for over a decade. The body snatchers too had
been put out of business. A new law decreed that the poor who
died in the workhouses would furnish corpses for scientific study.
The fear of the anatomist's art was not resolved by this measure;
it was simply concentrated in the vulnerable who ended their
lives on the parish, men and women who would now be full of
apprehension that dying in the workhouse might mean shameful,
horrible dissection, the felon's lot of old.[31]

Horwood's skeleton remained for a time in Smith's black
museum of 'memorabilia', the skull 'grinning the more horribly'
because it was kept with the paraphernalia of execution. The
remains then passed into the care of the university's medical
school. There the skeleton was kept in a cupboard, still with a

noose, perhaps the original one, round its neck. The book of skin, meanwhile, offered clues for John Horwood's descendant, Mrs Halliwell, whose genealogical searches had eventually uncovered a distant connection to the bones in the cupboard. She found that her great-great-great-grandfather had been John Horwood's brother. Knowing that John Horwood's parents had pleaded fruitlessly at the time of his execution for their son's body to be returned to them for decent burial, Mary Halliwell was moved to have him interred according to the rites he had been denied.

And so on 13 April 2011 John Horwood's bones were carried back to Hanham.[32] After the service Mrs Halliwell told the press that her wish was simply to 'lay him to rest as his parents wanted, and for him to be buried in a dignified way'.[33] Graveyard burial among the ancestors' bones is not such a preoccupation in a modern world in which so many lead itinerant lives and feel less attachment to any one place.[34] Belief in resurrection of the body, in any kind of afterlife, has fallen away as ritual tastes have altered. The idea that the body's integrity matters in death has lost much of its power; a measure of that change is that most people would now countenance cremation. And while the visceral horror of a gibbeting, punitive dissection and crossroads burial is as strong now as ever it was, the sensibility that allowed some of the dead to suffer these things as spectacle and warning is utterly alien. Ultimately it is the instinct to lay the dead properly to rest that bridges the years. Reverence, respect for their wishes and the idea that quiet rest should be the end of life are still powerful sentiments; so too are the kinds of emotions from which those instincts derive. Mrs Halliwell reflected that 'in a funny way during the procession I was imagining I was his mother' because, in burying him, 'I was doing his mother's job'. She added 'it touches me very much that things like that did happen, that mothers laid their sons to rest like that'.[35]

10

FIERY RESOLUTION

Across the waters of the Bristol Channel, some fifteen miles inland among the rising hills of South Wales, is Llantrisant. It is an ancient place, a market town built around its medieval church and castle. By the nineteenth century it was in the grip of steady transformation wrought by industrialisation. The population was rising, its streets were filling with chapels and coal and iron-ore mines were springing up in the countryside round about.[1] There, in the thickening dark of a winter evening, on Sunday 13 January 1884 the peace was broken. The sky above the town was lit up by a fire on the high ground of Cae'r-lan Fields. The flames were spotted a little after 7.00 p.m. by local men, Lewis Ajax and Uriah Wilkins, and crowds of people, many of them leaving chapel, converged on the spot. The sight that greeted them was strange indeed. An elderly man dressed in flowing white robes was presiding over a ritual centred on a blazing barrel part-filled with petroleum. Periodically he would kick the barrel to rouse the flames. Some of the onlookers thought they could see something inside. Sergeant Hoyle of the Llantrisant police then arrived, having seen the fire from the town below. He kicked over the barrel and out rolled the body of an infant, partly wrapped up in napkins. Another man, Albert Davies, caught it with a crook and dragged the burning bundle to the gutter of a hedge where he and others doused the flames. The crowd was now whipped up into a state of great excitement; the mood turned ugly. 'The women', recalled Albert Davies, 'were the worst.' There were shouts of 'lynch him' and 'burn him' and calls for the old man to be put in the burning cask. He was saved by the police. Myths were later spun round the figure of PC Francis who, it was said, leaped through the flames, his cape over his head, brandishing a truncheon to keep the crowd back.[2] In any event, the Llantrisant constabulary hustled the strangely dressed figure away and put him into the cells while they decided what was to be done with him.[3]

The man in the flowing robes was William Price, a local doctor. Born in 1800 at Risca, near Newport, he had trained as a physician in London, sitting in the capital's anatomy theatres through the bodysnatching age. Once qualified, he had come back to the valleys. A radical in politics and a reformer by inclination, he even played a part in a rebellion of working men in 1839 and had to flee to Paris when troops arrived to put an end to it. When he returned, he expressed his sympathies for working people in quieter ways as he treated them in practices in Nantgarw, Trefforest and Pontypridd. By the time he moved on to Llantrisant, in 1871, medical work had already won William Price a reputation for unusual generosity, for he was a rare doctor, willing to treat the poor irrespective of their ability to pay. He was also a man with long record of defying social convention in other ways, many of them much more eccentric to the eye of his neighbours. He was an evangelical anti-smoker in an age when many smoked, and was rumoured once to have thrown a man's pipe from a train when he refused to stop smoking in his compartment.[4] He was a vegetarian too, claiming that if man feasted on beasts he would, eventually, assume their 'habits and passions'. Above all, he was a Druid. Interest in things Druidical was piqued during his exile and it matured as he elaborated his own system of the cosmos. He began to preach to any who would give him a hearing and even to those who would not, haranguing passers-by in the public spaces of Llantrisant. Styling himself as the leader of the Druids in Wales, he donned white tunic, red waistcoat, green trousers and cultivated a straggling beard and hair worn in long plaits. He topped the outfit off with a fox-skin headdress, the tail and legs of which dangled round his shoulders 'like so many tassles'. This was the costume, so Price said, of a Druid people and the fox-skin was the mark of a healer.[5]

His beliefs moved him to flout not only sartorial but also moral conventions. He set up house with a woman called Ann Morgan and lived with her outside wedlock. When she died he caused a bigger scandal, taking up with Gwenllian Llewellyn, a farmer's daughter of just twenty-one. She gave him a child of his old age who they named Jesu Grist. All this was shameful in a land dominated by chapel, but the strange precepts that might have landed Price in prison or worse in an earlier age were tolerated in the late nineteenth-century valleys. Many in the communities that Price served saw the value of his attentive medical care. His morals might be suspect, his beliefs might be a mockery but, at worst, he was a harmless madman. Until, that is, little Jesu Grist died. For now Price marched onto Cae'r-lan Fields with the boy in his arms, determined, as his Druidical convictions decreed, to commit him not to a grave but to the fire.

What Price planned was almost unprecedented. For many centuries, cremation had no place in the British way of death. Thomas Browne observed in the seventeenth century that although the ancient people of Britain had chosen a 'fiery resolution' for their dead, since the coming of Christianity 'moist relentment' in sacred earth had prevailed. So it remained in the nineteenth century. Burning was uncustomary, perhaps illegal. True, a society dedicated to winning acceptance of cremation had been active since 1874 but it had made limited headway. Cremationists had tried a variety of arguments. Gesturing towards ever-expanding cemeteries, they suggested that the dead were driving out the living. Space could be saved and funeral costs would be reduced for the hard-pressed poor if cremation were adopted. But their evangelising was hampered by grass-roots religious opinion, the sheer weight of tradition and biblical authority itself, which seemed to tell firmly against burning dead bodies. In a bid to set cleanliness against godliness, they argued that cremation circumvented the vileness of the body's decomposition and so public hygiene would be improved too. They even built a cremator at Woking. But they had got no further than disposing of the body of a horse there in 1878. For although the technology worked perfectly well, attitudes in wider society were antagonistic. Local people were agitated about clouds of cremated remains floating over their heads and landing on their homes. Doctors, lawyers and politicians worried that cremation would be a godsend to any murderer eager to destroy evidence of the crime. And advocates of cremation had not always helped their cause. Sir Henry Thompson, president of the Cremation Society, had opined that the rendered dead might, with advantage, be spread on fields as fertiliser.[6] This sort of bright idea opened the cremationists to mockery as well as further arousing anxieties about the respectful treatment of the dead. So in 1884, there was little sense that the argument was moving in their direction or, indeed, that many in authority were listening to them at all. Then William Price entered the fray.

Price was put before the magistrates at Pontypridd Police Court. In a crowded room, the prosecutor, Mr Rhys, pointed out that anyone under whose roof a death occurred had an obligation to provide for the decent burial of the body and this Price had manifestly failed to do. He had tried to dispose of the body in full knowledge that the coroner wished to carry out an inquest. Rhys also laid on thick the argument that Price had outraged the decent folk of his town by his behaviour. Funeral rites chosen for the deceased must not 'do violence to the feelings and health of the living'.[7] The need to save Price from a lynching suggested that the feelings of many had indeed been violated. Price's incendiary activities had stirred up 'horror and disgust' in the onlookers. Any right-minded person must conclude that it was far preferable for the dead to be carried to the grave followed by mourning family, friends and neighbours in the traditional fashion rather than to be consumed by flames according to Price's 'new-fangled' pyre. Such practices must be stopped. Playing to the gallery, the prosecutor wondered where, if allowed in this case, it would all end. Perhaps with impromptu cremations in back gardens and vapours wafting under the windows of neighbours. The magistrate was persuaded. Price was bailed but would be sent for trial at the Assizes.

Judge James Fitzjames Stephen was to preside over the Winter Assizes for Glamorganshire in Cardiff Town Hall on 12 February 1884.[8] As the judge entered and the court rose, it was to a full house. Many women filled the seats to the left of the judge's bench and the balcony of the courtroom was 'thronged with a number of members of the softer sex'. They had not come to see the petty cases of theft – blankets, knives, cakes – with which the assizes were otherwise concerned. They had come to see the trial of William Price. He did not disappoint. When it was his turn, he emerged from under a blanket to reveal his customary white, red and green attire. Price would represent himself as he faced a series of charges. For the Crown was pursuing him on three fronts. Most far-reachingly, it was alleged that the very business of burning a body was an offence; bodies of the deceased must be buried with all due solemnity and not otherwise disposed of. But Price was also charged with preventing the coroner from carrying out an inquest and with giving rise to a public nuisance by way of the burning since 'divers unwholesome smells did arise therefrom, and the air was greatly corrupted and affected to the danger and common nuisance of all the liege subjects of our Lady the Queen there inhabiting and residing'.

From the outset, Price was helped by the judge. Stephen was unpersuaded that cremation was an offence in law. He had searched for precedents and found none; the closest cases he had come across touched the issue of a householder's obligation to bury one who died under his roof but these judgments were narrow and did not bear on Price's case. There was nothing in the case law to suggest that cremation was unlawful. He had consulted with the aptly named Lord Justice Fry upon the matter and Fry had agreed. And so, since no law forbade it, the assumption must be that burning a body was not in itself an offence and Stephen thought it was not his business to invent a new offence where none existed. In meditative mode, he reflected that all means by which bodies were reduced to their constituent elements were grisly if contemplated. 'Whether decay or fire destroys a body matters not' was an adage quoted by Thomas Browne in the seventeenth century from Lucan and this was a maxim that the learned judge borrowed now. Fire was quick, rotting in the earth was slow. One or the other was inevitable, both were horrible and yet neither, if properly concealed, need offend the public. And while religious feelings were closely engaged when considering the proper way to dispose of the dead, Stephen did not think that 'every practice that startles and jars upon the sentiments of the majority of the population is for that reason a misdemeanor in common law'. Stephen asked Price whether he wanted to add anything. But Price was quite content. He agreed, he said, with everything the erudite judge had been saying, prompting laughter in the court.

But this left open that matter of nuisance. To burn a body in a public square would indeed be an offence. To do so in a private place would not. The question was whether an open field and a fire visible from round about constituted an offence through the 'hideous smell' and 'horrible spectacle' visited on the public. The prosecution pressed the business of nuisance, claiming the fire was just 250 yards from a densely populated area. They called a witness, Ann Thomas, who said that scores of women got sick that evening from the vapours given off by the fire, she among them. Price pressed arguments used more widely by those who championed cremation, evoking the vileness of the buried body's decomposition and how the carcass would waste good land, polluting earth, air and water. Cremation was altogether the more hygienic end. And if anything on the hillside had given offence to sight, it was not his burning of the body on his own private land but the interfering trespassers who dragged the infant's body out of the barrel. The jury was sent out but could not come to a verdict. The trial on that count collapsed. The following day a new jury tackled the final question of whether Price had disposed of a body unlawfully before the coroner could carry out an inquest. This touched closely on a point raised by the enemies of cremation. It would be, they thought, a stratagem of the murderer whose crime might more easily go undetected if there was no body to exhume. But in Price's case there was scant suspicion that he had concealed an infanticide and the grounds for the coroner to have intruded in the case were then too slight. On that charge, too, William Price was acquitted.

Fickle opinion in the valleys now shifted. Men and women who had been ready to lynch Price a few days before cheered his return to Llantrisant. There was bunting in the streets and a flag planted where the pyre had been. This might, reflected sections of the press, be evidence of the law-abiding character of the Welsh, now happy to respect the decision of the court.[9] But there was still gossip about the doctor's intentions. Some thought he would quickly resume the cremation in the big oven of his house. Others, rightly, anticipated a spectacle. With the authority of the court behind him, on 14 March 1884 Price restaged the cremation of his son on the site of his original attempt. He built a structure of three hurdles, piled in half a ton of coal and lubricated the pyre with petroleum. The infant's body placed reverently in its midst, the fire was lit at 8.30 p.m. and burned for three hours. Cattle from the old man's fields came to the flames; his donkey came, braying as it gazed into the fire, as if privy to things human beings could not see. A crowd of up to three hundred local people gathered too, this time quiet, orderly and respectful but supervised by a large police contingent, nonetheless.[10] When the crowd had gone, the fire burned out and the ashes blown away in the wind, Price marked the spot with a tall pole topped by the figure of a moon. This, he resolved, would be the very place where his body too, when the time came, would meet its end in fire. In the interim, he announced plans to build a cremator at Llantrisant.

So, claimed one newspaper, 'all the fine sentiment about ancient Druidic customs ends in commercial speculation'. In reality, Price was anything but commercially minded; he baited his enemies with the idea for a while but it was quickly forgotten. But others could now follow where Price had led.

Thanks to 'a half crazy Welshman and the decision of an English judge', the legal obstacles in the way of cremation had been swept away. It might still be 'hedged in by inane prejudice and narrow-minded superstition', in the eyes of progressives in the press, but the way was nonetheless clear for the cheap and hygienic removal of the dead from the world.[11] William Harcourt, the Liberal Home Secretary, was less sanguine. He saw that only trouble could come out of the court decision since most members of the public thought the practice 'repugnant'.

Churchmen themselves were divided on the issue. A long, dense and complex lineage of discussion about the body's fate was there to guide them. Medieval theologians had picked over the issue of what happened to scattered bodies when God raised the dead.[12] They had probed the worst-case scenarios, wondering how people who had been eaten by animals, still worse by cannibals, might fare at the general resurrection. The answer was that such fates did not have any bearing on their eternal fate. The Creator's skills were sufficient to reconstitute the dead whatever mischance had overtaken their mortal remains. Nonetheless, the Catholic Church preserved, through the Middle Ages and beyond, a strong sense that the body still mattered after death. It would be needed again and mortal remains must be reverently treated. The living must ensure the dead were buried decently in hallowed ground. On this point the Catholic Church remained unyielding, bluntly forbidding cremation to its members in 1886.[13] The Anglican Church was full of more ambivalent feelings. Echoing medieval debates, Bishop Fraser of Manchester wondered whether opponents of cremation could really believe 'that it would be more impossible for God to raise up a body at resurrection, if need be, out of elementary particles which had been liberated by burning, than it would be to raise it up from the dust, and from bodies which had passed through the structure of worms'.[14] He argued in favour of the practice but in doing so, he made a straw man of his opponents' case. Those churchmen who worried about the spread of cremation did not think the divine plan would be frustrated by burning rather than burying a corpse.

Bishop Christopher Wordsworth of Lincoln, nephew of the poet William, was in the vanguard of the opposition and, in 1874, he took to the pulpit in Westminster Abbey and denounced cremation as barbarous. Had Christianity, he wondered, put out the pyres of pagans fourteen hundred years ago only to rekindle them in the great cities of the west on grounds of 'public health and public economy'? Of course the soul's fate was untainted by the body's end, but the scriptures made clear that burial and not burning was the proper way to treat the dead. And to burn the body offended against deep human sensations. It was an unnatural, a terrible thing to do. When we look upon a dead loved one, we see 'a calm beauty, a holy loveliness, spiritual, refined, almost angelic and divine, reflected like a gleam of light from the heavenly world'. To cast such a body into the flames would be to treat it 'as if it were a guilty thing for penal execution'. To cremate the corpse was, he hinted darkly, to send it the way of the sorcerer or the heretic or the husband-killer of ages past. Worse still, by endorsing cremation the Church risked sending out a dangerous message. Committing a body to the earth showed that although human beings were sinful things, destined to die and decay, through Christ there would be resurrection to new life. Wordsworth called up the image of faithful African bearers who had carried the dead body of David Livingstone out of the wilderness so that he might be decently buried and attacked those who would have reduced the great explorer to ashes the easier to transport him. Burying the dead was, he said, a confession of faith; it was a creed in deeds rather than words. And so, if cremation were taken up widely, 'one of the very first fruits of its adoption would be to undermine the faith of mankind in the doctrine of the resurrection of the body'. This in turn might 'bring about a most disastrous social revolution, the end of which is not easy to fore-tell'.[15]

William Price died full of years in 1893. He had lived into great old age and Gwenllian gave him more children, including another son who, again, they called Jesu Grist. Price said that he had no belief in life after death. When he was dead, he would be gone. He would live in these children, especially in the second Jesu Grist who had grown into a healthy boy. Nonetheless, he still had firm views about the fate of his body. Set in motion by his victory, cremations were well under way at Woking, still one of the few places in Britain where fiery exequies might be performed deco-rously.[16] But Price did not want to be spirited there when he was dead and said so.[17] He wanted to be burned in the fresh air so that his ashes could mingle with the elements. And so, as he had instructed, they built up his funeral pyre on the site where the moon on a stick had stood. So many people were expected that tickets for the funeral were issued and a major police operation organised to marshal the crowds. Twenty thousand people packed Cae'r-lan Fields to see the old man off. Clergy – almost certainly against the old man's wishes – officiated. But they faced something of a conundrum, for there was, inevitably, no printed rite for a pyre-side service. In the end, they adapted the ritual for burying a body at sea, substituting the words 'consigned to the fire' for the usual language of committal to the deep.[18] When the flames died down, what was left of the old Druid was scattered to the winds. Onlookers were not sure what to think. Some saw magic in his bones. A few even scrabbled in the ashes for a piece of him – whether for a souvenir, a lucky talisman or a relic with which to fend off misfortune.[19] More common was incomprehension about William Price's eternal fate. Newspaper reporters noticed people questioning what would become of him on the day of general resurrection. The issue at stake in the whisperings was not Price's 'infidel opinions' – whether these might send him spinning into hell – but the matter of resurrection itself. Anxiety about the body's unnatural disintegration, the separation and scattering of its remains still gnawed at some of the bystanders. How, they wondered, could William Price's particles be reassembled when the dead were raised from their graves?[20]

On 8 October 1966 an elderly woman travelled to Glyntaff cemetery not far from Llantrisant. She was Penelopen Price, the daughter of William, a woman who still enjoyed a certain celebrity thanks to memories of her father. Her task was to unveil three new stained-glass windows, which had been commissioned for the chapel there. The chapel had been built by the Victorians using the grey local stone and they had made it in the Gothic style; its arches, traceried windows, coloured glass and crenellations harked back to the Middle Ages, an age, so it seemed, of faith. Around the chapel was a burial ground, an average-sized cemetery opened in 1874 in the hills outside Pontypridd, one of many necessary cities of the dead to match the expanding cities of the living. By the time of Penelopen's visit, such cemeteries were commonplaces of the English landscape. But in long perspective they were aberrations, things of recent creation to solve a problem posed by burgeoning urban populations. Vast, spreading Victorian London had been prototypical.[21] During the late 1840s, after the capital was hit by cholera, it had become plain that its old churchyards could no longer cope with the number of corpses the city obliged them to accommodate. Scandal and anxiety about public health had ensued as news spread of miasmatic graveyards overloaded with the dead. This was stimulated in large part by the hectic prose of George Alfred Walker, 'Graveyard' Walker as he was known, who made it his mission to survey the old churchyards of London and then convey to the authorities why they needed to be shut up and new arrangements for disposal of the dead established.[22] He computed that 100,000 bodies had been packed into Bunhill Fields alone by the mid nineteenth century and worried about exposure to grave vapours; he even claimed cases of gravediggers killed by the 'effluvia' of corpses as they set about opening new graves. Cemeteries apart from the living, sculpted landscapes of trees and shrubs, were a serene and healthy counterpoint to these sepulchral horrors and, as the old burial places were closed, they started to spring up. Many began as private enterprises but steadily municipal authorities took the initiative and the dead were regimented by civic authority. No longer lying near at hand in places of habitual prayer, they were warehoused in great fields of bones, fields over which the Church had much slighter control. Some of the connections between the living and the dead, between parishioner and parish churchyard filled with the ancestors, broke or were refigured.[23]

Facilities for cremation had spread across England too in the wake of the Price case. Mindful of the acres of land they might otherwise need to set aside for cemeteries, local authorities could see virtue in cremation and began, again where private enterprise had led, to build their own crematoria. At first it was mainly agnostics and unbelievers who made use of them but eventually even eminent ecclesiastics were cremated as the Church came to accept that there was no conflict between the practice and Christian doctrine, though Roman Catholics remained conspicuously hostile to the idea. One of Christopher Wordsworth's successors at Lincoln had been cremated and even Archbishop Temple of Canterbury made that choice in 1944, his ashes being buried in the cloister garth of his cathedral. It was the working classes who proved most resistant to the 'new-fangled pyres'.

For generations, belief and ritual around the dead had converged on the idea that the body still mattered. Whispered worries about resurrection, determination to hold on to immemorial rites of burial when faced by death and the horror of consigning the loved one to the flames all played their parts in that resistance. Among the poor, meanwhile, a good send-off still meant burial with all the trappings of hearse, flowers, tea and stone.[24] Soon after the Price case, the *Scotsman* newspaper put its finger on one reason why there would be no sudden reformation of funerary manners. Burning might indeed be a better end than 'the cold and distant grave' but 'men continue to bury their dead because their fore-fathers did so'. They shrank, the reporter said, from appearing 'wanting in respect for their relatives' by subjecting their bodies to what many would consider to be a novel and indecorous experiment.[25]

But as Penelopen unveiled the Glyntaff windows in 1966, that structure of belief was on the point of collapse. The crematorium there had been opened in 1924, only the sixteenth in Britain and the first in Wales, but in 1968, cremation would, nationally, over-take burial as the means by which most people were seen out of the world. Arguments against cremation were ceasing to stack up; to voice them was to risk being branded old-fashioned, igno-rant and superstitious in a bright post-war world. At an earlier celebration of William Price in 1947, a Llantrisant newspaper correspondent had already claimed that 'traditional and senti-mental objections are rarely heard among enlightened people today'.[26] Arthur Pearson, the local MP, spoke during the same event about the 'great courage' of William Price in the face of 'such ignorance and superstition' about cremation. It was, he said, more 'economical and hygienic' and 'most consonant with modern standards of public health'.

For most people after the Second World War, the dead were no longer sleeping in the graveyard waiting for the moment when the last trumpet would waken them. Even churchmen, especially Protestant churchmen, were speaking less about the body's resur-rection and more about resurrection to eternal life: bodies were ceasing to be seeds ready to sprout again.[27] Shifting belief made cremation easier to accept but the spread of cremation reinforced new belief. For the funeral was indeed a kind of creed, not in words but deeds. Now it implied that if the dead were anywhere, they existed in spirit and had no more need of a body.

By the 1960s, elements of William Price's eccentricity had become part of the mainstream and something of the revolution Christopher Wordsworth had prophesied was almost complete. And so when Penelopen Price pulled the string that removed the covering from the Glyntaff windows, she revealed a design that sought to fit theology into this different pattern of belief. The dominant image was familiar. The central, and much the largest, panel showed Christ, resurrected, arms outstretched. The other lights were more unusual. To one side of the central panel was a pane containing a peacock, a creature whose flesh was, according to ancient myth, incorruptible. On the other was a phoenix, the legendary bird that rose again from its own ashes. The windows were a bid to make sense in coloured glass of the Church's teachings about death, teachings in need of new metaphors now that cremation was, for many, the gateway to resurrection and eternal life.

II

BEYOND THE VEIL

The road north from Hebden Bridge rises over moors, 'hilly and bleak as there are but few trees to arrest the wintry winds', passing isolated farms built from the local stone, a cold, grey millstone grit. This is Brontë country. The road continues through Haworth where the sisters lie buried in the church. When the Brontës were growing up in the rectory there, in the early decades of the nineteenth century, the working men and women of the moors still heard stories about the supernatural. Many of them heard hellfire sermons delivered by evangelicals, men of similar bent to Charlotte Brontë's creation Mr Brocklehurst who talked with a young Jane Eyre about the fate of the naughty child destined to be punished eternally in a pit of fire. They heard stories too about ghosts, though these were usually remote from the psychologised visions of the dead in the kinds of novels that the Brontës wrote. The ghosts of the folk stories did not fade when the percipient woke nor were they projections of inner mental states; they had an existence in the external world.

In 1826, Methodist preachers touring the local circuit, expounding the gospel to all who would hear it in cottages, barns or even in the open air, fastened onto such a story in an effort to call people to repentance. It concerned a blind farmer called William Clarkson. Around harvest time in 1825 he had fallen ill while away from home in Nidderdale. Taken to Pateley Bridge, he had asked for his will to be fetched but he proved too sick and too much encumbered by his blindness to make the changes he had planned before succumbing to his illness. This, it transpired, was the mainspring of future trouble for the living. For William Clarkson began to haunt his former landlord, William Mann, appearing to him first on the Grewelthorpe road and then, as he was asleep, laying a hand on the living man's face and pulling him from his bed. Mann was initially resistant to the idea of talking to the ghost and waited until it had come to him several times before asking what it wanted. But by then it was too late. Appearing one final time on a cold, clear night by the light of a full moon, the ghost explained that the time in which amendment could be made had passed. All he could do now was to warn William Mann to look to his own religious condition lest he too be lost.

The story recalls the Byland tales. The ghost haunted appointed places. It needed the help of the living but could not seek it until bidden. It was a menacing presence. It deprived William Mann of the hearing in his left ear – saying, 'I must have something from thee' – as a punishment for not offering help sooner. After seeing the ghost, Mann's 'flesh failed and sleep departed'. All this was skimmed over with a Protestant rhetoric. On the surface, Clarkson had been a good man but he had trusted too much in good works for his salvation and this explained his perdition. The ghost glowed with light like burning brimstone and left a tang of sulphur in the air when it had gone, such that none could doubt its fate. The story was taken seriously; indeed it was a small sensation and a filip to preachers on the circuit, keen to waken sleeping souls to the message of the gospels and warn of the dangers of hell. They wrote it up in detail and printed their findings in the pages of *Primitive Methodist Magazine*.[1] Testimony about Clarkson and the percipients was assembled too. The witnesses to the goings-on after this death were trustworthy men. William Mann was a religious and reliable man; his brother was a preacher. He had gone along with William to his final rendezvous with the ghost, watching from a distance as the two conversed. And although he had not seen the ghost directly, he insisted that he had still been able to discern a shadowy presence, out there in the moonlight.

These events played out against the backdrop of the Pennine Hills in the grip of industrial transformation and at a moment when a recognisably modern world was coming into being. The transformation becomes plain a few miles north of Haworth as the road descends and reaches Keighley. The town formed at the foot of hills almost at the point where the rivers Aire and Worth converge. Victorian buildings fill much of its heart; solid, with a touch of provincial grandeur about them, they too were built from the ubiquitous millstone grit. Keighley was a thriving industrial centre by the 1820s.[2] Cotton spinning, worsted production and machine-making had taken hold there and mills sprang up around the town. Powered at first by swift-flowing water from the streams off the moors, the jennies, looms and lathes were converted to steam power and Keighley came to be wrapped in the smoke of innumerable chimneys. The population expanded too, drawing people in from the surrounding countryside who were in search of opportunity. It doubled in size during the three decades after 1821 and there were more than 18,000 souls in the town by 1851. Back-to-backs were thrown up to house them and traders proliferated to supply provisions. No fewer than twenty-four inns and twenty-two beer shops catered for the needs of the flesh by the 1850s. Rather fewer chapels and churches catered to the spirit but there was still a plurality of places to worship. There were Anglicans, at St Andrew's, rebuilt in the Gothic style in 1846, and Methodists of several different factions were scattered about chapels in the town, the movement having split nationally along several axes. There had long been Baptists in Turkey Street and Quakers at Mill Hill, just off the High Street, and there had been a big enough Catholic resurgence, buoyed by immigration from Ireland, to give rise to a new church, designed by Augustus Pugin, architect of the Houses of Parliament, which opened in 1838 in North Street. Beyond the main streets, there were exotica too, most prominently the Swedenborgians in their temple on King Street, a group guided by the teachings of their founder, Emanuel Swedenborg, who claimed to have enjoyed visions of heaven in the eighteenth century.

Worshipping anywhere or nowhere, the everyday experience of townsfolk was reshaped by the great changes through which they lived as their lives were ordered by municipal powers. An Improvement Act of 1824 provided for the streets of Keighley to be newly paved, swept regularly and lighted by gas, oil or 'inflammable air'. The rivers were to be kept free of pollution: butchery was not to be undertaken in the street and no animals killed there, save only in the event of a traffic accident. Guns and squibs were not to be set off in the town and horses were not to be ridden 'furiously' within its limits. Householders were even enjoined to secure flowerpots to window ledges lest they fall on passers-by. Not all of these ambitions were carried through quickly but the streets already enjoyed the dim luminescence of some ninety-three gas lamps as early as November 1825.

As the fabric was improved by the authorities, minds were being nourished by private enterprise. A Mechanics' Institute brought lectures and library books within reach of respectable working men and the lower middle class, the sorts of people who could afford the joining fee and tuppence-a-week subscription. Sunday schools made up for limited public education with a diet of reading and scripture; one at Temple Row had over eight hundred children on its books by 1821. The town was being knitted more tightly into the wider world, too. In 1847 the railway reached Keighley and a wider reading public encouraged experiments with a local newspaper. Turning the pages of the *Keighley Visitor and General Advertiser* of the 1850s, is to meet a world infinitely more recognisable than that conjured up in the stories of hellfire and haunting of the *Primitive Methodist Magazine*. The library, it noticed, was open Monday, Wednesday and Friday evenings and boasted 2,300 volumes on all subjects, scientific, artistic and literary. Meanwhile 'Professor' Carrodus promised the latest hair-styling in an emporium that was the 'acme of fashion' and Morton's the photographer had harnessed collodion processes for the purpose of taking portraits. Naylor's, the druggist, purveyed 'patent medicines, drugs and trusses' and there were Torren's herbal pills too, all-purpose prophylactic and 'eighth wonder of the world', available to the discerning on application. That the 'progress' wrought by proliferating educational, technological and chemical wonders was also disorientating for those living through it was hinted at elsewhere in the paper's pages. In December 1853 the *Advertiser* carried a whimiscal piece remembering Christmas in 'Old England', a rural neverland before mill and manufactory invaded the Pennines.

Joseph Lawson, a rich Yorkshire cloth merchant, wrote in old age about similar changes in Pudsey on the edge of Leeds, the place where he had grown up in less favoured circumstances during the 1820s and 30s. He remembered a childhood dominated by poverty and hard grind. It was dominated, too, by chapel in a family brought up on the Bible, hymnal and Bunyan's *Pilgrim's Progress* and with a fear of hell, thanks to preachers who held the feet of their congregrations to the fire. His parents read lurid cheap prints for recreation, pamphlet confessions of murderers hanged at York and others retailing strange news from the invisible world, and they believed implicitly in ghosts, boggarts and spirits. But by the time Joseph Lawson was an old man that structure of belief had crumbled, swept away, he said, as railways, newspapers, education and gaslight conspired to destroy much of the village's traditional culture, a destruction of 'superstition' in which he gloried.

Lawson probably overstated his case because he was beguiled by the notion of progress and his own circumstances had altered so radically over a long life. He illuminated, nonetheless, how the generations born in the first half of the nineteenth century felt old ways of thinking and believing – about ghosts and spirits and the dead in general – had come under pressure from new ideas spread in the lecture hall, through books and newspapers or in the schoolroom. By 1850, it was becoming hard to imagine that a preacher would make much headway if he regaled his congregation with stories of ghosts attended by brimstone hues and sulphurous vapours. But traditional beliefs about ghosts and spirits did not abruptly die in mid-Victorian Keighley. They underwent a kind of metamorphosis.

Tucked away a short walk from the town's centre, across a beck, is Heber Street. Here, among Victorian terraces, engineering workshops and warehouses of similar vintage, is an unprepossessing building. It resembles a school and indeed it was built as a school, a Wesleyan Methodist one, but the inscription stone set into the apex announces that in 1895 this became a 'Spiritual Temple'. This little building stands for a story that put Keighley on the map of Victorian England. For, decades before this school was recommissioned as a church, the town was the heart of a new movement. That movement was spiritualism. It arrived in 1853.[3]

Its prophet was a man called David Richmond. He came to the town curiously dressed in Shaker garb. For although Richmond hailed originally from Darlington in the north-east, he had spent the last eleven years living in the United States, much of it among the Shakers. The movement, with origins in the Lincolnshire town of Boston, had spread to America where 'families' of believers sprang up, until there were some six thousand of them in the 1840s. Separated from the world, they marked themselves out through communal living, simple dress and spiritual ecstasies from which sprang their name. Richmond was notionally still attached to his Shaker 'family' when he came to Keighley but the story he told was not about them and their beliefs. It was an altogether stranger tale. In the winter of 1847 a man called John Fox, a farmer, had moved to the town of Hydesville in New York State with his wife and two of his daughters, Kate and Margaretta.[4] Soon after moving into their new house, the Foxes were disturbed each night by inexplicable noises, chiefly tapping and bumping. On 31 March, the noises reached a peak. The children said something supernatural was at work. They called it Mr Splitfoot, a New England name for the devil, and they, and their mother, began to interrogate the spirit, posing questions, which it answered with taps. Neighbours joined in the inquisition on subsequent nights and a system of communication – a sort of bespoke Morse code – linking sublunary and spirit worlds was opened up. The spirit, they learned, was not in fact the devil at all but the earthbound shade of a murdered peddler named Charles Rosna. He said he had been murdered and buried in the cellar and later, sure enough, the family claimed to have found hair and bones which seemed to bear that story out. For the moment the tappings and rappings were already making them famous. Kate, Margaretta and their mother moved in with the eldest Fox daughter, Leah, who lived at Rochester. The spirit moved with them and the phenomena continued. Leah, too, became part of the prototype spirit circle and the girls began to develop powers of mediumship allowing them to communicate more freely with the other world. A public event was staged in the Corinthian Hall of Rochester in November 1849 at which an astonished audience was treated to an extravaganza of sounds from the beyond. In the train of these manifestations, spirits stirred across America as others began to pay attention to the uncanny. Inspired by the example of the Foxes, imitators were soon trying their hand at mediumship, and the popular press and missionising converts were spreading the craze.

The Fox phenomenon had not appeared out of the blue; others had prepared the way. In the United States, Andrew Jackson Davis, the 'Poughkeepsie Seer', had visions that revealed the other world, and he had, the year before the Hydesville hauntings began, prophesied that spirits would make contact with human beings. In Britain, the novelist Catherine Crowe had made a splash with a widely read book, *The Night Side of Nature*, in which she said that modern people were too rationalistic, their souls were too much wrapped up in clay, to take account of the uncanny.[5] They needed to shed their prejudices and open their eyes. The Bible taught that there was a spiritual existence and so did intuition; many openly believed in ghosts and many more believed but would not voice their thoughts for fear of mockery. And there was a wealth of evidence to justify this belief: she looked to history, folklore, ethnography and science, contending that beliefs about spirits, ghosts, fetches and glimpses of the future life shared across time

– the Tedworth Drummer and the Sampford Peverell spirit among them – testified to occult truths about an unseen world. Crowe's star, briefly ascendant, faded when she went mad in the most public of ways. Thinking herself invisible, she tested the proposition and was found naked in an Edinburgh Street. When she emerged in 1857 from the asylum to which she had been committed three years before, she found that spiritualism was taking root in the soil her writing had helped to prepare.

That David Richmond could turn up in Keighley with his stories and curious clothes and not be drummed out of the town or laughed off as an eccentric may have owed something to others who had trailed theories about spirits, but it owed more to a prominent resident called David Weatherhead.[6] He was Keighley born and bred, the son of the landlord of the Commercial Inn, a rich grocer and a leading light locally.[7] He had risen to prominence in the febrile atmosphere of the 1830s and 40s, the 'Hungry Forties', when violence and fear of violence simmered under the surface of local politics. Legend had it that the yeomanry had even been called out during these years to break up a seditious gathering on the moors only to find on arrival that the crowd was of Methodists gathered at a camp meeting to hear the gospel. But Weatherhead's engagement in politics was not mythical. He had agitated against the New Poor Law, organised demonstrations and even refused to pay his dues to the rector, a figure he thought aligned with an oppressive establishment, leading to a spell as a guest of Her Majesty in a cell at York Castle during 1843. By the 1850s improving economic conditions helped draw the sting out of national and local politics and Weatherhead and his friends dedicated themselves to peaceable causes such as the cooperative movement, the education of working men and the encompassing idea of self-improvement. In this vein, he helped found a Working Men's Hall in Green Street. The hall was a centre of political activism and radical anti-religion, members being treated to iconoclastic lectures about the faults of the Churches, but when David Richmond came to town, to the astonishment of many, he was given the use of it.

On the surface David Weatherhead's readiness to heed his visitor's spiritual message seemed strange for a man who had set his face against the Church, but in 1853 Weatherhead was still raw with grief from the loss of his son just two years before. There was comfort in Richmond's story about a world beyond the grave and Weatherhead wanted to see for himself whether the spirits of the dead really could speak. So Richmond was given his chance. He held a 'demonstration' of spirit communication in the Working Men's Hall and many from the town crowded in to hear him, hard-boiled infidels among them. The effect, sympathisers subsequently claimed, was electrifying. Richmond won his audience to spiritualism in part by demonstrations of his powers as a medium, by bringing messages out from the spirit world, but he also did it by arranging the audience into their own 'circles'. In these little groups, gathered round tables, 'manifestations' began, the tables tipping and tilting in answer to questions as the participants joined hands around them.[8] Richmond did not stand before them as a new kind of priest. He was not equipped with occult knowledge or veiled powers which he planned to keep to himself; he appeared as a teacher who would show them how to liberate their own potential to communicate with the dead.[9]

One circle went on to produce especially astonishing results. John Hardacre, a medium in the making, led a group of thirteen men into contact with the spirit world using the art of table-tipping.[10] Through raps and taps and tilts, John Mason, a deceased preacher at the Swedenborgian temple, came through and began to communicate, laboriously tapping out a whole sermon over a series of sittings. That he was a Swedenborgian was perhaps material, for this group was nearest the spiritualists in their teachings. Their founder, Emanuel Swedenborg, had visions of a heaven finely divided from this world in which reunion, human love and spiritual progress were all possible and where there was no counterpoint in a fiery hell. On his death in 1772 the visions ceased; his followers did not admit the possibility of further revelations.[11] But now one of their number, so it seemed, was pushing through the veil. Mason preached, orthodoxly enough, on a Bible text fitting for the occasion. He chose from Revelation: 'And behold I come quickly; and my reward is with me, to give every man as his work shall be.'[12] He had a traditional message for the gathering too: they must all soon leave their natural bodies behind and so come to repentance while there was time. 'I tell you plainly,' said the spirit, 'that everything which has been given by the table, even the present sermon, has been given first from spirits in the spiritual world into the mind of the medium, and from thence through the motion of the table, to the minds of others.' By way of the medium, the spirits were also able to see into the lives of the living. And lest anyone think that the seance amounted to dangerous hocus-pocus, the spirit had further assurances. Not only had he taken Revelation as his text, he also warned that the Bible must be the fount of knowledge, since 'real information' came from no other source but this, and especially in matters touching 'eternal welfare'.

This did not allay everyone's fears. Some in the room were less immediately bothered by the morality of the spirit communications than by their authenticity. The sitters were aware of dissentient voices – some scientists had already argued that 'Animal Magnetism' or 'Electricity' in some way transmitted from the sitters to tables made them move, not mysterious powers of the air – but then Mason found a new way of proving himself.[13] Having already received pages of coherent prose from the hereafter, the company was treated to dialect verse. The spirit of Robbie Burns, no less, came through and favoured them with poetry. Warming to the Revelation theme, he began, 'When we wer in the world o' clay, we little ken'd how breef two'd be . . .' Three stanzas followed and, since no one in the room had command of the 'Scotch' tongue, even the doubters were won to the view that only a spirit could have rendered the lines. Although still a little worried about being mocked 'as a set of weak-minded and visionary individuals', they made a leap of faith, published the words of Mason and Burns in a pamphlet,

Table-Moving Extraordinary, and subjoined their names to the text. Spiritualism was catching light in the Pennines.

Something of its spread is revealed in the pages of the *Yorkshire Spiritual Telegraph*, a spiritualist newspaper published in Keighley between 1855 and 1858 and bankrolled by David Weatherhead. It encouraged readers to form their own circles, to commune with the spirits and to send in accounts of their experiences, which were duly published, crammed in small print into the paper's columns. A strange underside to the brightly lit, neatly paved Keighley of the civic imagination emerges from the *Telegraph*'s crumbling leaves. Spirits made solid wooden buffets shake. The dead tapped out tattoos on tables. Ghosts shook hands with men and women who had gathered in darkened rooms to commune with them. A Bingley man had a vision of the world beyond the grave. A medium in the same town communed with the spirit of Benjamin Franklin.[14] Sitters gathered round a Bradford table reached Pope Gregory the Great, the poet Alexander Pope, and George Fox, founder of the Quakers. Up to four hundred people gathered in the Working Men's Hall and heard from the spirits of Thomas Paine and Martin Luther, among others, being treated to comfort, reproof and prophecy. After one sitting in a private house, a table sprang spontaneously into life when the sitters had retired from it, a phenomenon attested by an affidavit signed by no fewer than six witnesses. Meanwhile, a 'frolicksome' Irish spirit caused a medium to ride the sideboard round the room as if he was mounted on a horse.

In Turkey Street, a spirit even counterfeited the Hydesville hauntings, bothering a family with its knocking. So loud was the noise that it sounded as if a joiner was driving nails into wood. Mother, father and children were perplexed; neighbours gathered to bear witness and the boy of the household saw a hand, glimmering 'like a glow-worm', beating on the bare boards of an upstairs room. The powers of the air, it seemed, worked through the daughter; the noises intensified in the fourteen-year-old girl's presence. And although some were sceptical, sixteen local people put their names to an affidavit attesting that supernatural forces were at work. 'The girl', the *Telegraph* reporter concluded, 'bids fair to be a very strong medium.'¹⁵ Others formed circles in which mediums heard voices from the beyond. They scrawled on blank paper, producing 'automatic' writings that could be interrogated for messages. Most commonly, adepts (or the simply curious) would 'try the table', sitters placing their hands on a small table and sensing its movements, propelled by spirits who by these gyrations answered the sitters' questions about the fate of dead loved ones and the topography of the hereafter. Since spiritualism came to the town, mocked a local newspaper columnist, no article of household furniture in the district had had any peace.¹⁶ By 1855 a 'Society for Investigating the Phenomena of Spirit Intercourse' had been established, members paying a penny a week and pledging that they wished to learn all the facts of spirit phenomena, would set no obstacles in the society's search for knowledge and withdraw 'peaceably' if dissatisfied with its work.

David Richmond's message had offered to the crowd in the hall – and to many beyond its walls – more than the excitement of the uncanny, it had laid before them in sketch a system of thought at once familiar and strange, drawing on familiar Christian ideas and ancient lore but recreating them. Man had a spiritual essence; the body was but an outer garment and 'conscious, individualised' existence continued when the body died. 'The disembodied', his followers argued, 'can and do communicate with those still in the flesh.' Churchmen had for centuries anathematised those who deliberately sought out the dead so as to speak with them. Some were still ready with anathemas. When spiritualists set up a circle in Carlisle, churchmen branded them necromancers and accused them of occult conjurations, quoting passages of scripture that branded their practices 'abominations'.¹⁷ Reverend N. S. Godfrey, the incumbent of Wortley, Yorkshire, went into print, denouncing table-tipping as a work of satanic agency. He, his wife and a curate had tried it for themselves but found that the table ceased to move the instant a small Bible was laid upon it. This, and a small avalanche of scriptural citation, was evidence enough for him to damn the new art as a black one.[18] The spiritualists, however, proclaimed that this kind of contact with the dead was not dangerous but beneficial; indeed it did 'incalculable good'.[19] Nor was it superstitious, it was scientific. Spiritualism was 'a positive, practical, teachable science'. It made sense, too, to a public acquainted with extraordinary technological innovation.[20] It was no accident that spirits spoke through systems of raps and taps. Although one middle-class medium thought that they did this for reasons of decorum – 'as if politely announcing themselves' – the spirits' choice of audible codes had more to do with Morse and the development of his code in the late 1830s and 40s.[21] Terrestial telegraphy was making commonplace the idea that people far apart on the earth's surface were able to communicate by means of dots and dashes and now spiritual telegraphy promised similar communication between worlds. Having conquered space, technology promised a conquest of new frontiers, of time and death itself.

Modern, scientific and full of solace about a happy life to come, spiritualism in the hands of Keighley people could be radical too. The 'incalculable good' of spiritualist communion stretched into politics. Here the movement touched different sensibilities. Although David Weatherhead and the secularists who first listened to Richmond were the last people Keighley folk expected to see converted, spiritualism's ministry was democratic. Mediums were born not made by laying on of hands. They might be poor men; they might well be women. They were 'untrained' and 'children of the people' – from families of miners and weavers and artisans. But 'their rude natural eloquence, heightened by the afflations of spirit intelligences that speak through their lips, produces a much deeper influence on audiences of their own class than the metaphysical arguments of more polished speakers could do'.[22] There was excitement, novelty, glamour, even danger, around early spiritualism; the movement was not only a way to truth, it was a means to achieve standing for those with little formal education, with few connections, without power.

And it could also be a faith for those who had turned away from the Churches, for those who sought a spiritual rationale for radical political ideas. The ringing endorsement of the grand old man of progressive politics, Robert Owen, helped its claims in this respect. An immensely prosperous industrialist, Robert Owen had poured his life and his fortune into working-class causes.[23] He had launched a series of model communities in Britain and the United States in which workers would live together harmoniously and he had campaigned for political and social reform. By 1853, when he was in his early eighties, he had seen these efforts to build a new Jerusalem in the here and now come to nothing; each of his model communities had failed. Then he paid a call on a medium called Mrs Hayden.

He met her one March morning at home in a bright room, frost still glistening outside. He had come simply to borrow a book so that he might learn something about spiritualism. Instead he was treated to an impromptu display of Mrs Hayden's powers. Strange raps filled the room with sound. The spirits, so she said, were present. And she duly interrogated them, proving to Robert Owen's satisfaction that she was indeed privy to knowledge from the other world. For, even though she had not met Owen before, she was able to learn the names of his parents and other personal particulars.[24] A convert, Owen began to attend seances with Mrs Hayden. He also proclaimed his new faith to the world. 'Strange and incredible as it will appear', he explained, 'communications most important and gratifying, have been made to great numbers in America and to many in this country . . . purporting to be from departed spirits.' And so, 'I have been compelled, contrary to my previous strong convictions, to believe in a future conscious state of life existing in a refined material, or what is called a spiritual state.'[25]

Some Owenites were appalled; for many, Owen's political philosophy had been intimately bound up with his rejection of religion and these revelations were a betrayal of the cause. But Owen saw in spiritualism a force that might carry political change

forward rather than retard it. 'A great moral revolution', he prophesied, 'is about to be effected for the human race.' He had
communed with the spirits, including the shades of Thomas
Jefferson and, more oddly, the Duke of Kent, and they had
confirmed him in his political opinions. The spirits, he was sure,
would galvanise change on earth with improving messages from
heaven. They were active, Owen contended, 'to arouse the attention of all to the deplorable condition of our race, to the unnec-
essary ignorance, poverty, crime, disunion, and misery now so
prevalent around the world', as well as to make 'immortality a
palpable fact'. Through their interventions they would encourage
the creation of a new government on earth founded on love and
wisdom.[26]

Keighley spiritualists seized on Owen's claims. Men, they said,
may live in a world 'marching from one discovery to another' and
may have reached 'the climax of refinement', but the powerful
were dead to the suffering of the poor and the Church was cold
to the needy. Spiritualism promised to change this, to bring about
the 'renovation and final redemption' of humankind through a
vision of happiness 'here and hereafter'.[27] Human weakness had
thwarted Owen's schemes for Utopian living but now moral regeneration would be stiffened with aid 'from the messengers of God'.
The spirits might guide him 'to establish on earth such social
institutions as shall resemble those in heaven'.[28] And so the *Spiritual
Telegraph*'s pages filled not only with tales of animated tables,
trances, voices and lights; they also bristled with radical political
commentary.[29] So incendiary were its opinions that only 'infidel'
booksellers, hostile to the Church and the political establishment,
would hawk its early editions; the more respectable kind would
not touch it at first but got over their nerves when the circulation
soared and the lure of profit trumped the demands of propriety.

Spiritualism was sleek, modern, progressive but it was full of
ancient wisdom too.[30] 'How much more pleasant', said an expo-
nent, 'is it that we can now sit down sociably around a table and
receive communications from friends and relatives . . . than meet

them in the character of ghosts, causing the very hairs of our head to stand erect?'[31] 'Weird supernaturalism' which held to exorcisms and wicked powers needed to be purged by the 'reason and light' of spiritualist teaching. But much in the old ghost lore survived. Haunting spirits were 'magnetically fettered' to the sites of their earthly offences; caught up still in the sounds and sights of their transgressions, 'remembrance of their evil deeds' became 'a hell in which they are compelled to re-enact the deeds that continually recur in their minds'. But there was hope for their eventual release from torment once they had served their time; to be a ghost was to undergo rehabilitation in an other-worldly reformatory. Some questioned why the dead were so suddenly garrulous, but the *Telegraph* pointed out that people had long 'been liable to a superstitious fear of seeing anything in the form of the dead'. The spirits had hardly been sleeping down the centuries but now fear was changed into a scientific understanding of their activities.

This was the view of Emma Hardinge Britten, another of the *Spiritual Telegraph*'s correspondents. An Englishwoman who had spent a good deal of her life in America, she was living in London for a time during the 1850s. She had a successful career as a medium, being mobbed by supporters and, from time to time, menaced by less sympathetic mobs. Luckily, on such occasions her spirit guide in the other world, a Red Indian called Arrowhead, was on hand to protect her. During one particularly tense affair at a hall in Glasgow, he stood before the lectern, unseen by the audience, waving his war hatchet above his head to stiffen her resolve.[32] For Mrs Hardinge Britten there had been many 'way marks' pointing to spiritualist developments in the modern age. 'Scientific spirits', she contended, had long been 'desirous of founding a spiritual telegraph between the mortal and immortal realms of being.' They had been behind notorious disturbances at Epworth parsonage, the home of Methodism's founder John Wesley, which had been visited by something resembling a poltergeist.[33] They had been responsible for the Sampford Peverell Sensation too. All the rattling of doorknobs, tapping on floorboards, strange lights and weird sensations in the house of Mr Chave were the work of attention-seeking spirits as they tried to open channels of communication between worlds. But only in the modern age had knowledge – of mediumship, table-turning and automatic writing – been won which allowed the living to make sense of these phenomena and speak properly to the dead. The narrow-minded rationalists who had mocked Reverend Colton's belief in the hauntings at Sampford Peverell had it wrong; modern discoveries had shown them to be authentic after all.[34] In the hands of women and men like Emma Hardinge Britten, ghost beliefs that had seemed on the point of eclipse could have a second life, retro-fitted into the spiritualist system.

For all these reasons, the message David Richmond proclaimed had taken hold in many homes in and around Keighley. But to the clear eye of a sceptic, such goings-on were putting the town on the map for all the wrong reasons. It was as if some had taken leave of their senses, and not least because spiritualism had made its greatest conquests among the sceptics and radicals. Soon after the publication of poetry by Robbie Burns in *Table-Moving Extraordinary*, an anonymous writer in the *Keighley Visitor and General Advertiser* hit back: Burns, he declared, must be turning in his grave now that such 'nursery-rhyme like' poetry was being ascribed to him post-humously. The pamphlet produced by the sitters was a teeming mass of superstition. Others took up the cudgels against them too. Those 'once notorious for believing nothing, [were] now equally notorious for believing everything'.[35] Even Keighley's secularist hall, a hotbed of radicalism, a veritable 'temple of unbelief', which made the godly shudder and cross themselves as they passed by, had been reborn as a 'Free Christian' church of spiritualism. A few hard-line infidels had even, it was claimed, converted after death, coming through during seances to confess their errors and preach the reality of an other world that they had scorned.

Despite the picture painted in hostile newspapers of epidemic credulity, more people were unmoved by the spiritualist message than accepted it. Some were actively hostile, and pioneering mediums might be in for a rough ride from an unconvinced audience, especially if they charged for their services and performed for a big crowd. That was the recurrent experience of the Davenport Brothers whose 'exhibitions' blurred the boundaries of mediumship, magic and escapology. On tour in the north, more than once their performances descended into minor riots as members of the audience suspected trickery. At one event the special box, integral to the act – which was at heart a rope trick – was smashed and the local constabulary and magistrates had, so to speak, to pick up the pieces. Sometimes the authorities even banned exhibitions in the interests of preserving public order.[36]

Violence against spiritualists and their fellow travellers was more usually verbal. A writer for the *Yorkshireman* railed against the *Spiritual Telegraph*.[37] For 'of all the phantasms generated in the heated brain of crazed enthusiasm, of all the juggles ever devised by designing impostors for the derision of ignorance', he contended, 'the grossest, most monstrous, the most abominable to reason and humanity is this latest the which is seriously and solemnly put forward for acceptance'. Spiritualism belonged in the same box as the 'rank grovelling superstitions of fetish worship' which Christian truth and imperial might had banished elsewhere in the world. Slyly, he also tainted it with a Catholic faith – 'the puerile and degrading forms of that religion which has faith in winking virgins and the doubtful bones of apocryphal martyrs' – banished by the bright light of Protestantism. Spiritualists said that their teaching was a cure for a materialistic age; for the plain-speaking Yorkshireman the cure was worse than the disease. They had succeeded only in 'carnalising' sacred mysteries. Even Greek religion had about it the beauty of rationality and naturalness; old superstitions about fairies, witches, goblins and ghosts were at least picturesque. But spiritualism was 'neither pretty nor poetical'. It was 'no less clumsy in shape than stupid in essence'. And yet the venom in the Yorkshireman's attack tells its own tale. The allure of spiritualism was strong enough, the minority drawn to it large enough, to make attacking it important. Spiritualist arguments did not sweep the board, in Keighley or anywhere else in the 1850s, but the new movement, built round the ties binding the living and the dead, had by the end of the decade established itself as a feature in the landscape of modern Britain.

When the Wesleyan school was acquired by the Keighley spiritualists in 1895, their movement's centre of gravity had long since shifted to London; the *Spiritual Telegraph* had closed down and been subsumed into a new publication printed in the capital. The early fervour in Keighley had cooled and the Spiritual temple had taken its place among the Anglican and Catholic churches, the Methodist and Baptist chapels, Quaker meeting house and Swedenborgian temple. Spiritualism now had its adherents across the nation. And not only 'earnest-looking sons of toil' among the working classes subscribed but also leisured ladies and gentlemen in middle-class drawing rooms.[38] It even won converts among leading scientists; for them spiritualism might be a plank to cling to if their materialistic explanations wrecked the ship of faith. Spiritualism also proved strong enough to survive a shock that might have killed it.

Two decades after the movement was born in Hydesville, New York State, two of the Fox sisters dropped a bombshell. The relationship between the three had become increasingly fraught as their fame grew; Leah had done especially well out of their celebrity but the other two sisters had lived troubled lives and were 'but poorly provided for with the world's goods'.[39] Margaretta and Kate had their revenge by pulling the house down round their sister's ears. Margaretta told a journalist that the Hydesville hauntings had been a fraud. They had begun as a means to frighten their mother – a nervous, superstitious woman – for their own mischievous amusement and then, when the neighbours were taken in too, the trickery gathered its own momentum.[40] The sisters' mediumistic powers, which had convinced both audiences and learned scrutineers, were entirely faked, nothing but 'humbuggery'. She even demonstrated the technique used to make the spirit sounds during exhibitions.[41] The sisters had no supernatural gifts, they simply had an uncommon power to make their toe joints crack very noisily. This was how they generated raps and taps, which they claimed to be communications by the spirits. Margaretta now attacked her old calling with evangelical zeal. 'I am here tonight', she told an assembled crowd, 'as one of the founders of Spiritualism to denounce it as an absolute falsehood from beginning to end, as the flimsiest of superstitions, the most wicked blasphemy known to the world.' God, she said, had wakened her conscience. Kate backed up her sister, portraying spiritualism as a blight. But too many people had invested too much; the spiritualist juggernaut was too powerful to be stopped. Angry letters were sent to the sisters by true believers who still held that spirit communications were 'a sure earnest of that reunion with those they loved for which the true heart most longs'. Another wondered that the 'glorious light' of the spirits could really be nothing but the gutter of candle called fraud.[42] In 1904 the *Boston Journal* reported the discovery of a skeleton in the wall of their old home, the 'Spook House' in Hydesville, by its current owner. This, it was contended, bore out the original testimony of the Fox girls from 1848–9 and corroborated the family's earlier claim that the bones and hair belonging to the troubled spirit of the house had been unearthed in the cellar. Despite themselves, regardless of their confessions, Margaretta and Kate Fox were still being held up as prototypical mediums. By then none of the sisters could gainsay the believer nor challenge stories about bones in the cellar. All three were dead. Leah had lived out her last years comfortably enough but Kate and Margaretta had died in poverty. Both had gone to paupers' graves.

The Plains of Heaven

Looking back from the moors, it is not easy to see Keighley as it was during the heady days of spiritualism. The Anglican church, shared now with the Methodists, still faces the Commercial Inn in the heart of the town and the Victorian skeleton of public buildings and spaces still exists. Brash, steel, glass and concrete shapes have intruded. Traffic clogs the old arteries. It is a typically hectic modern place. It is a cosmopolitan place, too, a town of many creeds and races, and while many of the Christian denominations that once dominated are dwindling, new faiths, especially Islam, have regenerated religion in the town. The mental world of men and women dead for a century and a half is harder to map than the town's Victorian fabric, something of which at least can be recovered from street plans and faded early photographs. The lives of the people of mid nineteenth-century Keighley were still structured round the shared stories of the Bible to an extent unfamiliar to most people today; even those who rejected the Church's claims about salvation and damnation had first absorbed them. Common experiences forged their thoughts too. Most would have seen a dead body at some point in their lives, many during childhood. It was a bid to proof them against death through early exposure but often, in practice, provoked only memories of the terrifying chill of the corpse as they had touched or kissed it.

Spiritualism's power lay not only in its validation of ancient claims about spirits and heaven, its modification of unpalatable ones about hellfire and damnation, but also its explanation of these encounters. A Keighley burial rite, a spiritualist rite, offered meditations on seeing the dead. The body was 'beautiful but in ruins'. It had 'the form of man but is a mass of insensible clay . . . calm, motionless and unfeeling but in outward appearances as perfect as it was a few hours ago'. What, its author wondered, wrought the change? Where had the spirit gone? The Bible sketched the outline of what to think about body and soul, this world and the next, as it had done for generations passed, time out of mind. These ideas the author largely embraced but he held that the mid Victorian generation was more fortunate than those that had gone before. Thanks to spirit communications, they had answers to these questions which possessed far greater clarity and assurance than those vouchsafed to the people of earlier centuries. Spiritualism drew on the Christian sentiment that man was at once a 'thing of clay' and 'a denizen of a brighter world'. Heaven would bring that divine illumination promised by scripture but it would also be, above all, a place 'where we shall meet again the objects of our love who are gone before us'. Death was but transcendence to 'another sphere' where existence continued as a real human being not as 'insubstantial vapour' or a 'a mere phantom'. The good would go to bliss and rest and the bad if not to hell then to a place 'where they cease to trouble'.[43] Where once the return of the dead had been feared, now it was known that spirits could be a help to the living, bringing solace and news from the invisible world. Spiritualism was a phenomenon of the moment that promised to rescue and improve on old truths at the very time they were threatened by modernity. Full of old things and new assurances, in the compound was its power.

As spiritualism was taking hold in the Pennines, John Martin's paintings were on tour in the north and, while Keighley itself was not on the paintings' itinerary, a circle of towns and cities roundabout were included, Leeds, Huddersfield and York among them. By September 1855 the triptych was on show in Bradford in the saloon of St George's Hall. Flyers boasted that two million people had already seen 'the most sublime and extraordinary pictures in the world', and added for good measure that the canvases were now valued at 8,000 guineas. Martin himself had been no spiritualist – he was dying before the movement had any real purchase – though it was said that as a young man he had dabbled with spirits in a search for knowledge of what lay beyond the grave. He had, so the story went, entered a pact with his apprentice-master in which it was agreed that whichever of them was first to die, he would send to the other some kind of sign of future existence. When his master died, Martin asked him to make his presence felt by opening and closing a door or causing a candle to burn blue. He even summoned his ghost when he was alone at night or the moors. Nothing happened and no one returned.[44]

Whatever the truth of that tale, some of the magic of John Martin's paintings came from the shapes they gave to fears and hopes, more especially the hopes, that people entertained thanks to Church teaching and Bible reading. In dim rooms by gaslight, the afterlife became a phantasmagoria in which horror and delight mingled. People wanted to see all three of the paintings but, by acclamation, it was the painting of heaven that most preferred. On their appearance at Newcastle, the *Gateshead Observer* recorded huge enthusiasm and noted that, of the triptych, the *Plains of Heaven* was the instant favourite. Ellen Wood folded a visit to the paintings into one of her novels and a child character spoke for most: 'One was called the *Plains of Heaven* and I liked that the best; we all did.' She explained why: 'Oh, you should have seen it! There was a river, you know, and boats, beautiful gondolas they looked [like], taking the redeemed to the shores of heaven.' These were 'shadowy figures in white robes, myriads and myriads of them, for they reached all up in the air to the holy city; it seemed to be in the clouds, coming down from God. The flowers grew on the banks of the river, pink and blue and violet; all colours but so bright and beautiful; brighter than our flowers here.'[45] Brighter than our flowers here: it was almost as if seers had stepped through the veil into the painting, into heaven itself, as they surveyed its terrain and they found there not whittled-down ranks of the elect but abundant crowds of souls.

Martin's painting of heaven floated in a sea of anticipation fed by books, which also lent form to these intuitions about the 'better place' people thought the dead had passed to. William Branks wrote about *Heaven Our Home*; the American author Elizabeth Stuart Phelps published *The Gates Ajar*, a peep into the hereafter which found a ready market on both sides of the Atlantic, selling some 180,000 copies in England alone.[46] Both books painted picturesque heavens in which families were gathered in, lost loves were recovered and marriages resumed. Both authors harnessed that widespread desire to be reunited with lost loved ones to be found in the more intimate reflections of men and women of all classes. The appeal of such books explains why Mrs Wood's words were prophetic. *Heaven* proved an enduring favourite and long after the other two canvases had ceased to see the light of day, it was being exhibited alone. Hellfire, judgement and lost souls tumbling into the abyss were fading from the preaching of many clergymen in late Victorian England. These hard, flinty doctrines were almost an embarrassment as liberal theology took hold in the Church. The paintings that depicted such things became an embarrassment too; a veil, or rather a dust sheet, was drawn over them.

As John Martin's paintings set out on their tour in the north-east, the artist was dying far away at Kirk Braddan on the Isle of Man. There, crippled by a stroke, he spent his hours gazing at sea and sky, unable to hold a brush. Through his art he had risen. He had dined with Charles Dickens; his work had been admired by the Brontës. The Academy never cared for his work but the crowd did. It did so because it spoke to them of familiar things, its power drawn from Martin's own formative years lived among stories of ghosts and goblins, Bible tales of hellfire, heaven and the end of the world. But even as Martin reworked the old prophetic story about the last things, he was aware of new ways of thinking which called the Bible into question. All the indications are that he had long ceased to believe in the literal truth of scripture. Telltale fossils had appeared in some of his biblical paintings calling attention to geology, a science which revealed that the earth was far older than scriptural computations. He had also, earlier in his career, drawn illustrations of dinosaurs for geological works, which intimated that the world was not God-made in days and then given over to man; there had, it seemed, been earlier inhabitants on its ancient surface. The Bible's narrative of past time was being opened to question and so too its claims for the future.[47] At the very moment that old truths seemed to emerge in sharper form, more solid and real in spirit descriptions of the hereafter and in Martin's magnificent art of heaven, the image they constructed was becoming brittle, apt to shatter.

A DARKLING PLAIN

Within a few years of the spread of spiritualism in the Pennines, an intimate but profound crisis was under way in the altogether different landscape far out to the east, in the fastness of southern Lincolnshire. The village of Sibsey, some five miles north of Boston and a similar distance from the northern shore of the Wash, lies in fen country. Unremitting in its flatness, the horizon is interrupted only by windmills and church towers; the earth is scored by a grid of drains, drawing off water and turning marshes into prime agricultural land. Trees shorn of leaves, skies iron-grey, squalls riding in on the north-westerly wind, it is a bleak place on an early winter's day, the sort of day when it never seems quite to get light. The houses of the village are dispersed, St Margaret's, the church, stands lonely in consequence. Although an ancient foundation, the building was much reconstructed in the mid nineteenth century, a beneficiary of the pious enthusiasm of the Victorians. In its windswept graveyard, sheltered a little by elderly limes, is the last resting place of one of the nineteenth-century incumbents, Frank Besant. He died here on 21 April 1913, aged seventy-six. His tombstone, a coped ledger, is inscribed with a line from the Song of Solomon, 'Until the day break, and the shadows flee away.'[1]

The epitaph is an appropriate one, for while Frank Besant served the parish from 30 December 1871 until his death, he lived out a long and troubled life there, a minor character in a story that exposed convictions which were the counterpoint of the

mid-century zeal that had seen his church rebuilt. His earliest
years in the village were marked by the most difficult of marriages.
For, a little while before he took up the living, he had married
Annie Wood who then became known to the world as Annie
Besant. Impeccably middle class by birth, superficially well
matched to the rector, Annie Besant would live a long life but
would find herself increasingly out of step with the conventions
of late Victorian Britain. She would become a campaigner for
causes not yet popular – birth control, socialism, union rights for
the likes of the London matchgirls, an India free from British
imperial rule. The events which launched her on that trajectory
took place in and around Sibsey. Under the open skies of the fen
country Annie Besant lost her faith.[2] The Christianity in which
she had been brought up crumbled away, feeding the dissolution
of a marriage to Frank, which became increasingly miserable. In
her loss of faith she was unusual but scarcely unique. Mid and
late Victorian England, for all the vitality of its churches, for all
the money lavished on stained glass and stone in rebuilding works,
had in its interstices a significant minority who were coming to
doubt Christian teaching about this world and the next which
had, broadly, held sway for generations.

Struggles and Flight

The crisis began beside a sickbed in April 1871. Annie and Frank's
daughter, Mabel, contracted whooping cough, an illness with a
significant mortality. She lay 'for seemingly endless hours' near
to death and shut up in the sickroom attended only by her mother.
Annie faced the struggle for her daughter's life fortified by the
Anglican faith in which she had been brought up. She had, in her
youth, been no lukewarm Christian and remembered herself as
the stuff 'of which fanatics are made'. In a more red-blooded age
she might have been a martyr. Such sentiments were at odds with
those of her mother who had embraced liberal theology and High

Church ritual. But, on her father's death, Annie had been entrusted to the care of a woman called Miss Ellen Marryat whose religion was evangelical and this had helped to fire her faith.[3] Evangelicalism was a powerful force in mid Victorian England. The many Protestant churchmen – Anglicans, Methodists, Baptists and others – who championed it recurred to teachings not so vary distant to those of Ralph Josselin, refitting them for a modern world. They lived lives shaped less intimately by divine interventions but still discerned a world shot-through by providence in which people must struggle against the snares of the devil and bear tests and temptations resolutely. There was no way out of man's sinfulness other than through Christ and for those who felt that inner conversion to his cause there was elated expectation of heaven's delights. But there was fear too, fear if one did not feel the joy of inner conversion or that the transformation was not perfect enough. For evangelical theology taught that hellfire waited for unregenerates and backsliders. It was an outlook to which John Martin's images of wrath and judgement made obeisance and it still resonated among many who viewed his paintings, schooled since childhood in a rhetoric of hellfire and damnation.

Such a theology should have forearmed Annie as she watched over Mabel. But rather than being strengthened in adversity, the claustrophobia and loneliness of the vigil encouraged her to question her beliefs. She wondered how it was that a loving God allowed such suffering to afflict a child. As she sat night and day nursing the child, her 'whole heart and brain revolted from the unutterable cruelty of a creating and destroying God'.[4] At the end of the ordeal, Mabel survived unscathed but Annie's Christianity did not.

The fens in the 1870s confronted Annie with a good deal more of the suffering that weakened her faith. Rural life in the flatlands of eastern England was no bucolic dream in the later nineteenth century. Some years after Annie had left, a resident of south Lincolnshire still endured a childhood of hard agricultural labour, walking to work in darkness, wading iced fens in winter, braving blizzards blown in off the North Sea. It was, she said, 'like heaven to me' when she found work at a factory in Leeds and moved away to the town. Some had despaired. A few used laudanum to escape their lives. A Crowland woman cut her throat when there was no money for her next fix and Frank Besant noted in his parish diary the presence of a tramp in the village who was insensible through opium-taking.[5] Annie saw the suffering first hand. Working among the poor of the parish, she nursed them during epidemics. There was fulfilment for her in snatching souls 'back to earth' when they had almost perished.[6] She saw too how Sibsey's people, most of them labourers, existed in 'cottages [which] were hovels, through the broken roofs of which poured the rain'. Therein 'rheumatism and ague lived with human dwellers' and periodically epidemic disease, notably typhoid, swept away many souls suddenly and terribly'. In one cottage riddled with the disease, a farm worker watched one child die and then saw his wife and remaining child lie convulsed by fever. When he returned home from his labours the whole family had to struggle on in a single room. And when night fell, 'the unhappy, driven man' had to lie down with his wife and living child on the same bed where the dead child awaited burial.[7]

These encounters sharpened Annie's sense of social justice and formed her political radicalism but they also whittled away her faith and pushed her further away from her husband. She could not speak about any of this to the people of the parish. For all their hardship, or perhaps because of it, unbelief sat uneasily with most of them. Their culture was saturated with stories about spirits. Fear of the devil and witchcraft still lingered. Rituals that helped the dead out of the world and prevented their return were commonplace. If the head of a household died, the bees would be told so that they did not abandon his heir and take good fortune with them. In some parts the feet of corpses were tied up as a precaution against wandering or pennies were popped into the mouths of corpses so that they might pay their way in the other world.[8] People who believed such things looked outside Frank's

church to others better able to guide them. The Primitive
Methodists had put down roots in the early nineteenth century.
With preachers, drawn from the ranks of ordinary folk, they
organised and explained a world of ghosts and spirits, conjurations
and exorcisms, appearances of the devil and divine interventions,
rather as Methodist preachers had in William Lovett's Cornwall.
They sweetened hellfire preaching with the prospect of a heaven
in which families would be reunited once more and so offered
glimmers of hope to those locked into brutal poverty. *Primitive
Methodist Magazine* told stories that brought comfort. One was of
a woman called Grace Rippingdale. Her son died young and, in
despair, she came to think that talk of a loving God was a delusion. The devil, so the article pointed out, had brought her low.
But on her own deathbed she had a foretaste of a world beyond
the grave. She saw visions of angels. So strengthened, she had
turned to Methodism at the last and so could be counted among
the saved.[9]

There would be no redemptive ending to Annie's time in the
fens. Set apart from the ordinary people of the parish by class
and education, she drifted away from her husband and his friends
too. Immersed in obscure theology, Frank kept company, insofar
as he kept company at all, with his fellow clergy. Annie found
them 'prim and Tory to an appalling extent'. Their horizons were
narrow, their politics unacceptable. They stood for the landholder
against the poor she was becoming keen to champion. There was
no society, no place, for her in Sibsey. The 'earnestly religious
soul' found every aspect of her Christian faith was coming under
challenge and looked for a spiritual refuge outside the parish,
turning at first to the ideas of the liberal-minded clergy of 'broad
church' Anglicanism. They talked more of the love and mercy of
God than his unsparing justice, imagined a heaven as the destination of many, perhaps most, souls and let hellfire fall out of their
preaching. Hell for them, if it existed at all, was not an inescapable
and sulphurous pit but a place of negation, a void, a place where
God was not. Or it might be a kind of reformatory, a refigured

purgatory in which sin was removed but by enlightened means rather than by fire. Such theology seemed to offer a scaffold for some of Annie's intuitions but, as she tried to adopt it, she found another obstacle. Ellen Marryat brought her up on the idea that the Bible was a tissue of literal truths and if the Bible was literally true, then it did indeed seem to ordain an eternal and fiery hell for the unregenerate. A figurative rereading of these passages was all very well, but then she wondered why the broader claims of the Bible should be trusted. Liberal theology seemed to license learned men to bend the words of scripture whichever way they would around changing moral convictions. The claims of the broad churchmen were fine ones but amounted, Annie came to think, to no more than 'skilful special pleading'.[11]

'Everyone who has doubted after believing', Annie recalled, 'knows how, after the first admitted and recognised doubt, others rush in like a flood.'[12] This is what happened to her now. She hated a God of punishment who demanded of Jesus a death-sacrifice to atone for the sins of men and women he had made frail. She still, for a time, loved the Christ she had come to know in her youthful devotions. But as she travelled to London to hear radical preaching and dabbled in alternative theology, she let go of the idea that he was divine. The final break with Christianity came a little later. Annie travelled to Oxford for a meeting. She had arranged to see Edward Pusey. As Regius Professor of Hebrew and the leading light of a movement dedicated to renewing the Church of England by rehabilitating many pre-Reformation rites and practices, he stood firmly for all the things she was coming to doubt. Finding her way among the colleges she reached Christchurch, where Pusey had his rooms. Entering, she saw little trace of the gentle smile that his friends thought a hallmark. For if ever Annie had intended that the meeting should help to allay her doubts, that notion quickly evaporated. Pusey was not prepared for the fiery Besant or expecting to engage her in intellectual debate. When she set before him her misgivings about Christian teaching he took this to be a confession and, when she persisted, construed it to be a sin. He brooked no discussion of her views about the nature of Christ and urged her to seek forgiveness through prayer. The interview ended in disarray. Annie left the study with a denunciation of her 'heresies' ringing in her ears. 'Out of such men', she concluded, 'were made the inquisitors of the middle ages.'

She returned to Sibsey but could not remain there long. Caught in a marriage to a man she had never really loved, her diminishing faith made it ever harder to play the part of the parson's wife. She nerved herself to go to services in her husband's church but she would no longer kneel at the rail nor receive wafers and wine from his hands. Doubt had destroyed the 'steady gleam of happiness' on the other side of the grave. It had removed the hope of better things beyond this world and robbed her of resources to bear the storms of earthly tribulation. It shipwrecked everything.[13] As others went up for communion, Annie slipped away. She finally left Sibsey for London in the summer of 1873.

No Rose-Water World

Only fragments of nineteenth-century Old Street remain today. There are some warehouse facades, the stuccoed front of the Hat and Feathers pub, a handful of eighteenth-century houses, the gaunt faces of St Luke's church, set back a little from the road. Bombing and redevelopment have seen off most of the Victoriana; much of the area round about is aggressively modernist in style. One of the vanished buildings came to play a central part in the middle years of Annie Besant's life. Number 142 is an Edwardian pile called Churchill House but in the 1870s a building known as the Hall of Science stood on the site.[14] It was unprepossessing, 'more a barn than a public building', and was ugly on the inside as well as the outside, so far as the respectable people were concerned. The Hall of Science was a venue for lectures expounding theories that were anathema to the religious. They unravelled the teachings of the Church, mocked the authority of the Bible and grounded morality in natural rather than super- natural reasoning. In a part of the city full of churches and missions to the godless working classes, the hall stood out. Here was no 'music or ritual to attract the sentimental or the weak'. There was no gospel and no free tea or cocoa, only a stronger ration of freethought for the price of a threepence entry fee.[15] The views articulated in this place were minority ones to be sure, but sprawling cosmopolitan London was a big and diverse enough place by the second half of the nineteenth century to supply doubters, unbelievers and fellow travellers enough to fill the hall. It was appropriate, perhaps, that it should stand a few hundred yards from Bunhill Fields, the burial ground of iconoclasts from an earlier ages, though preachers at the time pointed to St Luke's Asylum, a short walk away, as a more fitting propinquity. One man could draw the crowds to the hall better than others. He was a firm unbeliever, the iconoclast par excellence to his friends, a madman in the eyes of the devout. His name was Charles Bradlaugh.

Annie Besant decided she wanted to hear him after picking up a copy of the *National Reformer*, a periodical dedicated to radical politics and sceptical writing. She read it brazenly on a horse- drawn omnibus, and delighted in the mortification of an older male passenger who noticed what she was reading.[16] She made her way to the hall for the first time on Sunday 2 August 1873. The Sunday streets of that part of London were full of crowds. Some were rough-looking to the middle-class observer, hanging around on the corners; many were made up of the grindingly poor. Missions and ragged churches did a roaring trade, pulling in the indigent with a promise of a bellyful of breakfast. Others were inured to the sounds of church bells and Allelujah bands and waited for the doors of the public houses to open instead.[17] Amidst these working-class throngs, the Hall of Science found some of its constituency. Annie took a seat in the hall and Bradlaugh appeared on the rostrum. Tall, broad and useful with his fists, he was a bull of a man. Yet his features were sensitive, almost delicate. Dressed in black, priest-like, he spoke with the fervour of an evangelical.

Charles Bradlaugh had grown up in a tougher place than Annie Besant.[18] Born in 1833 in London, his family's fortunes spiralled downwards until they came to rest in Bethnal Green. There was usually little education to be had for such an early Victorian boy but he had natural talent and, making the best of what there was, studied hard at Sunday school. He might have turned into a very ordinary kind of believer, brought up in a Christian family and attending church. But his own intellectual curiosity changed that. In his spare time, the young Bradlaugh analysed one of the central texts of the Reformation, the Thirty-Nine Articles of the Church of England, and to his amazement, he found discrepancies between the Church's teachings and the Bible's words. He prayed for guidance and then laid his findings before his teacher, Reverend Packer. Packer was appalled. The young Bradlaugh was thrown out of Sunday school and Packer denounced the boy's dangerous unbelief to his father. But Bradlaugh's doubts only intensified. Aged sixteen, he left the family home for good. From there Bradlaugh trod a path every bit as unorthodox as Annie's, choosing a life outside the mainstream of a society where the great majority were at least passive believers. His choice brought not only social ostracism but also hardship. Few wanted to associate with an infidel, and when he set up as a coal merchant, a miller's wife said she would not have any fuel from him for fear her bread would reek of brimstone.[19]

Homeless and adrift in London, it was as if providence set him on a new course. He moved in with a widow, a woman called Eliza Sharples. She had previously lived 'in sin' with a man called Richard Carlile, a man who had been in his day a champion of anti-Christianity. He had risen to prominence from 1816 as a writer and publisher of blasphemous literature, which he sold in pamphlet form so it was available to the working man. For growing numbers of literate working men and women, committed to self-improvement, were reading widely and thinking radically.[20] In particular, they were devouring Thomas Paine's book, *The Age of Reason*, which attacked priestcraft and superstition, a work that Carlile helped to popularise. It was thought a dangerous book and Carlile a dangerous man by authorities unnerved by memories of a bloody revolution in France in which atheist values had been championed. They had him locked up in the 1820s for blasphemy and sedition. Not the least of the government's worries was that in chipping away at the edifice of Christian teaching about future reward and punishment he reduced the power of the poor to 'bear up against the pressure of misery and misfortune'.[21] But Carlile was unrepentant; the edifice of Christian teaching was a fiction. 'The whole substance of my creed', he explained, 'is that I believe in nothing supernatural.' He followed this up with blunt words about the proof texts of the Christian faith, claiming that 'every account that exists about the appearance of God or gods, an angel or angels, a spirit or spirits, to any man or . . . woman . . . is a fabricated and false account'. This world was all there was. The soul was an illusion. The mind was matter, 'mere pulsating sensation that cannot exist without the animal frame'.[22] Materialism could account for everything in the cosmos from planetary systems to the workings of the brain.

Scepticism of this kind was no invention of the nineteenth century; it was almost as old as the hills. The Psalmist of the Old Testament wrote that it was the fool who said in his heart that there was no God. There were hints in the Middle Ages that some were sceptics. Peter of Cornwall worried in 1200 that some did not believe in God, thought the cosmos was ruled by chance and did not believe 'in good or bad angels, or that . . . the human soul lives on after the body'.[23] These doubters need not have been fools. The monk and chronicler Thomas Walsingham wrote in 1381 that some thought 'a man's life ends, just like that of an animal, when it dies'.[24] In 1622 a Wiltshire gentleman called John Derpier made similar dark conjectures. There was 'no God and no Resurrection', he argued, 'and men died a death like beasts'.[25] In the seventeenth century, some divines, Joseph Glanvill among them, were becoming fearful of unbelief, whether scepticism about the resurrection of the dead or a broader rejection of Christianity itself, though here clerical fears probably magnified the extent of these sceptical reflections.[26] David Hume went further, going cheerfully to his deathbed in 1776 with no faith and no thought of a world beyond the grave. But Hume had refrained from sharing his unbelief with the lower orders; it was the property of intellectuals, its wider dissemination might be destabilising and it was not to be talked about in front of the servants.[27] Richard Carlile and men like him were changing that. They talked freely about doubt. They shouted it from the soapbox; they scattered it through the streets in pamphlets. This was the tradition into which Charles Bradlaugh stepped.

He moved freely among the heirs of Richard Carlile, rising steadily in their ranks. His prepossessing appearance, oratorical gifts and toughness all served him well in the rough calling he had chosen. And fortunately for him, the dangers of a prison sentence had receded somewhat since Carlile's heyday. George Holyoake, a middle-class man from Birmingham, had made religious scepticism a little more respectable and a little less threatening to the social fabric. By the 1860s he had also turned a loose congeries of ideas into a movement and called it secularism.[28] Its tentacles extended out into the provinces, especially into industrial Lancashire and Yorkshire, and a base had been found in London at the Hall of Science.[29] Bradlaugh went out on the stump to champion the secularist cause. He could often fill a local hall with converts and the curious but he drew hostile crowds too. Heckling was expected. Hymn-singing, breaking glass and a fist fight were common and all three in combination were not unknown.[30] As he rose to prominence in the movement, gossip and slander were drawn to him like wasps to jam. It was even said that in one address he challenged the Almighty to strike him dead in the next five minutes and then took out his watch to wait for the Deity's vengeance. But that gift for showmanship meant he could rouse an audience like few others. Cerebral Holyoake was soon in eclipse; in 1858 Bradlaugh became the movement's leader at the tender age of twenty-four.

Then, in the Hall of Science on 2 August 1873, his path crossed that of Annie Besant. She was at that time a striking woman with a 'slight but full and well-shaped figure', dark hair and fine, chiselled features.[31] After the meeting, she went to see him in his lodgings and a deep emotional relationship and intellectual connection formed. Quickly, Annie Besant's reputation rose in the Hall of Science. The pair and those around them were engaging in a novel enterprise: finding a way to live without religious belief. Central to the project was a rejection of the idea of an afterlife with all its compensatory and retributive dimensions. The poor would not inherit the earth in a second life nor would the wicked be punished in hell. So, as one campaigner explained, 'it is our duty to secure that happiness, virtue and freedom here, so long promised us hereafter'.[32] The rejection of Christian teachings triggered political radicalism. Men had to build the New Jerusalem in the here and now; they could not wait for it in the next world.

As they made a case for unbelief, the secularists acquired new intellectual armaments during the nineteenth century.[33] New forms of criticism, born in Germany, subjected the Bible to scrutiny that laid it bare as a composition of many men, stripping away the mystique of divine authorship. Biology framed explanations of life in material terms. Primitive forms of evolutionary theory, which restricted the need for divine involvement, circulated as early as the 1840s. They prefigured Darwin and prepared the way for the epochal shock that he would deliver, that man had risen from among the beasts rather than being made in the image of God to rule over them. Perhaps most powerfully, and as John Martin had noticed decades before, probing of fossil records and rock strata was showing that the world was infinitely older, perhaps millions of years older, than conventional wisdom suggested. By the time Annie Besant and Charles Bradlaugh were busy evangelising, few learned men believed Bishop Ussher's calculation that the cosmos had come into being in 4004 BC. The new science was beginning to dissolve man's specialness among the animals. It was cutting him loose in great tracts of time and space.

Ultimately, secularist lecturers fastened onto these ideas but most continued, even in the 1870s and 80s, to rely on older repertoires as they attacked conventional beliefs. A hostile witness said that in her lectures Annie Besant 'takes the Bible to pieces, and turns it inside out, and holds up to ridicule all its heroes and prophets, and kings and apostles, and Christ himself'.[34] This was an old-fashioned kind of attack on scripture, showing the audience the kinds of contradictions that she had seen as her own faith collapsed in Sibsey. Hell was one of her targets too. The doctrine was to Annie Besant one of the central horrors of traditional religion. It formed a confection of all the 'most loathsome, most revolting, the most treacherous, coarse brutal . . . fiendish cruelty, unsoftened by any remains of human feeling. 'Hear', she said, 'those yells of concentrated blasphemy and hate as they echo along the lurid vault of hell.'[35]

Even in the 1870s, she pointed out that hellfire preaching was far from dead and many sensitive souls were still traumatised by its effects. The old-fashioned teaching was pernicious and it continued to blight lives and 'blacken the earth with the smoke of torment'.[36] Annie's claims had some substance. Many churchmen no longer declaimed about eternal torment from their pulpits but others still conjured with hellfire. England's Catholics were especially likely to hear about it; it had never vanished from their church's preaching and mass-marketed cheap print gave it a new lease of life. Father Furniss, an English priest and missioniser, sold some four million copies of instructional pamphlets aimed chiefly at the young. In them, the aptly named author offered an account of what awaited the wicked that might almost have been plucked from the writings of medieval visionaries.[37] The young reader was told that in hell there was rain, but it was a rain of fire. There were thunderbolts, but they fell all the time and were made of fire. There was fog, but it was a fog of fire. Floods of fire would 'roll through hell like the waves of the sea'. And 'you may', Furniss noted, 'have seen a house on fire but you have never seen a house *made* of fire'. In hell there were such houses. Lest the reader's imagination became dulled to the pyrotechnics, Furniss added human interest. He described a girl tormented by a blazing bonnet that burned forever into her skull because 'in life she never thought of God' but only of pretty clothes. Then there was a youth whose blood boiled, singing in his veins with the sound of a kettle, because he wanted to go to dancing houses and public houses rather than spending his time in church.[38]

By the later 1870s, many leading Protestant churchmen were ready to smother hell's flames, seeing it in terms of separation from God, as a temporary fate akin to purgatory or seeing anni- hilation rather than endless suffering as the fate of the wicked.[39] When first sung in English in 1849, the hymn 'My God I Love Thee' promised sinners that they would 'burn eternally' but the 1876 version slid more quietly over the matter. Now they would be 'lost' eternally.[40] In medieval and early modern visions the elect were sometimes shown visions of hell so that they might see the suffering of the damned and then find their own joys redoubled; the Victorian devotional writer Edward Henry Bickersteth rendered the same idea with a more delicate image, suggesting that smoke from hell wafted endlessly through heaven to remind the saved of their happy estate.[41] But the new theology was still far from over-mastering its more terrifying antecedents. There were enough pale imitations of Father Furniss around for Annie and her peers in their pamphlets and preaching to be able to turn traditional hellfire rhetoric of the pulpit into a weapon against the churches. For the old view, deeply rooted in scripture and tradition, died hard. And while Annie Besant argued that human morality did not depend on promises of other-worldly reward or punishment, many, not least the Prime Minister William Ewart Gladstone, feared that if hell's flames were quenched the social order would crumble along with the infrastructure of supernatural deterrence. Hellfire preaching remained one way to shake the apathetic in a congregation too. The most popular preacher in late Victorian England, Charles Spurgeon, still conjured up – right down to his death in 1892 – visions of the jangling chains and agonised cries of lost souls of hell in an effort to call sinners to repentance.[42]

If hell was an easy target for the secularists, it was harder for them to release death fully from the grip of religious interpretation. The patternless-ness of human life could make it difficult for people to believe. The suffering and death of a child was especially unbearable. It could shake steadfast faith: even bishops in their correspondences struggled to see a benevolent God at work when they buried one of their own offspring.[43] But if deaths, especially untimely ones, shook faith then consolation in time of loss was hard to find in a godless world. In the face of death, the secularist message was bleak. George Holyoake warned that human beings were doomed to watch their loved ones suffer and die before their eyes, immune to all effects of prayer. There was no pattern to man's existence and 'no special providence smoothes his path'.[44] Men and women must place their faith in human ingenuity, in medicine, in science, in order to lighten life and stave off death. Trapped in a mine filling with firedamp, salvation came through the Davy lamp not through prayer. Science must be the providence of the human race. And when death came, it must be faced unflinchingly. Holyoake expected that he would gaze from his own deathbed across 'the dim sea of the future on which no voyager's bark is seen returning' but would put no trust 'in priestly dogmas [nor] paltry visions of gilt trumpets and angels' wings'.[45] An afterlife must be found in this world, in legacies of art or writing, a memory of virtue or in one's children.

This was a bitter pill. Secularism was never a mass movement in Victorian England and its limited consolations in the face of death played their part in limiting its appeal. Men and women who struggled to make ends meet in their daily lives, to raise themselves above bare subsistence, might have little time or inclination to listen to preaching.[46] What was true for the churches was true for the secularists too. The founder of the Salvation Army, William

Booth, pointed out that many of their halls of science were as empty as the chapels and churches. The menace to faith in the nineteenth century was lukewarmness and apathy; an irreligion built on indifference. But then when the numinous did break into the lives of such people, it was usually to the churches that they turned. The churches were everywhere; Christianity's infrastructure, supplied now by many denominations, was a national one. Religious teaching saturated society. Confronted by the terror, mystery and grief of death, it was still to the churches that the vast majority of people went. In many cases, they did this because this was what was done. The solid frames of ritual, as much as deep belief, offered support for men and women on their deathbeds and those left behind when they had gone: washing and readying the dead, the woman's work, then viewing, touching, kissing the corpse, neighbours gathering, a procession in a decent coffin, laying to rest in hallowed ground, the cadences of the burial rite, its language strange but the forms familiar, the cured hams and funeral biscuits of the wake. Such things attended the last rite of passage. Many of them had little to do with formal Church teaching, some were mere 'superstitions' in the eyes of the clergy, but all were woven into ways of facing death and taking leave of the dead that were, at root, religious.[47]

In the winter cold of January 1891, Charles Bradlaugh lay dying. The great infidel had acquired a certain respectability. He could look back on a successful parliamentary career, having won a Northampton seat and struggled for a long time with the authorities of the House to take it up without swearing the religious oath. His private life was more tortured. Estranged from his wife, Susannah Lamb, he had watched from a distance as she drank herself to death. Intimate for a time with Annie Besant, but eschewing an 'improper' relationship with her, they had drifted apart in his later years. She came to see him but stayed only a short time before saying her final farewell. As he waited for death, Bradlaugh knew that there was a final battle that he must win.

If his reputation was to survive him, he must die true to the values by which he had lived. The religious regularly published stories of infidel deathbeds attended by visions of angels and last-minute conversions or fraught with horror as the unbeliever sank into despair at the thought of annihilation.[48] 'Reason', they warned, was a 'hard bolster for the dying head'.[49] His enemies would do all they could to paint his final hours as ones of religious transformation. So his deathbed was guarded by his daughter, Hypatia, and he was tended by trusted nurses. He died at six thirty in the morning on 30 January. Dawn was breaking. When he was dead, there were indeed tales that he had undergone a deathbed conversion. One Mr Gray of Pershore Road, Birmingham, even said that Bradlaugh's spirit had returned, revealing through a medium a 'never-ending life in the glorious spheres of immortal bliss'.[50] But the truth was more prosaic. Hypatia and the nurses testified that Bradlaugh was steadfast in his beliefs right to the end. He had died a good secularist's death, his mind unclouded by any revelation.

To the City of the Dead

He was buried, as he wished, at Brookwood, London's great cemetery out to the south-west, beyond the city's sprawl, for here, Bradlaugh knew, he could rest in a patch of unconsecrated earth. Brookwood was already well established by this point, having been opened in 1854 to replace the overflowing churchyards of the capital which had recently been shut up.[51] It was to be the antithesis of these burial places of old with its open vistas, uncrowded plots, magnolias, rhododendrons and evergreen trees.

The sequoias planted there by the cemetery's founders around the time of its opening have since grown to maturity and the capital's suburbs have spilled outwards towards it. The bones of some 235,000 people lie in its earth. Different nationalities, denominations, religions have their own spaces. Cremated remains are scattered in glades and green burials take place in the woodland. Bradlaugh lies in plot 108 under a mature pine, a family grave. His monument is hard to find, swallowed almost by yew trees and a rhododendron. A simple pillar made from red granite and paid for by public subscription, it records the facts of his life and the motto *semper nobilis*.[52] The cemetery, strewn with windfalls after a gale, is empty and silent save for the occasional passing train. But on this same spot among younger trees on 3 February 1891, a huge crowd assembled to see the great iconoclast off. An unusual array of people attended his funeral. There were secular-ists, trade unionists, men and women from working-class commu-nities whose causes he had taken up, politicians including the young David Lloyd George, and many members of London's Indian community, Gandhi among them, grateful for his cham-pioning of their interests in the Commons. The infrastructure of late Victorian death got them to the graveside with special trains steaming out of the Necropolis station near Waterloo to one of the cemetery's own dedicated stations.

But the panoply of mortuary ritual to which many Victorians were firmly attached was abandoned for Bradlaugh. There were no horses with plumes, no solemn procession or elaborate flowers. Mourning blacks were exchanged for brighter colours. There were no prayers, no liturgy of any kind. He wanted none of these things. Much had changed between the death rites of Bradlaugh in 1891 and those surrounding his infidel forebear, Richard Carlile, who had been buried in 1843. He too had defied mortuary conven-tion, willing his body to medical science for dissection and demanding a non-religious burial. But when it came to his funeral amidst snow and slush on another February day, a clergyman appeared on the scene and insisted that a service be read. The old 'priest-hater' was sent to the grave in sure and certain hope of glorious resurrection.[53] At Bradlaugh's graveside there was no such intervention. The wishes of the deceased prevailed over those of the Church, the requirement that a burial service be read at burials having been abandoned in law in 1880.[54] Instead there was silence. No speeches were permitted. No words were spoken. There was nothing to be said in the face of death; Bradlaugh wanted only meditation. His body was buried, as he wanted, 'as cheaply as possible', being lowered into earth in a coffin made from papier mâché.[55]

Among the crowds at the funeral, one figure stood out. Black-bombazined and veiled, she wore a widow's weeds despite the injunction that those attending should abandon mourning colours. The woman was Annie Besant. It was a strange sartorial decision. Perhaps she could not quite shake off the conventions of her class or perhaps it was a token of feelings for a man she may once have wished to marry.[56] Nothing is clear about why she made her choice. But her incongruity symbolised how she had ceased to move easily in circles of infidels and unbelievers. For by 1891, Annie had abandoned secularism. Dabbling first with socialism, she then embarked on an onward journey through newer, stranger philosophies suffused with the supernatural. In a sense, Annie Besant's life was turning full circle, for as she stood at the grave-side in 1891, shut in behind her veil, she was coming to think once more that death was not the end of life. Intrigued by the idea that the spirits of the dead might commune with the living, her detractors said when Bradlaugh's daughter, Alice, was dying in 1888 she had gone to her so as to observe a soul's departure from the body. But if she found the phenomena of spiritualism 'indu-bitable', explanations in terms of communicating spirits did not satisfy her. She quickly left the movement behind.

When Annie penned her autobiography in 1893 she was settling into a new philosophy. She had been given a book to review, Madame Blavatsky's *Secret Doctrine*. The book was a sort of prophy-lactic against narrow rationalism, mingling Buddhist and Hindu ideas with insights about occult forces and hidden powers. Reading it led to another epiphany for Annie. 'In a flash of illumination,' she later recalled, 'I knew the weary search was over: the Truth was found.' She embraced wholeheartedly Blavatsky's theories, turning herself into a disciple of the Russian mystic. She found in reincarnation and karma ideas that promised social justice through cosmic mechanisms. Human beings, Blavatsky claimed, passed through many bodies, living, dying and being born again; where they began each new life was determined by how they had lived the last one. This was, in its way, an evolutionary principle for the human soul, a means by which there could be punishment and progress towards perfection. Secularists looked on aghast as Annie absorbed all this and proclaimed that during her years as an unbeliever she had been 'misled by the intellect to ignore the needs of the soul'. Bradlaugh's successor as the leader of the secularists, George Foote, dismissed her as too much 'at the mercy of her emotions' as she flitted between ideologies. But the leap into theosophy was no fad.[57] For the rest of Annie Besant's long life, theosophical teachings about spirit and matter guided her. Ever the champion of radical causes, she shuttled between India and Britain and became one of the leading proponents of Indian independence, her theosophy, an eclectic mix of eastern religions, cohering with much that she found attractive in the spirituality of her adopted subcontinent.

As Annie wrote her autobiography, she looked back on her life and felt that theosophy helped to make sense of it. Her brother, Alfie, had died young. In middle age she could still see the boy 'white and beautiful' in the coffin where she took her leave of him; she still recalled the 'deadly cold that startled me' as she kissed her brother goodbye. When her mother died, she remembered following the cortège into gloomy Kensal Green 'where her husband and baby son were already sleeping'. Whatever reason taught, she had struggled to leave and wept 'when we left her behind in the chill, damp earth with the rains of spring'.[58] Annie also remembered childhood encounters that added to her sense that human beings might be made of more than matter that would eventually be consigned to the cold ground. She had Irish blood flowing in her veins and tales of ghosts, the banshee and death warnings abounded on that side of the family.[59] Her mother had uncanny powers. When Annie's father died young her mother had been too traumatised to attend the funeral. Nonetheless, 'with vacant eyes and pallid face' she had 'seen' it all unfold in her mind's eye while sitting motionless in a chair at home. So clear was her second sight that she could find the grave unaided when she visited Kensal Green. And Annie even remembered 'vague misty presences' and dim apprehensions of spiritual forces from her own childhood; shadows of her mother's powers, perhaps, since her own 'Keltic' blood had been watered down thanks to her mother's marriage to an Englishman. None of this had made sense to her at the time, but in the blinding flash of theosophist revelation it did. Reflecting on her mother's vision of Kensal Green, she remembered how very improbable her claims seemed at the time. But she 'now knew' that 'conscious can leave the body, take part in events going on at a distance and impress on the physical brain what it experienced'.[60]

When Annie Besant was born in 1847, amidst the rose-filled gardens and middle-class respectability of Harrow, the course of her life was unimaginable. Then there were many kinds of Christianity in Britain, but it was still dangerous to dissent from the faith in radical ways. The threat of the prison cell still hung over the unbeliever. She died in 1933 as a devotee of a mystical philosophy, her body cremated on an open pyre in the city of Aydar in India. During her life, technology and politics had transfigured society and culture. New ways of believing had become possible as mystical theologies and new philosophies came into being, many absorbed from the empire back into the mother country. Unbelief, liberating and disorientating unbelief was not only accepted, it could be respectable, at least in learned circles. Annie Besant's was a singular life. And yet the forces that shaped it would work more powerfully and generally to make twentieth-century Britain more complex and diverse as religions and irreligion mixed. In some ways, Annie Besant revealed something of the future.

13

THE GLORIOUS DEAD

This book ends almost where it began. The galleries of Tate Britain and John Martin's paintings of the last things are exchanged for the nave of Westminster Abbey – a mile or so away on the same side of the Thames – the nation's church. Its origins are in the eleventh century, the England of King Edward the Confessor who planned it as his burial place. The present building swallowed its old self in the thirteenth century, during a great rebuilding funded by the largesse of King Henry III. Through the ages the bones of kings and queens, generals and admirals, poets and prelates have been laid down here and statues and memorials raised up and it is as close as anywhere is to being a national mausoleum. Mingled with the dust of generations, in the nave and close by the West Door, is an unusual body and a singular memorial: the Tomb of the Unknown Warrior. Where the exploits of the ancient dead, famous in their day, are now largely forgotten, the bones of this nameless man within are renowned. For the circumstances of his burial and the way he came to be celebrated remain powerfully emblematic. A soldier of the Great War, he was laid here in 1920 and a slab of highly polished black marble from Belgium was lowered over the grave the following year. This ordinary man, this Everyman, came to stand for much, as the dedication makes plain. The central inscription says that he was 'buried among the kings' as a symbol of the sacrifice made by a multitude killed on land and sea and in the air during the war. The Warrior died, the stone says, for God and King, for country and empire; for loved ones, for justice and for the freedom of the world. The words are consolations: proofs that all of the personal tragedies for which the tomb stood were not in vain; that death in the war to end all wars had served higher purposes, preserved abstract values with tangible meaning for those left alive in the world. The stone also makes other, older promises too, which might have made the loss of loved ones easier to bear. Pushed to the edges of the slab, forming a frame, are four phrases from scripture. Three hold out traditional hope of salvation: 'In Christ shall all be made alive' and 'The Lord knoweth them that are his' and the especially resonant 'Unknown and yet well known, dying and behold we live'. The fourth assimilates the war dead to Christ's teaching of the chiefest sacrifice that a human being might make, for 'greater love hath no man than this [that a man may lay down his life for his friends]'.

Still embedded today in national myth, this black slab remains one focus of ceremonies at Remembrancetide. Royal brides still lay their bouquets there as they leave the Abbey on their wedding days. The Warrior is a rare anonymous figure commanding a place in the sixty-one volumes of the *New Dictionary of National Biography*, which compasses the great and the good of British history. His entry in the *Dictionary* is doubly unusual since it tells not of a life but of an afterlife. The story is famous but it bears retelling because it is a clue to other narratives, personal, painful and far from anonymous, which the Great War set in motion and which, in one way or another, meet at this tomb.

The morning of 11 November 1920 was very still. Flags were motionless and smoke rose vertically. As the sun came up, frost yielded and people formed thickly along the processional ways or gathered at windows and on rooftops; latecomers were to be seen cutting across Hyde Park, some carrying flowers done up in newspaper. Just two days earlier, a senior officer, Brigadier General Louis John Wyatt, had entered a makeshift chapel at Saint-Pol-sur-Ternoise. Inside had been four (some said six) coffins draped in Union Jacks, the bodies inside each having been disinterred from the battlefields of the Great War, from Arras and Ypres, from the Aisne and the Somme. With a touch, the general had chosen one of them, anointing the man who would become the Unknown Warrior. Now at mid morning in the autumn sunshine, he would be laid to rest at the Abbey with the kind of ceremony once reserved for great commanders, for Horatio Nelson or the Duke of Wellington, or for royalty. The Warrior was for *The Times* correspondent 'a modern King Arthur', but for most he was simply an everyman, a bearer for hundreds of thousands of individual griefs, a signification of a general sacrifice.[1]

A little before ten o'clock, the pipes and drums of the military bands struck up, the six black horses drawing a gun carriage took up the traces and its wheels bit into sand scattered over the road. The procession emerged from Victoria into the public gaze. The coffin was covered with a Union Jack, and a trench helmet and bayonet had been laid on the lid. All along the route silent crowds pressed to watch, black-hatted women and hatless men. The gun-carriage wound its way from Grosvenor Place, down Constitution Hill, into the Mall and on into Whitehall.

The backstory of this ritual reached into a past when the war dead were treated differently, but its immediate roots were in the imagination of a military chaplain, David Railton. He had served in Flanders since the early days of the war, had buried his first casualty in the summer of 1914, trickling blue cornflowers into the grave after speaking the words of committal. By 1916 he had buried many more but, returning to his billet at Erkingham, a village outside Armentières, he stumbled one evening on a grave in a place that had once been a back garden but was now an improvised cemetery. The white wooden cross must have stood out in the twilight. On it, in thick black pencil, was the inscription 'An Unknown Soldier', with the regiment, the Black Watch, indicated in parentheses below. The spectacle impressed itself on Railton's memory, perhaps because of the uncommon peace of the moment; even the guns, he recalled, had fallen silent and the

only noise was of a card game under way in a billet. Soon afterwards he thought to write to General Haig, suggesting that an
anonymous body be taken back from the battlefields to be buried
with honour as a symbol of all who would not return.[2] For some
reason he did not write, or he did write and Haig did not respond,
but then, in August 1920, he reactivated the idea, writing to Herbert
Ryle, the Dean of Westminster, who quickly took up the cause
and wrote to George V. The king disliked the suggestion. He
reasoned that wounds that had begun to close in the wake of the
war would break open as all the pain and suffering successfully
borne or suppressed rose up again. But the Prime Minister, David
Lloyd George, thought differently. The war had compassed the
deaths of almost three-quarters of a million British men and he
saw that its scale and nature might demand a new kind of
commemoration.

Before 1914, wars had been fought far from home by profes-
sionals, men who took the Queen's shilling and knew that, if their
luck ran out, the price was that their bones would lie forever in
a foreign field. When Walter Scott saw the field of Waterloo, the
ground had been picked clean of things of value but the 'steaming
carnage' of human remains, miasmatic and dangerous, was still
there, barely concealed under mounds.[3] By the early twentieth
century, most received more reverent treatment than this but
soldiers still worried about decent burial.[4] There was also little
sense that if they died their countrymen would keep them in
mind; there was little by way of public obligation to remember
the men who laid down their lives in imperial wars. The Boer
War had given rise to some civic memorials but these were still
the exception rather than the rule.[5] If the war dead were remembered at all, it was usually by families and friends and by comrades,
in chapels and in great churches, filled with memorial plaques
and stones paid for by officers and men set up among fading
colours and falling spindrift. The Great War altered the calculus.
The motherland had made enormous claims on the young.
Conscripted, regimented, sent into battle and to their deaths; even

after death their bodies were regimented in military cemeteries, denied to families because repatriation on the scale the war demanded was impossible.[6] And if all could not be returned home the government was firm in its resolve that none should return. There could be no special dispensations for the rich who had the wherewithal to bring their dead home while the dead of the poor languished in the cemeteries of Flanders and France or further afield.[7] These circumstances demanded a new kind of symbolic response and so Lloyd George bent the king to his will. The press seized on the idea and *The Times* explained the rationale. The ceremonies would be 'impersonal, or, more truly . . . personal to all of us . . . They are a tribute to no single name, to no General whose genius inspired our Armies, to no warrior whose prowess won more renown among his fellows. They are a tribute to "the Glorious Dead", equal in their glory as in death . . . The Unknown Warrior is, in a special sense, an emblem of the "plain man", of the masses of the people.'[8]

At 10.45 a.m., the Warrior's cortège reached the Cenotaph, newly built and shrouded by flags, and paused there to be met by the king and clergy. There was a silence and then a hymn, before the Archbishop of Canterbury, the bald-headed and bushy-browed Randall Davidson, led the recitation of the Lord's Prayer. He had previously fought for these religious trappings against the Foreign Secretary, Lord Curzon, who had been put in charge of the ceremonies. He had argued that the national commemorations needed to appeal to all faiths and none. This attenuated Christianity of hymn and prayer had been the compromise. As Big Ben struck eleven o'clock, the king pushed a button and the swags fell away to reveal the Cenotaph beneath. An empty tomb, it stood for the absent dead in distant lands. Originally cobbled together out of plaster and wood by Sir Edwin Lutyens to form a centre point for the victory parade in July 1919, some had doubted its suitability then. Sir Alfred Mond had thought it 'too Catholic' a commemoration for British tastes but the public had warmed to it, and on the day of the parade people had laid wreaths all around the base.

So it was rebuilt in stone. Stark and modernist, there was nothing overtly religious about it. Its simple remembrance was of the glorious dead. The decision had been deliberate. Among the dignitaries gathered around it were not only the leaders of the many Christian denominations but also Hindus, Muslims, Sikhs and Jews. The Great War had truly been a world war. Many races and creeds had been drawn into it and men like Curzon held that the debt of the motherland lay not only to Christians but also to the Muslim, Hindus and Sikhs of the empire who had fought in the many theatres of battle.

As one commemoration played out at the Cenotaph, other rites had begun at the Abbey. One hundred holders of the Victoria Cross formed up there as an honour guard for the Warrior and one thousand women, widowed or robbed of their sons by the war, 'titled ladies next to charwomen', waited in the nave amidst solemn music and the glittering renown of those interred beneath the vaults. After opening hymns and sentences, the two liturgies, the novel one at the Cenotaph and its more ancient counterpart at the Abbey, began to converge. The congregation repeated the Lord's Prayer and then, as they finished, silence fell at eleven o'clock in the great church too, shutting each man and woman into a private world. The clergy moved into the nave and gathered at the graveside. Dean Ryle in a purple-and-golden cope met the coffin as it was brought in. The pall bearers included brass hats of navy, army and fledgling air force: Field Marshal Haig, Air Chief Marshal Trenchard and Lord Beatty, the First Sea Lord. There was the diminutive figure of Sir John French, too, a man trained up in the cavalry who had commanded the British Expeditionary Force in 1914, and a triumvirate of admirals, Meux, Madden and Jackson, who had entered the navy when many of its ships moved under sail.[9]

The hymns, readings and prayers that followed formed a shortened version of the burial service familiar to any in the congregation who knew the Prayer Book.[10] The words described a shape of traditional consolations. They promised regeneration: for even 'after my skin worms destroy this body, yet in my flesh shall I see God'. The warrior was laid in the grave 'in sure and certain hope of the resurrection to eternal life'. The words of the liturgy held out to the righteous hope of salvation, salvation achieved through trust in Christ. They would, as a reading from Revelation prophesied, stand before God's throne and serve in his temple; they would don white robes – robes washed bright and pure in the Lamb's blood. The language was rich in ancient images of heaven in which the dead lived again to worship God in eternity. Hymns, most of more recent vintage, offered other visions also figured in metaphors honed for generations. Heaven was an eternal home, a refuge from 'the stormy blast', a kingdom made ready for the elect. It was 'a sweet and blessèd country', a place of 'unspeakable joys', a 'light that shall never more fade'. One hymn, O Valiant Hearts, went further. It seemed almost to join Christ's sufferings to the agonies of the battlefields, making the war dead almost Christlike in their sacrifice. Christ had travelled through the world in 'the frailty of human clay'. He had suffered and died on the cross for humankind and this cross was now, still, the 'bright star' over and above the dark abyss of death and desolation. Those who had given their lives in the Great War – for family and friends, for king and country – had their Calvaries in Flanders; they too had 'drunk his cup of sacrifice', had suffered to redeem those left alive in the world, freeing them not from sin but from tyranny. The assimilation of fighting man to Christ savoured of things deeply unorthodox but the ideas were too powerful, the hymn too popular, to be forsaken, and, in Westminster Abbey on this most resonant of occasions, the Dean had found a place for it in the service.[11]

As the service ended, the body of the Warrior was lowered into the ground, into sands and river gravels undisturbed, so it was said, since the building of the nave, resting among the ancient and the honoured dead. The king scattered earth from the battlefields over the coffin, the service drew to a close and the congregation dispersed. Then ordinary men and women, especially women, began to queue in order to pay their respects at the grave, people whose stories of loss, most irrecoverable now, twined in some way round that of the nameless man in the grave. Filing in unbroken columns marshalled by mounted police, they continued to queue through the afternoon as fog began to fill Whitehall. They still queued as darkness fell and a chilly night set in.[12] The crowds waxed again at first light and more and more people came in subsequent days, a million or more in a kind of pilgrimage from the corners of the kingdom, 'from homes on the moors, cottages in Hampshire, from trim little houses in seaport towns and the two million houses of London'.[13] Most went first to the Cenotaph where many laid flowers – it seemed, said one newspaperman, that every fifth or sixth woman bore a bunch of white chrysanthemums. One elderly woman, so a policeman recalled, had come from Scotland carrying flowers that had withered during the journey. She would, she said, still lay them there in memory of her son since they were late blooms from a garden he had planted before the war.[14] From the Cenotaph the crowds went on to the Abbey and the Warrior's grave.[15] The unidentified man laid close to the Abbey's West Door had an extraordinary resonance; in burying the Unknown Warrior it was, as one Liberal politician observed, as if the nation had laid to rest 'every boy's father, every woman's lover, every mother's son'.[16]

For one widow who visited the Abbey it was indeed as if the freshly buried bones within were those of her missing husband. She explained the sensation in an anonymous account, privately printed and now rare, *To My Unknown Warrior*: it is so impassioned it is almost hallucinatory. She traced the emotions of the dead man's family, turning first to her husband's father. He had made sacrifices for his boy, had invested so much emotion in him, and had been ambitious for him too. As he made ready for the service at the Abbey he fussed about exactly how he should be dressed, a sign of the nerves that always struck on important occasions, but beneath it all there was pride in his son's sacrifice. He could find some solace in the 'honour, glory and splendour' of the funeral and for a moment the sting of death was drawn. His boy had 'done well', he had made his mark and he would rest among the bones of kings.

The boy's mother was reticent in her grief, concealing it under a 'twisted smile', which formed on her lips when she was deeply moved, or by a bubbling laugh, which she used to smother emotion. Only occasionally had she let down her guard to the writer in the months since her son's death. 'Sometimes,' she had explained, 'without warning, something quite unexpected gets past one's guard and cuts through all our defences.' It had happened on Good Friday. She had been to church as she always did and sat through the Passiontide service. Usually she was moved to pity by the gospel words describing Christ crucified, but this time the words that moved her left her cold. In her mind's eye all she could see was a dead soldier hanging 'broken' on the wire in no man's land. Only when she heard words from the lesson, a phrase that she had previously scarcely noticed before, did she begin to recover her balance. The words were 'I know not where they have laid him', spoken about the fate of Jesus's body when it was taken down from the cross. Memories of her lost son then flooded in. Christ's burial, not his passion, spoke most deeply to her grief because her son's body was lost somewhere in France. Nourished on the lessons of many Eastertide services, the bereaved mother was left contending with them to make sense of her loss. But consolation of a kind came, so the anonymous writer claimed, after the Abbey service and the burial of the Unknown Warrior. Then the dead man's mother was full of thankfulness that her boy had, in some sense, been 'found' and buried. It mattered, the writer said, for a mother to have a tangible thing, a thing to touch and feel, which connected her to the baby to which she gave life, had held and nursed, even if that thing was a cold stone or a cross over a grave. That, she intimated, was the part of the Westminster tomb in the thoughts of mothers whose sons would be forever missing.

Many other stories twined round the Warrior's grave. A Cumbrian woman, a working-class woman who lived much of her life in Kells near Whitehaven and latterly moved to Durham, had lost her son in the Great War too. Something of her story was told by Jack Lawson, another son who became a Labour Member of Parliament in the years after the war.[17] His mother was descended from 'a race of giants', the Grahams of Cockermouth. Flinty and tough, she was undemonstrative of her maternal love, making him wonder if she loved him at all, but she had struggled for her children, to put clothes on their backs and food on the table. She gleaned coal washed up on the beach, staggering home up the hill like a strange beast of burden, and if her sons were in harm's way she fought for them, literally if need be, once setting about a man in the street who had beaten her son and vanquishing him in a fist fight. She edged into the winter of life as the Great War broke out and while in material terms the family was more comfortable by then, the war destroyed her inner peace. In February 1916 she received a telegram saying that the youngest son, William, was dead, killed, it later emerged, by a sniper's bullet as he tried to pull a wounded man from a shell hole. With tense mouth and dry eyes, all she could say to Jack was that her 'babby' was gone. Seemingly stone-hard, she never wept, an image 'of inarticulate suffering, defying description', and confined herself to her room for days, which turned into weeks. Eventually she recovered a little. Domestic routines reasserted themselves. She might from time to time alight on an item of her son's clothing, using it as a prop, a way to speak about him, but she never recovered fully. When she herself was dying the pain came back. Jack listened at her bedside as she called the dead boy's name, holding out her arms as if to cradle a baby who was not there. Whether cenotaphs, war memorials or a Westminster grave brought any consolation to this woman is impossible to guess but it was for countless women like her that they were made.

The unanswered need, that the dead be brought home, led many to seek out surrogates for a body, a funeral and a grave to tend. There might be a photograph of a grave on the mantelpiece; the army's Grave Registration Committee had advertised the availability of such photographs to relatives should they wish to apply.[18] There might be a boxes of cemetery earth or soil from the battlefield. There were mementoes, things from the dead man's pockets – his watch, photographs, a cigarette case, a lighter – effects returned by the military in a brown paper parcel, secondary relics in the body's absence.[19] Many travelled to find, see, touch and lay a wreath on the grave. If they chose, as many did, to make this pilgrimage soon after the war, they needed to steel themselves for a glimpse of its horrors. William Ewart, a former lieutenant in the Scots Guards, travelled back to the Somme with his sister Angela Farmer in October 1919 to search for the resting place of her husband, Jack.[20] They looked out over undulating ground framed by 'wintry skeletons of trees', shattered houses, and huddles of grey crosses, inscribed but many without names. The impedimenta of war was still to be seen everywhere, wire, dug-out frames, ammunition boxes and heaps of shells and rifles turning to rust. There were signs of life as it was once lived, dented helmets, shreds of uniform, bully-beef tins and a marmalade pot, biscuit tins and even an officer's quarters, with the remains of soap and water in its basin and shaving tackle strewn about on the floor. It was 'a reality forever fled'. Scraps of letters and even a woman's decaying photograph hinted at the inner lives of men who had once lived in the trenches, headed over the top and had 'long since gone to dust'. The scenes called to mind too Jack's final days, 'the waiting hours by night, the lurid dreams, the stricken, weary eves that must have haunted his last hours'. When he committed memories of the journey to paper, Ewart remembered the incongruity of seeing all this in autumn sunshine; nature acted not in sympathy or antipathy to the terrible sights but simply with indifference. He remembered too the urgent need to find Jack's body. He could not explain why this mattered so very much. It was 'as though some magnet, some occult, refined sense drew us on'. He knew the reality of the grave, that there remained within only 'a skull, a few bones, a wisp or two of hair, a shred or two of khaki cloth' and yet, against the force of reason 'to that we cling'. The pair walked the battlefield all day, lost track of time and were caught out by the fading light. As they travelled away, Ewart saw three crosses silhouetted on a hill, and found in this some glimmer of consolation.[21]

The trauma of the war had no precedent. At the very moment that death rates among children had dipped such that more had survived infancy, the war had swept away much of the healthy generation.[22] Through the war years, families had lived in anxiety, fearing black-edged notifications of the death of sons, husbands, fathers. If the notice came, grief had to be held in, borne with fortitude, assuaged with the knowledge that a loved one had made a sacrifice for king, country and family. The rituals of death were attenuated; so many had been killed that mourning blacks lost their distinguishing character.[23] There could be no funeral, no rituals of the grave in which the living could take leave of the dead, for the dead were not returned. And for many, for perhaps a third or more of the dead, there was no grave.[24] Entombed by explosions, swallowed in the mud, atomised by shells, they would never be found and would receive none of the grave's rites. For some this still savoured of the horror and stigma of a pauper's fate, the corpse laid in an unmarked grave, or shivered by explosives rather than being cut up by a surgeon's blade; now the horror had been visited on ordinary men, even on members of the elite, who had gone as volunteers or conscripts in a spirit of service.[25] For others it mattered that bodies lay in unhallowed earth. And for many there was simply an ineffable sense that the body mattered, that taking it back and laying it to rest mattered. Those charged with bringing the Unknown Warrior back to England grasped that. They considered but ruled out cremating the remains before bring them home, seeing that people would forge imaginative connections more readily with a body that was entire and intact. Only through traditional rites could pain be eased. The widow who wrote *To My Unknown Warrior* knew this because she had experienced the sensation. At the end of her little book, having fathomed the emotions of her dead husband's family, she noted, 'Of myself, I do not write.' Even under the cover of anonymity, she could not, or would not, articulate her grief. It would be soothed not with words but with deeds, in silences and rituals, the rituals so long suspended but now, symbolically and imperfectly, completed in the Warrior's burial.[26]

To many, open to the Christian promise in the liturgy and hymns of the burial service, there was more consolation to be had than this; the Warrior's grave was the way to life beyond death. Leslie Sanders was killed in action on 10 March 1917 when a shell exploded in his dug-out. He was twenty-five. He had already been wounded and shell-shocked in the fighting for Hill 60 near Ypres but had gone back to the Front, winning a commission in due course. His mother, Agnes, published some of his letters, obituaries and writings, unable to believe that his glittering life was over. 'Why was a life of promise not allowed to come to fruition?' she asked in her preface, wondering at the purpose of so much waste. Grief was sharpened by an awareness of her son's faded religious convictions. He had, indicated one of his obituarists, 'fought the battle of belief' and won but his letters were run through with doubts. Soldiers often wrote letters home that were full of reassurance that if death took the writer then there would be a reunion in heaven, an expression of faith sometimes made even by those who did not believe it. But Leslie Sanders did not hide his agnosticism. He wrote to his mother in February 1915 of 'the poppied sleep, or else whatever good or evil fate there be in store'. He answered her reproaches, saying that though he might not believe in God or heaven or hell, his philosophy was no narrow materialism; his was still a life structured by virtue.

When he was killed, his parents received a bundle of his papers. There were prayers among them, but doubting prayers, one of which appealed to an 'unknown God', a God 'to whom many bear confident witness'. Not the writer. Sanders implored that God reveal his presence, that he make himself known. There were more letters too for his mother and father, letters to be opened when he was dead. They said nothing about heaven but spoke instead of the motherland, his lodestone when faith had slipped away. To be one of those who 'in their bodies' honoured the nation with the greatest sacrifice was a privilege; in this his parents should find their consolation.

Condolence letters that came subsequently to his mother and father were full of warm appreciations of the endeavours of their son; of his fortitude, valour and patriotic spirit. The writers stepped delicately round notions of blissful rest or meeting again; the doubts that Leslie Sanders had articulated were widespread enough by the time of the First World War to make correspondents wary of invoking them, perhaps because they had doubts of their own, perhaps because they feared embarrassment or deepening grief with comforts that would sound hollow.[27] There was not enough consensus about the last things out of which to build consolations. But for Agnes Sanders happy memories and patriotism were not enough and Christian consolation still had the power to heal. She did not rail against a God who allowed men to make a hell in this world and squander so many lives nor did she retreat into stoicism before her son's death. Instead she tried to convince herself of a deeper meaning. Beyond the pain, the aching eyes and empty arms, she foresaw that 'there is no death'. Her son still lived 'a vivid, radiant life free from all fetters and time and sense'. He would, she said, 'live and work and love' in paradise 'as he could not do in this life' and his family, left behind in the world, would be 'content and glad and proud'.[28]

On Armistice Day 1922 a woman called Ada Deane made a remarkable discovery. She had taken a photograph of the scene at the

Cenotaph at the exact moment of the silence. On developing it
in her improvised darkroom – the kitchen table covered with a
drape – she had found, she said, not only images of the living,
heads bowed in contemplation, but also a gaseous penumbra in
which were visible the faces of the dead.[29] Many already imagined
that the victims of the Great War in some sense 'dwelt' in the
places consecrated to their memory; one newspaper correspondent
even imagined the heavy scent of flowers laid at the Cenotaph
assuming the form of men remembered there. Mrs Deane's photograph turned this into a literal rather than a symbolic truth. Many
mocked it but images like this were persuasive enough for Mrs
Deane to have made a business out of them. She had begun as a
charwoman in Islington, but with the aid of her brother who was
a chemist, she had successfully fused together photography and
mediumship.[30] Spirit photographs had been produced by others
long before the war, usually portrait shots in which ectosplasmic
likenesses of loved ones floated around the sitters, but the war
brought new markets.

Spirit photography was but one element in a larger renaissance
of spiritualism. Spiritualism had waxed again during the war as
the Churches, especially the Church of England, struggled to
make sense of the violence. It was hard to construe the horror
and chance of the battlefield in terms of divine providence;
Flanders could hardly be figured as test or chastisement and to
many made a mockery of a loving God. And if big explanatory
shapes for the war eluded Anglican divines, they had difficulty,
too, finding a place for the dead in prayer. The Catholic Church
with its notions of purgatory and intercession allowed its members
to reach out to the dead, but Anglicans had fewer resources with
which to satisfy the bereaved and some, to the alarm of the clergy,
looked outside its traditions.[31] They looked to the spirits for intel-
ligence of missing men, to find where the dead lay or to discover
if they were still alive in another world.

One family who turned to the spirits for consolation was that
of a soldier called Raymond Lodge. A member of the comfortable

classes, he had volunteered for military service in 1914 and was commissioned as a junior officer, serving at the Front near Ypres. His life in the trenches was one of scant pleasures eagerly seized – apples and butter sent out by his parents, Sir Oliver and Lady Lodge, a 'ripping present' of figs and dates shared with friends, of roses in the mess away from the line – and trauma too. His unit was short of morphia for the wounded. He saw men die, and buried and then reburied them when shells blew apart their graves. He learned to distinguish the smells of horse-flesh and human flesh as it rotted near the surface. Sometimes he tried to eat but found he could smell only the corpses he had buried earlier in the day.[32] At night he tried to study the constellations using a planisphere sent out by his father as, around him, Very lights flickered in the sky like astral signs. By day he watched Ypres turned into a 'a city of ruins and the dead' in which even the graveyards had been crumped into non-existence. Raymond's war was one of machines and mathematical calculation, of troop movements and shell trajectories precisely described, but superstition bled through it nonetheless. There were tales of angels and ghosts. Men kept charms and amulets for luck and attended to premonitions and dreams as they struggled to make sense of the strange elections by which some men survived as others perished. Raymond wrote his war, detailing it in his letters which streamed from the Front. Then just as he noticed that the blackberries were 'coming on' in the early autumn of 1915, the letters stopped. Raymond Lodge's luck had run out. Somewhere on Hooge Hill, on 14 September, a shell exploded and a splinter hit him, killing him instantly.

Sir Oliver Lodge was a distinguished scientist, professor of physics at Liverpool University and a man who would head the new university at Birmingham. And yet even before the war began he had been open to ideas about spirits, one of a number of senior scientists ready to give credence to spiritualism. He had even served as President of the Society for Psychical Research between 1901 and 1903, an organisation dedicated to exploring occult sciences. When Raymond was sent to Flanders, these scientific predilections melded with apprehensions about dreams and signs and what they might mean. Once he woke sure that his son was in great danger but felt that 'they', unseen spirits, were watching over him. The presentiment was almost true; he questioned his son in letters and Raymond revealed that he had been enduring 'a hell of shrapnel' around the time of his father's vision but had escaped unscathed.[33] There were no portents, only stark telegrams when Raymond was killed, one bringing the news and another conveying the sympathies of the king and queen. They left life 'irretrievably darkened'.[34] But then, a short time after Raymond was killed, Lady Lodge came to her husband with news of an uncanny experience. She had gone down to London in the company of an elderly French acquaintance who had been staying with the family. There the two women had joined a sitting with a medium, a woman called Mrs Leonard. The ostensible purpose was that the friend might make contact with her own sons, both of whom had been killed in the war. But in the seance room another spirit came through. Lady Lodge was confident in her anonymity; she had no reason to think that the medium knew anything about her or her family. So she was astonished to recognise the figure of Raymond in one of the spirits Mrs Leonard was able to 'see'.

Sir Oliver followed her to London to meet the medium for himself. He went alone and, he thought, anonymously, to Mrs Leonard's flat, though it later transpired that Mrs Leonard had guessed who he was, having heard the name 'Lodge' in a 'French sentence' that had passed between his wife and her friend during their visit. The medium entered a trance and soon a figure appeared. He would not 'build up' in the way other spirits did; he had not, the medium surmised, learned how to do this properly since he was new to the spirit world. He was of 'medium height' and 'well built'. He had brown hair 'short at the sides', a 'nice-shaped nose' and 'good-sized mouth'. Some information was a little more circumstantial. His eyes, she averred, were grey. Mrs

Leonard's control, a girl called Feda, brought more news. The spirit did indeed seem to be Raymond and he was mingling with others with whom he had struck up friendships. There were, it seemed, many things to learn in the spirit world and there were jobs to do too. His own work took him back to the Front. Those who died in the war were gripped by fear when they first woke up again and some even tried to carry on fighting; Raymond was one of those charged with soothing and guiding them. He too was still 'getting his bearings' in this strange terrain and though he had not thought when he first 'waked up' that he would be happy there, now, he said, he was.[35] In the last moments of Mrs Leonard's trance, images of Raymond yielded to a mystical vision, a black cross falling through the air, twisting and falling, but with brightness beyond – a sign of sacrifice, perhaps, but also an earnest of hope. Then the spell broke and the vision faded, leaving the medium exhausted. Sir Oliver took his leave. He enjoined Mrs Leonard not to tax herself with too many sittings but she said that there were 'so many people who want help now' that she must hold as many as three seances in a day, despite the strain on her nerves.

There followed many sittings, which led to an ever strengthening belief among the Lodges that Raymond was not dead but had simply entered 'another realm of service' in the other world. Slowly but steadily, they accumulated knowledge of the spirit world in which he dwelt. The soul there was an itinerant. The world beyond was one of progress and upward striving. Bonds of affection survived death; new ones might be forged and Raymond was even glimpsed in the company of a pretty girl who, as the medium put it, 'belonged' to him. He wore his own clothes, or aerial versions of them, until he had settled in and then he exchanged them for white robes. People lived in houses whose bricks were made from 'emanations from the earth'. As flowers died and decomposed on earth so they were recomposed in the hereafter; the process revealed a general law, for even decayed wool from the 'earth-plane' was reconstituted as a kind of otherworldly worsted. There were creature comforts in the hereafter, spirits in 'Summerland' were furnished with whisky and cigars. There was work there too, 'fifty times more interesting than on the earth-plane'. Some of it lay in spreading, via mediums, the happy truth about future life among those left behind in the world. This was in some ways a recognisably Christian place – Christ was there, although Raymond had not met him yet – but there was no fiery hell. Re-engineered as a fire-less purgatory, hell was 'more like a reformatory' than the traditional place of eternal suffering.[36]

For Sir Oliver, these messages from the dead needed to be read critically, measured against each other, as if they were travellers' tales from an unknown land. Then the contours of the afterlife could be mapped with confidence.[37] Of the existence of such a place, he was not in doubt. It did not matter that some mediums were fakes and some mercenary; there was a sufficient body of powerful testimony to show that some were not. Nor did it matter that the dead were sometimes wrong about the afterlife or contra-dicted each other; death did not bring sudden illumination. The dead, like the living, were mere 'fallible gropers after truth' in an other world characterised by ongoing work and personal develop-ment. If one medium genuinely communicated with a single spirit once, then that fragile proof was enough to secure all of Sir Oliver's hopes.

So much is known of Raymond because Sir Oliver published his letters from the Front and his dispatches from the afterlife; that act was a catharsis for his family and a comfort to others. His messages were attractive ones. His hell-less other world promised not only happy activity and reunion but also communications that might break through the 'impassable' barrier of death. Raymond disavowed, too, the idea that the body 'mattered', trying to free the bereaved from the ancient assumption that it did. Although his soul had loitered for a time around the shell of his former self – a circumstance that made cremation a most cruel and dangerous thing – he had soon forsaken his body; now he did not care where it rested in the cold Ypres clay or whether there were flowers on his grave. Love, the adamantine substance in human nature, mattered and this ensured that bonds between human beings survived death. That was the idea on which the Lodges fastened. Behind it all – the very public memories of his son, the semi-public world of sittings and seances – there was a private world of spirit communications in the Lodge household motivated by love and pain. Lady Lodge lived in hope of direct communication with her son – that Raymond would visit her in the quiet of the evening or in dreams, that he might in some way 'get through', as if by way of an unreliable telephone line, so that she might once again hear his voice. At Christmas 1915, the Lodges had a place set in the hope that his presence might be felt during Christmas lunch. In the afternoon, they gathered around a small table and had one of their many private sittings so that they might hear from him. Thousands and thousands of the war dead would, Raymond had said, rejoin their families that day.[38] Generations had held that spirits had special power around Christmastide; the ghosts of the glorious dead would, for a day, come home. Sentimental, mawkish, ludicrous, perhaps, in its evocation of cigars and whisky in Summerland, Sir Oliver Lodge's comforting vision was the object of withering scorn but his book, *Raymond*, was a best-seller nonetheless.[39]

The war memorials built after the Armistice were more tangible and less controversial ways to address pain than the claims in Sir Oliver Lodge's *Raymond*. They are omnipresent: in town squares and on village greens, churches and churchyards, in schools and railway stations, universities and factories and even on hill and mountain tops, high places consecrated to the memory of the dead.[40] Their makers turned usually to traditional shapes and Christian idioms as they struggled to make sense of loss.[41] At St Ives in Cornwall a Celtic cross was set up 'in proud and grateful memory' of the dead. At Seamer there were simple plaques in a memorial hall and replicas in the medieval church, and at Earls Colne a squat cross was set atop a slender pillar. Keighley was rare in choosing a secular monument, an obelisk topped by a woman holding a laurel, a symbol of peace and victory recalling nine hundred sons of the town and locality who died in the war. Wenhaston's memorial recalled far fewer, only twenty-five men of the small rural parish. But among them were two Spoores, two Ebbs, two Robertses and four Coopers, the reiterated surnames clues to the scale of the trauma, to families shattered and bodies buried far away, swallowed by the sea, atomised on land. The memorials answered the need to bring the dead back and keep their memory alive even if there was no body. Creations of communities rather than the state, war memorials were stone successors for shrines of flowers which had appeared during the war, spontaneous commemorations established in many streets where men had died.[42]

The Great War and its bequest of suffering knitted together the people of the disparate places in this book through a common experience, which defined one generation and marked others. The war memorials are tokens of this. In time memories settled. The battles – Mons, the Marne, Loos, the Somme, Cambrai, Passchendaele – were woven into a fabric of modern myth. The generals who had commanded the armies died and were absorbed in the myth themselves although, unlike earlier commanders, their reputations tended to shrink as the perspective lengthened rather than being puffed up. The ordinary dead of the war, or at least those who could be found, were paraded a final time, their bodies laid in orderly rows topped by white stones, identical in form. The cemeteries in which they lay, each with a Cross of Remembrance and Stone of Sacrifice, were turned into English gardens, filled with roses and familiar shrubs.[43] At home, the dead found a place in space and time and language, being recalled faithfully at Remembrancetide, a time of lengthening nights, falling leaves and frosty air, a time when medieval men and women had also turned their minds to saints and souls and ghosts. The coincidence was appropriate. Remembrance rites and war memorials were at the heart of a new reciprocation between living and dead which the Great War had made. 'We are more than beasts', wrote *The Times* reporter on 12 November 1920, 'because we willingly die for each other, and in that is our hope of immortality.' The hope the correspondent conjured with may have been the traditional one of life after death. It may have been something else, an immortality in this world. His words were nicely, perhaps studiedly, ambiguous. In any event, the glorious dead had given life itself and the living owed them everything: that was the golden thread running through all of the rites commemorating them. The debt could no longer be discharged through prayer for their souls; it could be discharged only through memory, through remembrance, reckoned now as a sacred duty.

EPILOGUE

The Great War did not revolutionise the way that the living imagined the dead. The rituals, public and private, the letters and memoirs of the bereaved, expose to view transitions already under way. The other world had thinned. Its punitive dimensions were attenuated as hell receded, at least in most Protestant preaching. The brilliance of the Martinesque heaven faded too. It was ceasing to hold out the promise of life in a resurrected body, becoming a land where spirits might mingle, a place of rest, or simply 'a better place' to which the dead would go, free from sufferings and anxieties of this world. But the old Bible narratives about the dead were still available in 1920. Taught in school, sung in church, prayed in many homes, they were a resource from which those torn open by grief could seek healing, if sometimes through symbols and metaphors rather than literal belief. Christianity was still the point to which most returned as they struggled with mortality and eternity even if they were not churchgoers during their lives; for even if Christianity's consolations were half believed or scarcely believed at all, its familiar rituals were the framework in which grief and loss and memory were worked out. But the forces that would, for better or worse, unmake that imaginative world are visible in 1920 too. There were some, still a minority, who had turned away from religion; others were born into different faiths, many arriving on British shores as migrants from the empire. The outlines of a more plural and cosmopolitan kind of Britain are clearly visible in these early decades of the twentieth century. The inscription on the Unknown Warrior's grave was, in this respect, a portent. Composed by Dean Ryle, the message at the centre of the slab spoke of sacrifice for king, country, family and freedom, as if these were the ideas around which the nation might most easily unite. The scriptural verses were pushed to the edges.[1] A world of movement, migration, exchange, of many faiths in close proximity, would in time further transform the religious life of the nation and erode the broad consensus that once existed about the fate of the dead.

Beyond the Abbey's West Door is the turbulent motion of London. The city is filled with people of all faiths, little faith and no faith at all. Religion for many, perhaps for most, people in Britain today has become less a matter of inhabiting a tradition, more a matter of personal election. Individuals are able to pick their faith, even to pick and choose articles of moral teaching and elements of belief to form a bespoke religion of their own. Many of these articles and elements are Christian but it has still become possible for commentators to speak of a 'post-Christian' Britain, a place in which people make use of fragments of belief but live their lives within no compelling system. This transformation is the second of the two revolutions in thinking about this world and the next that bracket this book, the first being the Reformation. And the first, it seems, may have things to teach about the second. For in the Reformation what stands out sharply on first inspection are the disjunctions: the Reformation saw purgatory abolished. It decisively fractured a medieval relationship, construed in the language of prayer, in which the living reached out to help the dead on their journey into the afterlife, souls that, for a time at least, were still close and in need. Meanwhile, deprived of their purgatorial rationale, ghosts were cut loose from theology, left wandering as counter-cultural presences. But the discontinuities are in some ways deceiving. There was more continuity after the Reformation than there first appears, and not only in continuance of covert prayer for the dead, communions conceived as votive masses or subversive bell-ringing to comfort souls on All Souls' Night. Obligations to hold the dead in memory, to honour them with an elaborate tomb or a wooden cross, outlasted Reformation zeal. Presentiments that the dead were still close at hand persisted too in rituals that implied spirits hovered round bodies, in stories about ghosts, in fuzzier sensations that dead loved ones were still, in some way, close.

Ours is a very different world to that of the Reformation; the analogy breaks down soon after it is made, for we exist in circumstances of diminished collective belief very different to those of the sixteenth century. And yet for many, the emotional need for a narrative about the dead remains. For while mysteries for which religion furnished explanations have tended to dissolve – or seem to dissolve – in the modern age, the mystery of death and the intuition that human beings might be greater than it has proved more resilient. Some look to new religions for a narrative that makes sense of this but many, still, as they think about death and the dead, hold on to flotsam and jetsam of Christianity; even if they do not ostensibly 'believe', they still cling to planks that remain after the shipwreck of faith. The language of heaven is still alive in memorial notices and cards attached to funeral flowers alongside more ambiguous ideas of peace and rest and freedom from pain. Most still choose a funeral that is religious; this is the most enduring of the Christian rites of passage when baptism and church marriages have long since lost their place. And in coping with a death, ritual is often of more immediate use to us than contemplation. Rituals around the dead sometimes make sense outside the structures of conscious belief; for there are things that simply are done around the dead, and for the dead, because they are things handed down, hallowed by long use.

These continuities may be very transient.[2] Soon even these fragmentary beliefs and rituals may well pass; the very desire to find a narrative for the dead may vanish too as the people of a post-Christian Britain accommodate themselves fully to life without the hope of post-mortem existence. To enter into such conjectures about the future is to venture from history into prophecy and that is dangerous ground, no place for the historian.

For few, one suspects, in the early nineteenth century would have foreseen that notions of spirit contact would be revitalised mid century as spiritualism, formed at a juncture of radical politics, ancient belief and cutting-edge science. If history does not replicate itself nor is its course tidy or linear.

Looking back on the people whose stories form this book – some infinitely remote and obscure, others closer and in sharper focus, but all forever receding – what connects us to them is not so much abstract theologies or systems of reason that blow about in the breeze. For on this count Thomas Browne was right. Other men's religions are indeed often madness to us. But many of the emotions and sensations that animated those beliefs, loves and hatreds, hopes and fears at work inside and underneath them, they are still familiar things; they connect us to the men and women that this book has tried to bring, fleetingly, back to life.

NOTES

Prologue

1   Revelation 6:17. The painting describes the moments after the angel had broken the sixth of seven seals which punctuated the events of the Apocalypse.

2   The paintings formed the climax of an exhibition exploring the art of John Martin which began at the Laing Gallery in Newcastle, near to the place of Martin's birth, and then transferred to Tate Britain. I was able to see the paintings in both locations and my remarks here draw on both viewings. See *John Martin: Apocalypse*, ed. M. Myrone (London, 2011); B. C. Morden, *John Martin: Apocalypse Now!* (Newcastle-upon-Tyne, 2010).

3   T. Balston, *John Martin, 1789–1854: his life and works* (London, 1947), pp. 15–16; M. Adams, *The Prometheans: John Martin and the generation that stole the future* (London, 2010).

4   *A Descriptive Key to the Three Grand and Solemn Pictures, namely the Last Judgement, The Great Day of His Wrath and the Plains of Heaven Painted by John Martin KL, Historical Painter to His Majesty the King of the Belgians.* I am grateful to the staff of the Department of Prints and Drawings at the British Museum for finding one of the few extant copies of this pamphlet for me to consult.

5   Revelation 21:4–5.

6   W. Feaver, *The Art of John Martin* (Oxford, 1975), p. 203.

7   *John Martin*, ed. Myrone, p. 183.

8   Some rough and ready measures: religious marriage fell from 88 per cent to 39 per cent between 1900 and 1997 in England and Wales. The baptism rate in the Church of England fell from 61 per cent of births in 1900 to 19.8 per cent in 2000. Churchgoing on any given Sunday fell from around 25–30 per cent of population in 1900 to just 7.5 per cent in 1998. For a digest and discussion of the statistics see C. Brown, *Religion and Society in*

Twentieth-Century Britain (Harlow, 2006), pp. 4ff. The timing, nature and extent of dechristianisation during the nineteenth and twentieth centuries have been the subject of much debate, for which see H. McLeod, *Secularisation in Western Europe, 1848–1914* (Basingstoke, 2000) for an overview. Different perspectives: A. Gilbert, *The Making of Post-Christian Britain: a history of the secularization of modern society* (London, 1980); C. Brown, *The Death of Christian Britain: understanding secularisation in Britain 1800–2000* (second edn, London, 2009); H. McLeod, *The Religious Crisis of the 1960s* (Oxford, 2007); G. Davie, *Religion in Britain since 1945: believing without belonging* (Oxford, 1994); S. Bruce, *God is Dead: secularization in the West* (Oxford, 2002).

9   For surveys dealing with these issues see data at: http://www. theosthinktank.co.uk/comment/2009/04/13/four-in-ten-people-believe-in-ghosts; http://www.brin.ac.uk/figures/#Changing Belief [accessed 25/7/2010].

10   The observation about 'hellfire and harps' is that of compilers of the Mass Observation survey *Puzzled People: a study in popular attitudes to religion, ethics, progress and politics in a London borough* (London, 1947), which discovered widespread belief in the afterlife – still running at around half the population – but fuzziness and confusion about its nature.

11   C. Merridale, *Night of Stone: death and memory in Russia* (London, 2000), p. 51.

1 The Strange Isles

1   The exact whereabouts of Baret's bones are uncertain as the upperworks of the tomb have been moved and hence are no longer aligned with the mirrors in the roof. For this issue and the life of John Baret generally see M. Statham, 'John Baret', in *The Ricardian* (2003).

2   *Thomas Carlyle, Past and Present*, ed. C. R. Vanden Bossche, J. R. Brattin and D. J. Trela (London 2005), pp. 50–2.

3   For the setting see R. Dinn, 'Death and Rebirth in Medieval Bury St Edmunds', in *Death in Towns: Urban Responses to the Dying and the Dead, 100–1600*, ed. S. Bassett (Leicester, 1992); M. Statham, in 'The Medieval Town of Bury St Edmunds', *Bury St Edmunds: medieval art, architecture, archaeology and economy*, ed. A. Gransden (British Archaeol. Soc. Transactions, 1998); M. Bailey, *Medieval*

Suffolk: an economic and social history, 1200–1500 (Woodbridge, 2007), esp. pp. 116–51. For religious life in a larger East Anglian town see N. P. Tanner, *The Church in Medieval Norwich, 1370–1532* (Toronto, 1984).

4 Baret's father left him money in his will of 1416 to buy sheep and it is quite likely that much of Baret's mercantile cash came, directly or indirectly, from the wool trade. Norfolk and Suffolk produced perhaps a quarter of England's cloth in the later Middle Ages with special concentrations in the Stour valley and Lavenham areas and significant activity around Bury St Edmunds too.

5 John Baret's will is printed in *Wills and Inventories from the Registers of the Commissary of Bury St Edmunds*, ed. S. Tymms (Camden Society, 1850), pp. 15–44 (hereafter cited as 'Baret's Will'). On wills and pious provision generally see C. Burgess, 'By Quick and by Dead: wills and pious provision in late medieval Bristol', in *English Historical Review*, 102 (1987).

6 Baret left many gifts in his will to the monks of Bury. The abbot and his successors 'for ever' had a set of fine rosary beads and a ring and a cup, and other named monks received gifts too, one getting his 'best powder box of silver' and a pair of silver gilt spectacles.

7 For the late medieval religious setting: G. McMurray Gibson, *The Theater of Devotion: East Anglian drama and society in the late Middle Ages* (London, 1989), esp. ch. 4; E. Duffy, *The Stripping of the Altars: traditional religion in England c.1400–c.1580* (London, 1992), chs 9 and 10; A. Brown, *Church and Society in England 1000–1500* (Basingstoke, 2003), ch. 5; M. Aston, 'Death', in *Fifteenth-Century Attitudes: perceptions of society in late medieval England*, ed. R. Horrox (Cambridge, 1994); R. Horrox, 'Purgatory, Prayer and Plague, 1150–1380', in *Death in England: an illustrated history*, ed. P. Jupp and C. Gittings (Manchester, 1999); T. S. R. Boase, *Death in the Middle Ages: mortality, judgment and remembrance* (London, 1972).

8 G. R. Owst, *Literature and Pulpit in Medieval England: a neglected chapter in the history of English letters and the English People* (Oxford, 1961), p. 518.

9 *The Alphabet of Tales: an English 15th-century translation of the Alphabetum Narrationum of Etienne de Besançon*, ed. M. M. Banks (Early English Text Soc., 1904–5), p. 206.

10 Owst, *Literature and Pulpit*, pp. 171–2.

11 'Baret's Will', pp. 16–19.

12 This promise was a theologically dubious one but was far from

being unique. On indulgences see R. N. Swanson, *Indulgences in Late Medieval Engand: passports to Paradise* (Cambridge, 2007), esp. pp. 107, 162, 409 for John Baret's case.

13 'Baret's Will', pp. 37–8.

14 For example: *Fasciculus Morum: a fourteenth-century preacher's handbook*, ed. S Wenzel (Philadelphia, 1989), pp. 719–21. We cannot know how John Baret died. The reconstruction offered here draws on priests' manuals, sermon materials and literature, particularly the works of Baret's acquaintance John Lydgate. It is therefore a composite image of a medieval deathbed.

15 *Disce Mori* was a learned riff on a popular theme. The *ars moriendi* were texts that instructed the faithful in the art of dying using a mix of Latin or vernacular instruction and woodcuts. See Duffy, *Stripping of the Altars*, pp. 313ff; and for *ars moriendi*, P. Binski, *Medieval Death: ritual and representation* (Cambridge, 1996), pp. 39ff.

16 *The Arte and Crafte to Lyve Well and to Die Well*, Wynken de Worde (1505), fol. lxxxxviii; for general discussion of the medieval deathbed see R. Wunderli and G. Brose, 'The Final Moment Before Death in Medieval England', in *Sixteenth-Century Journal*, 20 (1989).

17 *The Vision of Edmund Leversedge: a 15th-century account of a visit to the other world*, ed. W. F. Nijenhuis (Nijmegen, 1991).

18 *Arte and Crafte*, fol. iiii. The dying were thought quite likely to glimpse visitors from the other world, whether angels or demons, and the literature of advice for the dying tried to fortify them against the fear and despair that might be induced by demonic visitors. When the great baron William Marshal was dying in 1219, the unusually circumstantial account of his last hours includes mention of Marshal seeing white-robed visitors in the death chamber who went unnoticed by those gathered around him. See *History of William Marshal*, ed. and transl. A. J. Holden, S. Gregory and D. Crouch, 3 vols (London, 2002–6), vol. 2, pp. 440–1.

19 Some of the details here are drawn from *The Testament of John Lydgate*, in *The Minor Poems of John Lydgate*, ed. H. N. MacCracken (Early English Text Soc., 1911).

20 McMurray Gibson, *Theater of Devotion*, p. 74; D. Pearsall, *John Lydgate* (London, 1970).

21 *Testament*, in *Minor Poems of John Lydgate*, ed. MacCracken.

22 *The Dance of Death*, ed. F. Warren and B. White (Early English Text Soc., 1931). Lydgate's was not an original work but a

translation from a French poem. He had seen the *Danse Macabre* at Les Innocents during a trip to Paris shortly after it had been painted in 1424.

23 For such tombs see P. M. King, 'The Cadaver Tomb in England: novel manifestations of an old idea', in *Church Monuments*, 5 (1990); for medieval memorialisation generally see N. Saul, *English Church Monuments in the Middle Ages: history and representation* (Oxford, 2009), pp. 311–34; and for Baret's tomb see D. Griffiths, 'English Commemorative Inscriptions', in *Memory and Commemoration in Medieval England*, ed. C. Barron and C. Burgess (Donington, 2010).

24 'Baret's Will', p. 24. Another, grander, family of gentle status which was extinguished in the main line and went to elaborate lengths to secure a place in local memory, this time through memorial brasses, is discussed in N. Saul, *Death, Art and Memory: the Cobham family and their monuments, 1300–1500* (Oxford, 2001).

25 See Dinn, 'Death and Rebirth', p. 154.

26 *Suffolk in the Sixteenth Century: the breviary by Robert Reyce*, ed. Lord Francis Harvey (London, 1902), pp. 24–7.

27 At Lavenham, for example, there are graves of Springs and Branches, families whose merchant-money was lavished on the local church. The church still contains the wooden parclose of the chantry where a priest was paid to sing daily for the soul of Thomas Spring III. Not strictly 'wool' churches, as they are often called in guidebooks, such grand East Anglian churches were built more usually with the profits of the cloth trade.

28 See K. Whale, 'The Wenhaston Doom: a biography of a sixteenth-century panel painting', in *Proceedings of the Suffolk Institute of Archaeology*, 39:3 (1999).

29 The psychostasis was quite an unusual feature in English fifteenth- and early sixteenth-century Doom scenes, which is one reason why Whale suggests a Netherlandish connection for the painting. See Whale, 'Wenhaston', p. 310; more generally see S. G. F. Brandon, *The Judgment of the Dead* (London, 1967), pp. 118–30.

30 On purgatory see J. Le Goff, *The Birth of Purgatory*, transl. A. Goldhammer (London, 1984). And for visions of the other world in the Middle Ages see A. Gurevich, 'The Divine Comedy Before Dante', in *Medieval Popular Culture: problems of belief and perception*, transl. J. Bak and P. Hollingsworth (Cambridge, 1988); G. R. Keiser, 'The Progess of Purgatory: visions of the afterlife in later Middle English literature', in *Analecta Cartusiana*, 117 (1987); C. Zaleski, *Otherworld Journeys: accounts of near-death experience in medieval*

and modern times (Oxford, 1987); A. Morgan, *Dante and the Medieval Other World* (Cambridge, 1986).

31   See for example 'A Revelation Shown to a Holy Woman', in *Yorkshire Writers*, ed. C. Horstmann (London, 1895).

32   For this: *St Patrick's Purgatory: two versions of Owayne Miles and The vision of William of Stranton together with the long text of the Tractatus de Purgatorio Sancti Patricii*, ed. R. Easting (Early English Text Soc., 1991).

33   *Vision of Edmund Leversedge*, ed. Nijenhuis, p. 52.

34   *Arte and Crafte*, fol. lxxii.

35   *The Gast of Gy: a Middle English religious prose tract*, ed. R. H. Bowers, Beiträge zur Englischen Philologie, 32 (1938), p. 23.

36   *Arte and Crafte*, fol. lxxxxv.

37   *Visio Thurkilli relatore, ut videtur, Radulpho de Coggeshall*, ed. P. G. Schmidt (Leipzig, 1978).

38   Owst, *Literature and Pulpit*, p. 319.

39   *Arte and Crafte*, fol. lxxxxvi.

40   *Arte and Crafte*, fol. lxxxix; *Alphabet of Tales*, ed. Banks, pp. 216–17; *The Golden Legend: readings on the saints by Jacobus de Voragine*, transl. W. Granger Ryan, vol. 2, p. 290.

41   *Arte and Crafte*, fol. lxxxxv.

42   *Vision of Edmund Leversedge*, ed. Nijenhuis, p. 67.

43   'That cryst schale come on domesday, Wyth his woundes fresch and rede, To deme the quyke and the dede', J. Mirk, *Instructions for Parish Priests*, ed. E. Peacock and F. J. Furnivall (Early English Text Soc., revised edn, 1902), pp. 16–17.

44   D. M. Hadley, *Death in Medieval England: an archaeology* (Stroud, 2001), p. 90.

45   *Lay Folks' Catechism*, ed. T. F. Simmons and H. E. Nolloth (Early English Text Soc., 1901), p. 27. The body was bound up with the sense of identity in the Middle Ages and people expected to preserve their individuality after death. For conceptualisations of the resurrection body see C. Bynum, *The Resurrection of the Body in Western Christianity, 200–1336* (New York, 1995).

46   *English Mystery Plays: a selection*, ed. P. Happé (Harmondsworth, 1975), p. 635.

47   *Ordynarye of crystyanyte or of crysten Men* (Wynken de Worde, 1502), pt 1.

48   *English Mystery Plays*, ed. Happé, pp. 635–6.

49   Whale, 'Wenhaston', p. 302.

50   *English Mystery Plays*, ed. Happé, pp. 642–3. The pattern for this

was biblical, especially Matthew 25, which warned that on his return Christ would say to the wicked, 'I was hungry and you gave me nothing to eat, I was thirsty and you gave me nothing to drink, I was a stranger and you did not invite me in, I needed clothes and you did not clothe me, I was sick and in prison and you did not look after me.'

51 *Speculum Sacerdotale*, ed. E. H. Weatherby (Early English Text Soc., 1935), pp. 112–14. For the same image of Christ showing his wounds see also *English Mystery Plays*, ed. Happé, pp. 641–2. It has been suggested that the missing words on two scrolls in the Wenhaston Doom, addressed to the risen souls, would have been '*Venite Benedicti*' (Come ye blessed) and '*Discedite Maledicti*' (Depart ye cursed). See Whale, 'Wenhaston', p. 304.

52 *Golden Legend*, vol. 1, transl. Ryan, p. 12.

2 *Spirit of Health or Goblin Damned*

1 *Bede's Ecclesiastical History of the English People*, ed. B. Colgrave and R. A. B. Mynors (Oxford, 1969), pp. 286–7.

2 The monasteries had, at the height of their powers, been instrumental in transforming these parts of Yorkshire. They had developed sheep ranches and agro-industrial enterprises, carving out new roads to serve the sheep economy and quarrying stone on a large scale for their building works. See *A Historical Atlas of Yorkshire*, ed. R. A. Butlin (Otley, 2003), pp. 100ff.

3 On the region see R. Muir, *The Yorkshire Countryside: a landscape history* (Edinburgh, 1998), chs 10–12; *A History of Helmsley, Rievaulx and District*, ed. J. McDonnell (York, 1963), chs 5–7; G. Frank, *Ryedale and North Yorkshire Antiquities* (York, 1888), ch. 8.

4 Monks were less inclined to trust stories told by women; their stories were often denounced as old wives' tales among the men of a monastic community.

5 *The Foundation History of the Abbeys of Byland and Jervaulx*, ed. J. Burton (York, 2006), p. xiv.

6 For this story and others from Byland Abbey, discussed below, see 'Twelve Medieval Ghost Stories', ed. M. R. James, in *English Historical Review* (1922), and for an accessible translation, albeit with several local place names rendered inaccurately, *Medieval Popular Religion, 1000–1500: a reader*, ed. J. Shinners (Peterborough, Ont., 1999), pp. 229–37.

7   *Foundation History*, ed. Burton, p. 17.

8   This image of the living and the dead was painted on the walls of Pickering church some twenty miles east from the site of the alleged Byland haunting and is still there to be seen, in fragmentary form.

9   *The Dialogue on Miracles by Caesarius of Heisterbach (1220–1235)*, transl. H. von E. Scott and C. C. Swinton Bland, 2 vols (London, 1929), vol. 1, pp. 355–7.

10   R. C. Finucane, *Appearances of the Dead: a cultural history of ghosts* (London, 1982); J. C. Schmitt, *Ghosts in the Middle Ages*, transl. T. L. Fagan (London, 1998); ed. H. Ellis Davidson and W. Russell, *The Folklore of Ghosts* (Cambridge, 1981); J. Simpson, 'Repentant Soul or Walking Corpse? Debatable Apparitions in Medieval England', in *Folklore*, 114 (2003); C. S. Watkins, *History and the Supernatural in Medieval England* (Cambridge, 2007), ch. 5.

11   *Lay Folks' Catechism*, pp. 62–4.

12   Mirk, *Instructions*, pp. 3–4. The mother's life should be sacrificed even if the child would only live long enough to hear the words of baptism and be sprinkled with water.

13   Glimpses of domestic life in medieval Yorkshire come from extensive archaeological investigations at Wharram Percy, a deserted village on the wolds some twenty miles from Byland, for which see J. G. Hurst and P. A. Rahtz, *Wharram: a study of settlement on the Yorkshire wolds*, 3 vols (London, 1983–7).

14   'Visitation Returns of the Diocese of Hereford in 1397', ed. A. T. Bannister, *English Historical Review* (1929).

15   *The Armburgh Papers: the Brokeholes inheritance in Warwickshire, Hertfordshire and Essex, c.1417–c.1453. Chetham's Manuscript Mun. E 6.10(4)*, ed. M. C. Carpenter (Woodbridge, 1998), p. 62.

16   There are other candidates for the place that the Byland monk called Kirby but Cold Kirby, given the topography detailed in the story, seems much the most likely location.

17   The Latin here is *exsufflauit*.

18   William of Newburgh, *The History of William of Newburgh*, in *Church Historians of England*, vol. 4, pt 2, transl. J. Stevenson, pp. 656–61.

19   This is a penitential, a handbook to guide priests as they heard confessions, composed by Bartholomew of Exeter, for which see C. Platt, *The Parish Churches of Medieval England* (London, 1981), p. 49.

20   Mortuary biology suggests that some bodies decay in strange ways when laid in the grave, the chemistry of soil elements,

moisture levels and air penetration all combining to determine the fate of the corpse. See P. Barber, *Vampires, Death and Burial: folklore and reality* (New Haven and London, 1988); and for what follows see important discussion of the archaeology, on which I draw here, in J. Blair, 'The Dangerous Dead in Early Medieval England', in *Early Medieval Studies in Honour of Patrick Wormald*, ed. S. Baxter, C. E. Karkov, J. Nelson and D. Pelteret (Burlington, 2009).

21 M. Merback, *The Thief, the Cross and the Wheel: pain and the spectacle of punishment in medieval and renaissance Europe* (London, 1998), pp. 148–9.

22 For a comment on the supernatural associations of ancient sites in the West Country see P. Marshall, *Mother Leakey and the Bishop: a ghost story* (Oxford, 2007), pp. 229ff, and more generally for his vivid exploration of a story which claimed a place in local folklore.

23 T. Parkinson, *Yorkshire Legends and Traditions* (London, 1888), pp. 218–20; *County Folk-Lore, ii, examples of printed folk-lore concerning the North Riding of Yorkshire, York and Ainsty*, ed. E. Gutch (Folklore Soc., 1901), pp. 36–7.

3 The End of the Iron World

1 The chapter's title comes from a remark made by John Hales, clerk of the exchequer, to Protector Somerset, architect of the Edwardine Reformation. He claimed that 'the people have great hope that . . . the iron world is now at an end and the golden is returning again'. For which see *England's Long Reformation, 1500–1800*, ed. N. Tyacke (London, 1998), p. 17.

2 A. G. Dickens, 'Some Popular Reactions to the Edwardian Reformation in Yorkshire', in *Reformation Studies* (London, 1982).

3 He wrote with the benefit of hindsight as well as with a Protestant axe to grind, this version of *Acts and Monuments* being published in c.1570 when Elizabeth I and her brand of Protestantism were becoming established. For which see Dickens, 'Popular Reactions', p. 30.

4 Foxe also talked up the danger to social order posed by rebellion by suggesting that a 'fantastical prophecy' had circulated which said 'that there should be no king reign in England, the noblemen and gentlemen to be destroyed, and the Realm to be governed by four governors to be elected and appointed by the Commons'.

5   For the impact of the Tudor reformations on beliefs about the dead see particularly P. Marshall, *Beliefs and the Dead in Reformation England* (Oxford, 2002); D. Cressy, *Birth, Marriage, and Death: ritual, religion, and the life-cycle in Tudor and Stuart England* (Oxford, 1997), chs 17–20; R. Houlbrooke, *Death, Religion, and the Family in England, 1480–1750* (Oxford, 1998).

6   John Stow, *A Survey of London*, ed. C. L. Kingsford, 2 vols (Oxford, 1908), vol. 1, pp. 327–30; V. Harding, *The Living and the Dead in Paris and London, 1500–1670* (Cambridge, 2002), pp. 86–93

7   For destruction at St Paul's see Marshall, *Beliefs and the Dead*, pp. 104–7; Duffy, *Stripping of the Altars*, p. 304; S. Brigden, *London and the Reformation* (Oxford, 1989), p. 423.

8   *The Yorkshire Church Notes of Sir Stephen Glynne (1825–1874)*, ed. L. Butler (Woodbridge, 2007).

9   For a summary of the evolution of Luther's thought and its increasing radicalism see Marshall, *Beliefs and the Dead*, pp. 47–8.

10   Brigden, *London and the Reformation*, pp. 82–128 ; *Long Reformation*, ed. Tyacke, esp. the editor's introduction.

11   Marshall, *Beliefs and the Dead*, pp. 48–51.

12   Another in the standard repertoire of arguments against purgatory by its antagonists made much of the conflicting views about the place and nature of purgation. Although there was much precision in the medieval theology, there was also a mass of contradiction too between different visions and versions of the teaching. This purgatory's antagonists began to expose ruthlessly to view.

13   F. Drake, *Eboracum: or The history and antiquities of the city of York, from its origin to the present times* (London, 1736).

14   E. Duffy, *The Voices of Morebath: reformation and rebellion in an English village* (London, 2001), pp. 87ff.

15   A. Kreider, *English Chantries: the road to dissolution* (Cambridge, Mass., 1979), pp. 93–124.

16   Duffy, *Voices of Morebath*, pp. 106ff.

17   Kreider, *Chantries*, pp. 150–3.

18   D. MacCulloch, *Tudor Church Militant: Edward VI and the Protestant Reformation* (London, 2001), pp. 4–5.

19   Marshall, *Beliefs and the Dead*, p. 91.

20   MacCulloch, *Church Militant*, pp. 81ff for details.

21   I Edw. VI in *Statutes of the Realm* (London, 1963), vol. 4, pp. 24ff.

22   C. Cross, 'The Dissolution of the Monasteries in Sixteenth-Century York', in *Yorkshire Archaeological Journal*, 80 (2008);

C. Cross, 'The End of Medieval Monasticism in the North Riding of Yorkshire', in *Yorkshire Archaeological Journal*, 78 (2006); *Victoria County History of the County of York*, vol. 3, ed. W. Page (London, 1974).

23 D. M. Palliser, *The Reformation in York, 1534–1553* (York, 1971), p. 18; for the background of intercessory institutions founded in York in the later Middle Ages see R. B. Dobson, *Church and Society in the North of England* (London, 1996), esp. chs 11 and 12, which examine chantry foundations.

24 Dickens, 'Popular Reactions', pp. 30–1, 35 n. 4; C. J. Kitching, 'The Chantries of the East Riding of Yorkshire at Dissolution in 1548', in *Yorkshire Archaeological Journal*, 44 (1972).

25 Palliser, *Reformation in York*, pp. 22–3.

26 For the role of guilds and chantries in providing pastoral care in places where parochial structures were otherwise inadequate, especially in sparsely populated areas where parishes were large, see B. Kümin, *The Shaping of a Community: the rise and reformation of the English parish, c.1400–1560* (Aldershot, 1996), pp. 138–9, 159–67, 181–2.

27 Dickens, 'Popular Reactions', pp. 24–5. See also on nearby dissolutions D. Lamburn, *The Laity and the Church: religious developments in Beverley in the first half of the sixteenth century* (York, 2000); P. Marshall, *The Face of Pastoral Ministry in the East Riding, 1525–1595* (York, 1995).

28 F. Rose-Troup, *The Western Rebellion of 1549* (London, 1913).

29 R. Steele and J. L. L. Crawford, *Tudor and Stuart Proclamations 1485–1714* (Oxford, 1910), pp. 36–8.

30 Duffy, *Voices of Morebath*, p. 134.

31 For the bitter experience of past rebellions, royal pardons and subsequent repression see M. L. Bush, *The Pilgrimage of Grace: a study of the rebel armies of October 1536* (Manchester, 1996); Kreider, *Chantries*, pp. 105–17, 129.

32 D. MacCulloch and A. Fletcher, *Tudor Rebellions* (London, 1997), p. 39ff; C. S. L. Davies, 'Popular Religion and the Pilgrimage of Grace', in *Order and Disorder in Early Modern England*, ed. A. Fletcher and J. Stevenson (Cambridge, 1985); Palliser, *Reformation in York*, p. 11. The chilling words about 'experiments' are those of the Duke of Norfolk who was involved in the business of suppression.

4 *Fire and Fleet and Candlelight*

1   A. G. Dickens, 'The Last Medieval Englishman', in *Reformation Studies*, p. 246.

2   'Robert Parkyn's Narrative of the Reformation', ed. A. G. Dickens, in *Reformation Studies*, p. 293.

3   Dickens, 'Robert Parkyn's Narrative', p. 295.

4   For the notion that Parkyn's probably stood for the views of many priests – and lay people too – in a changing world see P. Marshall, *The Face of the Pastoral Ministry in the East Riding, 1525–95* (York, 1995), pp. 7–8.

5   Dickens, 'Robert Parkyn's Narrative', p. 287.

6   *Tudor Treatises*, ed. Dickens, pp. 63–4; and for the 'signs of death' see Duffy, *Stripping of the Altars*, p. 312.

7   Dickens, 'Last Medieval Englishman', p. 276.

8   Dickens, 'Robert Parkyn's Narrative', p. 303.

9   Marshall, *Beliefs and the Dead*, p. 111.

10 M. Sherbrook, 'The Fall of Religious Houses', in *Tudor Treatises*, ed. A. G. Dickens (York, 1959), p. 138.

11 Duffy, 'The End of it All', in *The Parish in Late Medieval England: Proceedings of the 2002 Harlaxton Symposium*, ed. E. Duffy and C. Burgess (Donington, 2006).

12 Palliser, *Tudor York*, p, 236. A shadowy figure in many ways at work in the 1670s and 1680s, it was said that he sympathised with the religion of Rome.

13 Bush, *Pilgrimage of Grace*, pp. 44–6, 107–8, 249–50, 280–1, 343–4, 386–7.

14 Marshall, *Beliefs and the Dead*, p. 100; Duffy, 'The End of it All', pp. 390–4.

15 Sherbrook, 'Fall of Religious Houses', p. 139; for context see E. Shagan, *Popular Politics and the English Reformation* (Cambridge, 2003).

16 Sherbook may have begun composing his account earlier than this, perhaps in the late 1560s.

17 Sherbrook, 'Fall of Religious Houses', p. 125.

18 Dickens, 'Robert Parkyn's Narrative', pp. 307–8.

19 Dickens, 'Last Medieval Englishman', p. 251.

20 MacCulloch and Fletcher, *Tudor Rebellions*, pp. 39ff; Palliser, *Tudor York*, pp. 244ff.

21 Borthwick Institute, Probate Register 19, fols 54v–55r (dated 16 March 1569). He seems to have been buried, on the basis of

evidence in the parish register, at Adwick on 24 March.

22   Dickens, 'Last Medieval Englishman', p. 278; on wills more gener-
      ally during this period of change see also Houlbrooke, *Death,
      Religion and the Family*, ch. 5.

23   For many of these continuities – bell-ringing, candles, unauthor-
      ised prayers, dirge-like psalm singing, the cortège pausing for
      prayer at wayside crosses, the use of *De profundis* and the singing
      of the Lyke Wake Dirge, see Houlbrooke, *Death, Religion and the
      Family*, ch. 9.

24   Palliser, *Tudor York*, p. 232. Note that during the 1560s and 1570s
      the Elizabethan regime moved against the plays.

25   Some of the Wintringham glass is medieval but much is neo-
      medieval Victorian replacement.

26   Palliser, *Reformation in York*, pp. 28–9; L. C. Attreed, 'Preparation
      for Death in Sixteenth-Century Northern England', in *Sixteenth-
      Century Journal*, 13 (1982).

27   Palliser, *Tudor York*, p. 228.

28   Cressy, *Birth, Marriage and Death*, p. 398ff.

29   Marshall, *Beliefs and the Dead*, pp. 134–5; also Houlbrooke, *Death,
      Religion and the Family*, p. 39, for scattered but widespread evidence
      of lay prayer for the dead in the late sixteenth and early seven-
      teenth centuries, which leads him to believe that the practice
      never completely lapsed.

30   Marshall, 'Pastoral Ministry', p. 8. 'Minds' were still being
      requested into the 1580s. On this see Cressy, *Birth, Marriage and
      Death*, pp. 398ff.

31   J. C. H. Aveling, *Northern Catholics: the Catholic recusants of the
      North Riding of Yorkshire, 1558–1790* (London, 1966), p. 23; R. Hutton,
      The Rise and Fall of Merry England: the ritual year 1400–1700 (Oxford
      1994), p. 305.

32   Brigden, *London in the Reformation*, p. 32.

33   Palliser, *Tudor York*, pp. 248–58.

34   Notably Lancelot Andrewes and John Cosin. See Marshall, *Beliefs
      and the Dead*, pp. 180–7; also Cressy, *Birth, Marriage and Death*, ch.
      18.

35   J. Brand, *Observations on Popular Antiquities: chiefly illustrating the
      origin of our vulgar customs, ceremonies, and supersititions*, 2 vols
      (London, 1813), vol. 2, pp. 288ff; J. Harland and T. T. Wilkinson,
      Lancashire Folk-Lore (London, 1867), pp. 270–4; *North Riding*, ed.
      Gutch, p. 307; C. Burne, *Shropshire Folklore: a sheaf of gleanings*
      (London, 1883), p. 308.

36   H. Lees, *English Churchyard Memorials* (Stroud, 2000), pp. 45–6.

37   Brand, *Popular Antiquities*, vol. 2, pp. 288ff; A. R. Wright, *British Calendar Customs: England*, ed. T. E. Lones, 3 vols (Folklore Soc., 1838), vol. 3, p. 134; P. H. Ditchfield, *Old English Customs Extant at the Present Time: an account of local observances, festival customs and ancient ceremonies yet surviving in Great Britain* (London, 1896), pp. 276ff.

38   From *lich*, which has Old English roots and indicates something pertaining to a corpse, as in the lychgate or lichgate, a covered gate at the churchyard entrance where mourners and coffin awaited the clergyman.

39   For the dirge see Marshall, *Beliefs and the Dead*, pp. 138–9; A. Shell, *Oral Culture and Catholicism in Early Modern England* (Cambridge, 2007), pp. 68–9.

40   Marshall, *Beliefs and the Dead*, p. 135; John Aubrey, *Remaines of Gentilisme and Judaisme*, in *Three Prose Works*, ed. J. Buchanan-Brown (London, 1972), pp. 176–8; Brand, *Popular Antiquities*, vol. 2, p. 274; R. Blakeborough, *Wit, Character, Folklore and Customs of the North Riding of Yorkshire* (London, 1898), pp. 122–5; *North Riding*, ed. Gutch, ch. 9.

41   Marshall, *Beliefs and the Dead*, pp. 138–9.

42   D. Woolf, *The Social Circulation of the Past: English historical consciousness 1500–1700* (Oxford, 2003), p. 358 ns 22–3; A. Walsham, *The Reformation of the Landscape: religion, identity and memory in early modern England* (Oxford, 2011), p. 479; W. Brockie, *Legends and Superstitions of the County of Durham* (Sunderland, 1886), pp. 232–2.

43   The survival of this song far beyond the Reformation, even if its meaning had been lost at the point of recording, suggests a slow decay of old ideas about purgatory; the Reformation came not as a sudden change, but a process in which relationships between living and dead were slowly adjusted as the generations passed. See Shell, *Oral Culture*, pp. 68–9.

43   Mrs Gutch thought that the routes by which the dead were carried to church in North Yorkshire were respected for similar reasons, noting the belief that the dead would not rest if taken to church by the wrong route. See *North Riding*, ed. Gutch, p. 307. For funeral rites more generally see J. Litten, *The English Way of Death: the common funeral since 1450* (London, 1991).

44   J. C. Atkinson, *Forty Years in a Moorland Parish* (London, 1891), pp. 215ff. He draws here on childhood experiences from Essex too

but his point is that similar beliefs persisted in Danby even though they had died out in many other places by the time he was writing. On Atkinson see W. J. Shiels, 'Church, Community and Culture in Rural England: J. C. Atkinson and the parish of Danby', in *Christianity and Community in the West: essays for John Bossy*, ed. S. Ditchfield (Aldershot, 2001).

45 Atkinson, *Moorland Parish*, pp. 70–1.

46 Atkinson, *Moorland Parish* pp. 58–9; and for other similar observations see Brand, *Popular Antiquities*, vol. 3, pp. 81–3; Henderson, *Northern Counties*, p. 273; *North Riding*, ed. Gutch, p. 104.

47 Aubrey, *Remaines*, p. 179; Brand, *Popular Antiquities*, vol. 2, pp. 246–8 (citing Aubrey) and pp. 288–9 (citing Thomas Pennant who noted a similar custom in Wales); S. O. Addy, *Household Tales with Other Traditional Remains* (London, 1895), pp. 122–6; E. Porter, *Cambridgeshire Customs and Folklore* (London, 1969), p. 26; Burne, *Shropshire Folklore*, p. 306; E. Leather, *The Folk-lore of Herefordshire* (Hereford, 1912), p. 121.

48 Brand, *Popular Antiquities*, vol. 2, p. 232; *North Riding*, ed. Gutch, pp. 300–1; Brockie, *Legends and Superstitions of Durham*, p. 203; Blakeborough, *Wit, Character, Folklore and Customs*, p. 122; W. Henderson, *Notes on the Folk Lore of the Northern Counties of England and the Borders* (London, 1879), pp. 39–41; J. Nicholson, *Folk Lore of East Yorkshire* (London, 1890), p. 5. For the practice of leaving doors open during a funeral in the twentieth century see D. Clark, *Between Pulpit and Pew: folk religion in a North Yorkshire fishing village* (Cambridge, 1982), p. 130.

49 Aubrey, *Remaines*, p. 115; and for later practices and explanations see J. Brand, *Observations on Antiquities: including the whole of Mr Bourne's Antiquitates Vulgares* (Newcastle, 1777), p. 23; Brand, *Popular Antiquities*, vol. 2, p. 234. Many of the folklorists who report the ritual suggested that it was dying out. See *North Riding*, ed. Gutch, ch. 9; Brockie, *Legends and Superstitions of Durham*, p. 200. Note also Henderson, *Northern Counties*, pp. 39–40, who claimed to have seen it done. Burne, *Shropshire Folklore*, pp. 298–9, explained that the rite was often thought to stop the body from swelling but speculated that some still did it to keep evil spirits at bay.

50 *North Riding*, ed. Gutch, ch. 9; Addy, *Household Tales*, pp. 122–6; Blakeborough, *Wit, Character, Folklore and Customs*, p. 120; Nicholson, *East Yorkshire*, p. 5; Brand, *Popular Antiquities*, vol. 2, p. 231.

51 Many of these rituals were far from placebound and similar ones

were to be found in parts of rural France. For which see T. A. Kselman, *Death and the Afterlife in Modern France* (Princeton, 1993), ch. 2.

52   J. Sykes, *Slawit in the 'Sixties: reminiscences* (London, 1926).

53   This early evidence comes from Shropshire, for which see Mirk, *Festial*, ed. Erbe, p. 270. For the inception of All Souls' Day see R. Hutton, *The Stations of the Sun: a history of the ritual year in Britain* (Oxford, 1996), pp. 371–9; and for souling see R. Hutton, 'The English Reformation and the Evidence of Folklore', in *Past and Present* (1990).

54   Souling had, by the early nineteenth century, been refigured as a form of sociability: it was fun for children or a mechanism by which the poor encouraged the rich to give charitably and the richer sort cooperated in what became for them an exercise in magnamity, reinforcing their status. But the very survival of the custom in such forms suggests a slow transformation after the Reformation in which, for many decades, it preserved older connotations of helping the dead. Its later manifestations are discussed in B. Bushaway, *By Rite: custom, ceremony & community in England, 1700–1880* (London, 1982) pp. 182–7.

55   Atkinson, *Moorland Parish*, pp. 231–3. In Yorkshire, the funeral hymns might be reprised during the next Sunday service after the funeral according to Nicholson, *Folk Lore of East Yorkshire*, p. 8; Brand, *Popular Antiquities*, vol. 2, p. 314; in nineteenth-century Herefordshire there was a 'mouzend', the month's end after a funeral, and the 'deathzear', a year after a death. In some places, special rituals attended these moments. In South Wales families might absent themselves from church on the month's end and in some parts of Wales families might, for some Sundays after the burial, kneel on the grave of their loved one and say the Lord's Prayer. See Brand, *Popular Antiquities*, vol. 2, p. 307; T. M. Owen, *Welsh Folk Customs* (Cardiff, 1976), pp. 185–6.

5 *Sure and Certain Hope*

1   *The Diary of Ralph Josselin, 1616–1683*, ed. A. Macfarlane (Oxford, 1991), p. 76.

2   Earls Colne had some 240 dwelling places and around 1,100 souls in *c*.1671.

3   For a study of similar religious values in a small-town setting see

D. Underdown, *Fire from Heaven: the life of an English town in the seventeenth century* (London, 1992).

4   *Diary of Ralph Josselin*, pp. 221–2.

5   *A Sermon Preached at the Funeral of Mrs Smythee Harlakenden, Wife to William Harlakenden Esquire, June 28. 1651* (London, 1652), A3v.

6   *Diary of Ralph Josselin*, p. 222.

7   Ibid. p. 31.

8   A. Macfarlane, *The Family Life of Ralph Josselin, A Seventeenth-Century Clergyman: an essay in historical anthropology* (Cambridge, 1970), pp. 68–78, 170–3.

9   *Diary of Ralph Josselin*, pp. 61, 339, 404, 349. For the attention given to wonders of these kinds see A. Walsham, *Providence in Early Modern England* (Oxford, 1999).

10 An early indication of this train of thought appears in 1650, *Diary of Ralph Josselin*, pp. 219–20.

11 For such images of life's fragility in poetry see D. Stannard, *The Puritan Way of Death: a study in religion, culture and social change* (Oxford, 1977), p. 56.

12 *Diary of Ralph Josselin*, pp. 202.

13 For what follows, Ibid., pp. 203–5.

14 Ibid., p. 203.

15 Ibid., p. 205.

16 Ibid., p. 262.

17 Ibid., p. 221.

18 For medieval ideas of heaven see J. B. Russell, *A History of Heaven: the singing silence* (Princeton, 1997).

19 *Diary of Ralph Josselin*, p. 567.

20 Macfarlane, *Family Life*, p. 91.

21 J. Casey, *After Lives: a guide to heaven, hell, and purgatory* (Oxford, 2009), ch. 13; C. McDannell and B. Lang, *Heaven: a history* (London, 2001), chs 5 and 6.

22 *Diary of Ralph Josselin*, p. 481 (13 June 1661); more generally see P. Marshall, 'The Company of Heaven: identity and sociability in the English Protestant afterlife', in *Historical Reflections / Reflexions Historiques*, 26 (2000).

23 *The Diary of Bulstrode Whitelocke, 1605–75*, ed. R. Spalding (Oxford, 1990), p. 385.

24 Ibid., p. 62

25 *Two East Anglian Diaries, 1641–1729*, ed. M. Storey (Woodbridge, 1994), pp. 184–5.

26 Ibid., pp. 150–1. He refers here to three babes only; his troubles

were not yet at an end. About loss and grief more generally in the early modern family see K. Thomas, *The Ends of Life: roads to fulfilment in early modern England* (Oxford, 2009), p. 230; A. Lawrence, 'Godly Grief: individual responses to death in seventeenth-century Britain', in *Death, Ritual and Bereavement*, ed. R. Houlbrooke (London, 1989).

27   R. Baxter, *The Saints' Everlasting Rest, or, A treatise of the blessed state of the saints in their enjoyment of God in glory*, ed. W. Young (London, 1907), pp. 37–9; P. C. Almond, *Heaven and Hell in Enlightenment England* (Cambridge, 1994), ch. 3.

28   Other divines agreed. The saved, said Robert Bolton, 'shall not know our old acquaintance by former stature, feature, favour: so vast a distance and difference shall be betweene a mortal and a glorified body . . . Our mutual knowledge of one another in heaven shall not be in the outward and worldly respects, but divine and spiritual, as we know them in Christ, by the illumination of the spirit', *Mr Bolton's Last and Learned Worke of the Foure Last Things* . . . (London, 1633), p. 149.

29   *Saints' Everlasting Rest*, ed. Young, p. 136.

30   Ibid., p. 53.

31   Thomas, *Ends of Life*, p. 228.

32   *Harlakenden Funeral Sermon*, A3r.

33   On thin congregations see *Diary of Ralph Josselin*, p. 95.

34   *Harlakenden Funeral Sermon*, 4.

35   C. Haigh, *The Plain Man's Pathways to Heaven: kinds of Christianity in post-Reformation England, 1570–1640* (Oxford, 2007), p. 79.

36   Ibid., p. 79.

37   Houlbrooke, *Death, Religion and Family*, pp. 46 and 55. Similar sentiments were expressed in the nineteenth century. In 1861, a shopkeeper took issue with the hellfire theology of a missioner, saying that God must be 'very cruel to act like a tyrant to send to hell more than half the human race'. Why make them, he wondered aloud, if only to damn them? See D. M. Lewis, *Lighten Our Darkness: the evangelical mission to working-class London, 1828–60* (London, 1986), p. 141.

38   *The Diary of Samuel Pepys: a new and complete transcription*, ed. R. Latham and W. Matthews, 11 vols (London, 1970–83), vol. 4, pp. 86–7. See on Pepys also Houlbrooke, *Death, Religion and Family*, pp. 54–5.

39   For the background: Marshall, *Beliefs and the Dead*, pp. 152–6, 200ff; Haigh, *Plain Man's Pathway*, p. 41.

40 Macfarlane, *Family Life*, p. 82.

41 For the life and death of Venetia see K. Digby, 'A New Digby Letter Book "In Praise of Venetia"', ed. V. Gabrieli, in *The National Library of Wales Journal*, 9–10 (1955–6); K. Digby, *Loose Fantasies*, ed. V. Gabrieli (Rome, 1968); John Aubrey, *Brief Lives: edited from the original manuscripts and with an introduction*, ed. O. L. Dick (London, 1949). For the portrait see N. Llewellyn, *The Art of Death: visual culture in the English death ritual c. 1500–c.1800* (London, 1991), pp. 31–2.

42 Aubrey, *Brief Lives*, ed. Dick, p. 260.

43 C. Gittings, 'Venetia's Death and Sir Kenelm's Mourning', in *Death, Passion and Politics*, ed. A. Sumner (London, 1995).

44 Aubrey, *Brief Lives*, ed Dick, p. 258.

45 For this see ibid., p. 99.

46 'In Praise of Venetia', pp. 122, 453, 137.

47 Gittings, 'Venetia's Death', p. 59.

48 Ibid., p. 61.

49 C. Gittings, 'Sacred and Secular 1558–1660', in *Death in England*, ed. Jupp, pp. 164–6; for instances of unusually deep grief see Thomas, *Ends of Life*, pp. 218ff.

50 *Harlakenden Funeral Sermon*, p. 31.

51 Macfarlane, *Family Life*, p. 167.

52 'In Praise of Venetia', p. 100.

53 Ibid., p. 139.

54 John Donne quoted in P. Marshall, 'The Company of Heaven: identity and sociability in the English Protestant afterlife', in *Historical Reflections/Reflexions Historiques*, 26 (2000).

55 'In Praise of Venetia', p. 455.

56 Gittings, 'Venetia's Death', p. 63.

57 A. Powell, *John Aubrey and his Friends* (London, 1963), pp. 169–70.

58 Wesley's Chapel, established by John Wesley himself, founder of Methodism, as the chief church of his movement in the capital was built in 1778 opposite the City Road entrance to Bunhill Fields. It stands there still today.

59 'Upon the Death of My Husband', in *Eighteenth-Century Women Poets: an Oxford anthology*, ed. R. Lonsdale (Oxford, 1989), p. 50.

60 Elizabeth Singer Rowe, *Friendship in Death: in twenty letters from the dead to the living. To which are added, thoughts on death* (London, 1728), p. 84.

61 Letter to Lady Hertford, quoted in *British Novelists, 1660–1880*, ed. M. C. Battestin (Detroit, 1985), pt 2, p. 409.

62   Rowe, *Friendship in Death*, p. 82.

63   Ibid., pp. 82, 11, 71, 14–15, 36.

64   Ibid., p. 71.

65   Others offered similar visions of heaven, which were also popular. One of the most prominent, Isaac Watts, composed *Death and Heaven; or the last enemy conquered and separate spirits made perfect* (1722) and was buried at Bunhill. For eighteenth-century notions of a 'companionate' heaven structured by human experiences rather than theocentric in conception, that is organised around worship of the divinity, see McDannell and Lang, *Heaven*, pp. 181–227.

66   On funeral sermons see Marshall, 'Company of Heaven', p. 318; for widespread expectations of reunion after death and the fate of the married in particular see Houlbrooke, *Death, Religion and Family*, pp. 45ff.

6 A New America?

1   John Gerard, 'Catalogue of Martyrs', in *Unpublished Documents Relating to the English Martyrs: English Martyrs, vol. 1 1584–1603*, ed. J. H. Pollen (London, 1908), pp. 288–9. For ghosts in post-Reformation England see K. Thomas, *Religion and the Decline of Magic: studies in popular beliefs in sixteenth- and seventeenth-century England* (London, 1971), pp. 701–24; Marshall, *Beliefs and the Dead*, ch. 6; and for a longer view, O. Davies, *The Haunted: a social history of ghosts* (Basingstoke, 2007).

2   Marshall, *Beliefs and the Dead*, p. 235.

3   K. Thomas, *Religion and the Decline of Magic: studies in popular beliefs in sixteenth- and seventeenth-century England* (London, 1971), p. 703. More's claim is striking as he was, in other respects, quite ready to believe that spirits had power to appear on earth since he was one among a number of late seventeenth-century scholars keen to probe the workings of the invisible world.

4   Marshall, *Beliefs and the Dead*, pp. 234–42.

5   Thomas, *Religion and the Decline of Magic*, p. 706.

6   The essential discussion, on which I draw here for the course of events, is M. Hunter, 'New Light on the Drummer of Tedworth: conflicting narratives of witchcraft in Restoration England', in *Historical Research*, 78 (2005). The story of the drummer was made famous by published narratives, especially those of Joseph

Glanvill, of which more below, but Michael Hunter's researches have uncovered a cache of earlier documents, including letters from Mompesson to an Oxford divine, William Creed, which offer insights into the case at an earlier date and unmediated by Glanvill. For an account of these documents see Hunter, 'New Light', pp. 315ff.

7   For the context of belief in supernatural phenomena see A. Walsham, *Providence in Early Modern England* (Oxford, 1999); W. E. Burns, *An Age of Wonders: prodigies, politics and providence in England, 1657–1727* (Manchester, 2009); P. Marshall, *Mother Leakey and the Bishop: a ghost story* (Oxford, 2007); V. Jankovic, 'The Politics of Sky Battles in Early Hanoverian Britain', in *Journal of British Studies*, 41 (2002).

8   *Letters of Philip, Second Earl of Chesterfield: to several celebrated individuals of the time of Charles II, James II, William III and Queen Anne with some replies* (1829), pp. 24–5.

9   Aubrey, *Three Prose Works*, ed. Buchanan-Brown, pp. xxix–xxxv.

10 *Diary of Samuel Pepys*, vol. 4, pp. 185–6.

11 Joseph Glanvill, *A Blow Against Modern Sadducism* (London, 1668); Almond, *Heaven and Hell*, pp. 34–6.

12 Hunter, 'New Light', p. 334.

13 Suggested by a letter Joseph Glanvill sent to him, which mentioned that Baxter was 'desirous of a particular account [of the story of the drummer] that you might publish the relation', dated 21 January 1663. For which see *Calendar of the Correspondence of Richard Baxter*, ed. N. H. Keeble and G. F. Nutall, 2 vols (Oxford, 1991), vol. 2, p. 37.

14 J. Webster, *The Displaying of Supposed Witchcraft* (London, 1677), p. 278.

15 Joseph Glanvill, *Saducismus Triumphatus, or, Full and Plain Evidence Concerning Witches and Apparitions* (London, 1682), fol. Aa4r.

16 *Letters of Philip, Second Earl of Chesterfield*, p. 25.

17 *Saducismus Triumphatus*, fol. Aa2r-v.

18 Ibid., pp. 1–2. [Henry More's preface].

19 Hunter, 'New Light', p. 325.

20 For learned fears about spreading atheism and the use of ghost stories and the like to confound sceptics see C. Koslofksy, *Evening's Empire: a history of night in early modern Europe* (Cambridge, 2011), pp. 238–47; E. Cameron, *Enchanted Europe: superstition, reason and religion, 1250–1750* (Oxford, 2010), pp. 262–82.

21 *Saducismus Triumphatus*, fol. 118ff.

22 Ibid., prefatory matter [by Henry More].

23 Ibid., fol. 3r.

24 Ibid., fols 238–40.

25 Increasingly, behind expressions of scepticism might lurk awareness of naturalistic explanations, for example in the field of
optics, which framed alternative accounts of why people
thought they saw apparitions. There also remained, of course,
blunter doubts about simple trickery and imposture. For the
new science and its ramifications: S. Clark, 'The Reformation
of the Eyes: apparitions and optics in sixteenth- and seventeenth-century Europe', in *Journal of Religious History*, 27 (2003);
also his *Vanities of the Eye: vision in early modern European culture*
(Oxford, 2007), ch. 6.

26 *Diary of Samuel Pepys*, vol. 2, p. 68.

27 Ibid., vol. 9, p. 495; vol. 8, p. 553.

7 The Sampford Peverell Sensation

1 C. S. Watkins, *History and the Supernatural in Medieval England*
(Cambridge, 2007), p. 61.

2 *Medieval Popular Religion*, ed. Shinners, pp. 220–1.

3 *Sampford Ghost!!! A Full Account of the Conspiracy at Sampford
Peverell, near Tiverton, Devon, Containing the Particulars of the
Pretended Visitation of the Monster, the Affadavit of Rev C. Colton and
the Circumstances Concerning the Detection of the Plot as Detailed in
the Taunton Courier* (Taunton, 1810), pp. 3–5. This tract reprints
with additional material a series of local newspaper articles dealing
with hauntings. For the background of eighteenth-century ghost
beliefs see S. Handley, *Visions of an Unseen World: ghost beliefs and
ghost stories in eighteenth-century England* (London, 2007).

4 *Sampford Ghost!!!*, p. 3.

5 Ibid., pp. 5–7.

6 Ibid., pp. 8–10; Caleb Colton, *Sampford Ghost: a plain and authentic
narrative of those extraordinary occurrences, hitherto unaccounted for,
which have lately taken place at the house of Mr Chave in the village
of Sampford Peverell in the county of Devon* (Tiverton, 1810).

7 For what follows: *Sampford Ghost!!!*, pp. 12ff.

8 A conjuror by this name was active in the Herefordshire/
Gloucestershire area in the 1790s. For which see O. Davies, *Cunning
Folk: popular magic in English history* (London, 2003), p. 47.

9   Aubrey, *Remaines*, p. 201

10   *Sampford Ghost!!!*, pp. 12ff..

11   Caleb Colton, *Sampford Ghost: stubborn facts against vague assertions, being an appendix to A Plain and Authentic Narrative . . .* (Tiverton, 1810), p. 19.

12   Print had long been a friend to wonder tales and ghost stories. A version of the Tedworth tale had been put into a pamphlet with an eye to circulation for profit before Glanvill was writing it up and, in the eighteenth and nineteenth centuries, newspapers readily published stories on ghost sensations, sometimes being open-minded about a story but sometimes seeking to explode the tale. On literature in which ghost stories circulated see T. Watt, *Cheap Print and Popular Piety, 1550–1640* (Cambridge, 1991); Handley, *Unseen World*, ch. 4.

13   Lovett was one of many working-class men, and some women, who engaged in autobiographical writing during the nineteenth century. A magisterial study of working-class ideas that makes use of these sources is J. Rose, *The Intellectual Life of the British Working Classes* (London, 2001); there is also important discussion in D. Vincent, *Bread, Knowledge and Freedom: a study of 19th-century working class autobiography* (London, 1981). The same sources can be used to reconstruct aspects of belief about the invisible world too and a number are used below.

14   Richard Polwhele, *Traditions and Recollections, Domestic, Clerical and Literary*, 2 vols (London, 1826), vol. 2, p. 605.

15   Richard Polwhele, *The History of Cornwall*, ed. A. L. Rowse (Dorking, 1978), p. 58.

16   *Life and Struggles of William Lovett, in his pursuit of bread, knowledge and freedom with some short account of the different associations he belonged to and of the opinions he entertained* (London, 1967), pp. 8–11.

17   The young William Lovett was not free from night fears even when he entered the village. After his mother remarried, the family was broken up and he moved into a new cottage with his grandmother. He found that his bedroom overlooked the village's 'haunted house', a place where many of the occupants had been given a scare by an invisible resident. So nervous was he of seeing it for himself that he would enter his bedroom with closed eyes to avoid catching a glimpse of the ghost through the window that faced the door.

18   Henry Bourne, *Antiquitates Vulgares, or, the antiquities of the common people, giving an account of several of their opinions and ceremonies* (Newcastle, 1725), p. 102.

19   Richard Hunt published detailed accounts of Cornish folklore in
      1865 based on stories he had begun collecting during walking
      tours of the county, the first of these being in 1829. His ambition
      was to set down 'every ancient tale of its people' and he claimed
      to have found a landscape crusted with stories. He presumed
      them to be immemorial and was surprised to find that, on a
      second visit, many tales had died out or evolved and new ones
      had sprung up. The 'lore' of the 'folk' proved a good deal more
      complex, often less antique, and more mingled with printed tales
      than he and other folklorists of his day bargained for. See Richard
      Hunt, *Popular Romances of the West of England* (London, third edn,
      1881); a study of this folklore exploring continuities is T. Brown,
      *The Fate of the Dead: a study of folk eschatology in the West Country
      after the Reformation* (Cambridge, 1979).

20   William Bottrell, *Stories and Folk-Lore of West Cornwall* (London,
      1880), pp. 152–4; M. A. Courtney, *Cornish Feasts and Folklore*
      (Penzance, 1890), pp. 79–81.

21   The earliest stories of John Tregeagle were told by Richard
      Polwhele at the beginning of the nineteenth century. A hard-to-
      find digest is B. C. Spooner, *John Tregeagle: man and ghost* (Truro,
      1935). See also A. L. Rowse, 'Jan Tregagle: legend and history', in
      History Today, 15 (1965); Hunt, *Popular Romances*, pp. 132–42;
      outlines are to be found in J. Westwood and J. Simpson, *The Lore
      of the Land: a guide to England's legends from Spring-Heeled Jack to
      the Witches of Warboys* (London, 2005), pp. 94ff and see index
      entries for many locations with Tregeagle legends attached to
      them.

22   *The Compleat Servant Maid: or, the Young Maiden's and family
      Companion* (London, 1729), p. 11. Joseph Addison described how,
      one winter's night, he sat in a chair eavesdropping on young
      girls gathered around his landlady's fire in conversation with
      her daughters about spirits and apparitions. Others also worried
      that exposure to supernatural tales filled children's heads with
      stories that they could not easily escape in later life. John Locke
      had been concerned about this in the seventeenth century and
      held that if such silly stories were abandoned, fear of the night
      might be ended as well. J. Locke, *Some Thoughts Concerning
      Education* (London, 1693), p. 159; J. Locke, *An Essay Concerning
      Human Understanding*, ed. P. N. Nidditch (Oxford, 1975), pp. 397–8;
      A. Fox, *Oral and Literate Culture in England, 1500–1700* (Oxford,
      2000), pp. 188–97.

23 A witness, albeit a slightly later one, is Joseph Hammond, *A Cornish Parish: being an account of St Austell, town, church district and people* (London, 1897), who has a number of stories of fetches and men dead before their time.

24 Most prominent here, though Lovett does not name it, was the wreck of the frigate HMS *Anson*, which had foundered in 1807; a hundred or more men died almost within reach of shore. A later nineteenth-century churchman, the eccentric Reverend Hawker of Morwenstow, recalled the horror of burying bodies of sailors washed up on the shore of his parish on the north coast of the peninsula, an experience that drove him close to madness. See P. Brendon, *Hawker of Morwenstow: portrait of a Victorian eccentric* (London, 1975).

25 For the Methodist context see M. R. Watts, *The Dissenters, vol. 2: the expansion of evangelical nonconformity* (Oxford, 1995); D. Hempton, *The Religion of the People: Methodism and Popular Religion c.1750–1900* (London, 1996). Also see J. Rule, 'Methodism, Popular Beliefs and Village Culture', in *Popular Culture and Custom in Nineteenth-century England*, ed. R. D. Storch (London, 1982); J. C. C. Probert, *Primitive Methodism in Cornwall* (Redruth, 1966).

26 Polwhele, *History of Cornwall*, pp. 139–40.

27 Rose, *Intellectual Life*, ch. 3; also D. Vincent, *Literacy and Popular Culture in England, 1750–1914* (Cambridge, 1979), chs 1 and 5.

28 The picture William Lovett paints of rural ghost belief in the first half of the nineteenth century is confirmed by many other writers who also tended to agree with him that education was emancipating the working classes from such convictions. See, for example, the remarks of Samuel Bamford, *The Autobiography of Samuel Bamford*, ed. W. H. Chaloner, 2 vols (London 1967), vol. 1, pp. 27ff.

29 T. Oliver, *Autobiography of a Cornish Miner* (Camborne, 1914), pp. 85–6; J. Harris, *My Autobiography* (London, 1882), pp. 39–44.

30 Tom Tremewan, *Cornish Youth: memories of a Perran boy* (Truro, 1968); others told similar stories of supernatural pranks which relied for their effect on a reservoir of beliefs about ghosts. Revd J. H. Howard remembered some decidedly uncharitable entertainments of his youth. He was a member of a gang who used to meet in the churchyard and dress up as ghosts to frighten passers-by at night. J. H. Howard, *Winding Lanes: a book of impressions and recollections* (Caernarvon, n.d.), p. 26.

31 Bamford, *Autobiography*, vol. 1, pp. 37–8.

32 Woolf, *Social Circulation of the Past*, pp. 361–2.

33   She used the fictional village of Lark Rise as a receptacle for her memories of the Oxfordshire countryside but her story was not a placebound one.

34   F. Thompson, *Lark Rise to Candleford: a trilogy* (London, 1945), pp. 66–7, 489–90.

35   Ibid., pp. 66–7.

36   Sykes, *Slawit in the Sixties*, pp. 11–12.

37   H. Snell, *Men, Movements and Myself* (London, 1936), p. 4. John Wilson told similar stories of a haunted landscape in which he feared as a youth walking to work. See J. Wilson, *Memories of a Labour Leader* (London, 1910), pp. 76–81.

38   J. Briggs, *The Night Visitors: the rise and fall of the English ghost story* (London 1977), who notes the particular popularity of the genre in the period 1850 to 1930; S. McCorrister, *Spectres of the Self: thinking about ghosts and ghost-seeing in England, 1750–2000* (Cambridge, 2010); E. J. Clery, *The Rise of Supernatural Fiction, 1762–1800* (Cambridge, 1995).

8 *Among the Tombs*

1   John Jope Rogers, *John Knill, 1733–1811* (n.d.); B. James, *John Knill: his life and times* (Redruth, 1981); J. H. Matthews, *A History of the Parishes of St Ives, Lelant, Towednack and Zennor* (London, 1892).

2   Cornwall Record Office, Truro, CA/B42/66–7.

3   Ibid., P91/25/1.

4   Samuel Pepys bequeathed 128 rings at a total cost of £100, three qualities of ring being produced and dispensed according to rank of the recipient. For which see N. Llewellyn, *The Art of Death: visual culture in the English death ritual c.1500–c.1800* (London, 1991), pp. 86–7; B. S. Puckle, *Funeral Customs: their origin and development* (London, 1926), pp. 268ff.

5   Atkinson, *Forty Years in a Moorland Parish*, pp. 223ff.

6   Knill was born in Callington, Cornwall, after his parents settled there. For a discussion of the charitable activities of others without children see Thomas, *Ends of Life*, pp. 257–8.

7   2 Samuel 18:18.

8   A fashion for burial in such stately pavilions had been set by the aristocracy in the mid eighteenth century and now the idea was trickling down to men like Knill who were of middling rank. Charles Howard, a religious sceptic, set a trend for

mausoleum-burial outside churchyards when he was installed in the particularly grand one designed by Vanbrugh and Hawksmoor for his Castle Howard estate in 1738. By 1760 there were some twenty free-standing mausoleums in England. For which see H. Colvin, *Architecture and the After-Life* (New Haven, 1991), pp. 283–326.

9 Cornwall Record Office, Truro, BIVES/139 [Accounts, Trustees of John Knill's Charity for Gluvian Richard, Mawgan in Pydar].

10 *Victoria County History of Cornwall*, vol. 2, ed. N. Orme (Woodbridge, 2010), pp. 2ff.

11 Matthews, *History*, p. 56, citing Bishop Stafford's Register entry of 27 September 1409.

12 W. Lack, H. M. Stuchfield and P. Whittlesmore, *The Monumental Brasses of Cornwall* (London, 1997), pp. 121–2; P. Cockerham, *Continuity and Change: memorialisation and the Cornish funeral monument industry, 1497–1660* (Oxford, 2006), p. 1462.

13 John Weever, *Ancient Funerall Monuments within the united monarchie of Great Britaine, Ireland, and the ilands adiacent, with the dissolued monasteries therein contained: their founders, and what eminent persons haue beene in the same interred . . .* (London, 1631); R. Lindley, *Tomb Destruction and Scholarship: medieval monuments in early modern England* (Donington, 2007), pp. 4–52, 113–24. On aspects of the Cornish experience: A. L. Rowse, *Tudor Cornwall: portrait of a society* (London, second edn, 1969), pp. 295–300; R. Whiting, *The Blind Devotion of the People: popular religion and the English Reformation* (Cambridge, 1989), pp. 101–4.

14 Houlbrooke, *Death, Religion and the Family*, p. 348; Thomas, *Ends of Life*, p. 246.

15 F. B. Burgess, *English Churchyard Memorials* (London, 1963), p. 220; also Thomas, *Ends of Life*, p. 247.

16 The description is that of Matthews, *History*, pp. 66–8.

17 Thomas, *Ends of Life*, pp. 235–62; Marshall, *Beliefs and the Dead*, pp. 265–308; Houlbrooke, *Death, Religion and the Family*, ch. 10. The essential work on post-Reformation tombs is N. Llewellyn, *Funeral Monuments in Post-Reformation England* (Cambridge, 2000).

18 J. Polsue, *A Complete Parochial History of the County of Cornwall: compiled from the best authorities & corrected and improved from actual survey*, 4 vols (Truro, 1867–73), vol. 1, p. 254.

19 Thomas Browne, *Urne Burial* in *Sir Thomas Browne: selected writings*, ed. G. Keynes (London, 1968), p. 151.

20 Matthews, *History*, p. 110.

21   Ralph Bigland, *Historical, Monumental, and Genealogical Collections relative to the County of Gloucester*, 2 vols (London, 1791–2).

22   As William Beard does at Standish in Gloucestershire, for which see Lees, *Churchyard Memorials*, pp. 104–5.

23   J. Hervey, *Meditations Among the Tombs: tending to reform the vices of the age, and to promote evangelical holiness* (London, 1746), p. 52. Hervey wrote many works in a similar vein, aiming to 'bait the gospel hook agreeably according to the prevailing taste' through religious musings inspired by flower gardens, starry heavens and winter scenes and the like. His *Meditations on the Tombs*, ostensibly about Kilkampton, was in fact a composite of several graveyards.

24   *The Oxford Book of Death*, ed. D. J. Enright (Oxford, 2008), p. 332.

25   Hervey, *Meditations*, p. 92.

26   The motif was an old one, pre-dating Christianity. 'Death', John Aubrey observed, 'comes even to stones and names', echoing the classical writer Ausonius. For which see G. Parry, *The Trophies of Time: English Antiquarians of the Seventeenth Century* (Oxford, 1995), p. 276.

27   Polsue, *Parochial History*, p. 259.

28   William Godwin, *An Essay on Sepulchres, or a proposal for erecting some memorial of the illustrious dead in all ages on the spot where their remains have been interred* (London, 1809), pp. 40–1. He noted that three-quarters of tombstones in a churchyard belonged to the last twenty or thirty years yet speculated that the 'passion for tombstones' was probably no less great in past ages, surmising earlier ones were weathered away and cleared.

29   Parry, *Trophies of Time*, p. 276.

30   On monumental symbolism see Burgess, *Churchyard Memorials*, pp. 167ff.

31   Matthews, *History*, pp. 81ff.

32   The inscriptions that follow were recorded in Matthews, *History*, pp. 78–87.

33   Matthews, *History*, p. 94. She was related to a Captain Thomas Cundy of St Ives, also buried in the churchyard, who had been killed fighting French pirates.

34   Houlbrooke, *Death, Religion and the Family*, pp. 332ff.

35   See V. Harding, 'Burial on the Margin', in *Grave Concerns: death and burial in England 1700–1850*, ed. M. C. Cox (York, 1998).

36   Lees, *Churchyard Memorials*, p. 23; Llewellyn, *Funeral Monuments*, p. 148.

37   Polwhele, *Traditions and Recollections*, vol. 2, pp. 579–80.

9 Added Terrors

1   http://www.thisisbristol.co.uk/news/LAID-REST-190-YEARS-LATE/article-3448698-detail/article.html [accessed 17.5.2011].

2   The gatehouse of the gaol still stands, sandwiched between the quay where the city's M-Shed museum is located and facing the 'New Cut'. The gaol was, in effect, built on a prison island formed beween the Cut and the River Avon proper. It held prisoners until 1883. In spring 2012 hoardings promised that the site would be redeveloped and houses built there.

3   Bristol's first newspaper had been published in 1702, among the earliest to appear outside London.

4   Bristol Record Office, 35893/36 [where a microfiche copy is available for consultation]. This is the core of the documentation used to reconstruct the events below. Some of it is printed in *Notes and Queries*, 2nd ser, 39 (1856), pp. 150–1. Another surgeon at the infirmary, Dr Estlin, also took notes on the case and these are to be found in BRO 35893/32/a. For discussion of medicine in Bristol during this period, including the activities of Richard Smith and his fellow anatomists and aspects of the Horwood case itself, see M. E. Fissell, *Patients, Power, and the Poor in Eighteenth-Century Bristol* (Cambridge, 1991).

5   Prosecution witness depositions and contemporary newspaper reports detail this alleged background of intimidation and assault and the former are to be found in BRO JQS/P/464.

6   A sketch map of the crime scene is included among Richard Smith's bound papers.

7   Some accounts suggest that she went to Bristol the day after the attack but Dr Estlin, one of the doctors who attended her, notes that this was mistaken and that at the trial it emerged that five days had elapsed between her injury and arrival in the hospital.

8   BRO JQS/P/464.

9   This is how his obituarists characterised him. He rose eventually to become Master of the Rolls. Extracts from the obituaries are among Richard Smith's papers dealing with the case.

10 The indispensable account of capital punishment in this period is V. A. C. Gatrell, *The Hanging Tree: execution and the English people 1770–1868* (Oxford, 1994).

11 Fissell, *Patients, Power and the Poor*, pp. 168–9.

12 The events were recorded in *Farley's Newspaper*, 25 April 1752,

and printed in *The Annals of Bristol in the Eighteenth Century*, ed. J. Latimer (Bristol, 1893), p. 56.

13   In general as well as specific terms. Horrible punishments had long been visited on a select few of the dead – on the bodies of rebels, for example – and well beyond the point at which life was extinguished. When Henry VIII let repression loose in the north in the aftermath of the Pilgrimage of Grace, ringleaders were dismembered and their remains exhibited at York. The corpses of the regicides who had signed the death warrant of Charles I were dug up and burned after the Restoration of the monarchy; even death, it seems, was not to be allowed to cheat King Charles II of his vengeance. See Marshall, *Beliefs and the Dead*, pp. 122–3; Josselin, *Diary*, p. 479; for another case Tyacke, *Long Reformation*, pp. 6–7.

14   Dissection was practised in late thirteenth-century Bologna and was authorised by Clement VI in the aftermath of the Black Death of 1347–8; there was further refinement of the Church's position in 1482 by Pope Sixtus IV.

15   See Fissell, *Patients, Power and the Poor*, pp. 167–9.

16   See R. Richardson, *Death, Dissection and the Destitute* (London, 1987), pp. 3–29.

17   At Aberystwyth a woman who took her own life so as to cheat the executioner was laid under sand on the shoreline. Caught between land and sea she would lie in an in-between place, trapped between worlds and thus, perhaps, prevented from rising. Burying her there also consigned her memory to oblivion; the grave would soon be undiscoverable on a featureless beach, swept from memory by the tides. For which see *Gentlemen's Magazine* 54.5 (Nov 1784), p. 868; also Puckle, *Funeral Customs*, pp. 152ff, 208.

18   Weever, *Funerall Monuments*, p. 22.

19   Only in 1823 was staking ended and then, allegedly, only because George IV's coach was held up while a suicide was being interred at a crossroads.

20   *Annals of Bristol*, ed. Latimer, pp. 192–3; R. A. Houston, *Punishing the Dead? suicide, lordship, and community in Britain, 1500–1830* (Oxford, 2010); M. MacDonald and T. R. Murphy, *Sleepless Souls: suicide in early modern England* (Oxford, 1990); for early rites see A. Murray, *Suicide in the Middle Ages: volume 2, the curse on self-murder* (Oxford, 2000), esp. ch. 1.

21   The Brislington Case was detailed in the *Bristol Mirror*, 1828; a brief account of contraptions designed to frustrate the body snatchers appears in R. Richardson, 'Why Was Death So Big in

Victorian Britain?', in *Death, Ritual and Bereavement*, ed. Houlbrooke, pp. 109–10.

22 The five men were taken to the Lamb Inn and held there for a time and the sexton's son, Mr Ward, was subsequently arrested too on suspicion of being their accomplice. The case was heard at the Wells Quarter Sessions but was considered serious so the judge reserved sentence until he had taken advice from the Judge of Assize.

23 *Bristol Mirror*, 1828.

24 A claim also made about a Devon grave which pre-dated the age of bodysnatching: the grave of Richard Cabell (d. 1677) of Buckfastleigh was said to have an iron grille to stop him rising. For which see M. Bailey, *Churchyards of England and Wales* (Bristol, 1987).

25 *Bristol Mirror*, 1828.

26 For this case see Bristol Record Office, BBM 8, with newspaper clippings, broadside, a poster offering a reward for information about bodysnatchers and other ephemera inserted between pp. 39 and 40 and pp. 53 and 54; for discussion of this see Fissell, *Patients, Power and the Poor*, pp. 165–6.

27 Cited in T. Marshall, *Murdering to Dissect: grave-robbing, Frankenstein, and the anatomy literature* (Manchester, 1995), pp. 178–9; and for the durable horror of dissection see J. Sawday, *The Body Emblazoned: dissection and the human body in Renaissance culture* (London, 1995).

28 Marshall, *Murdering to Dissect*, pp. 29–31.

29 The M-Shed Museum, located between the New Cut and the River Avon and adjacent to the Cumberland Road site where Horwood was executed at the New Gaol.

30 The inscription, explaining that the book is bound in Horwood's skin, sits in an inner frame in the shape of a gallows; binding and decoration alike were done with considerable attention to detail.

31 The essential work, the argument of which I draw on here, is Richardson, *Death, Dissection and the Destitute*, esp. ch. 12; also T. Laquer, 'Bodies, Death and Pauper Funerals', in *Representations*, 1:1 (1983).

32 http://www.thisisbristol.co.uk/news/LAID-REST-190-YEARS-LATE/article-3448698-detail/article.html [accessed 17.5.2011].

33 See: http://www.upi.com/Top_News/World-News/2011/04/14/Young-man-hanged-in-1821-gets-burial/UPI-93351302760652/#ixzz1MiXbYjBq [accessed 17.5.2011]. Paradoxically, John Horwood's rest is now less likely to be disturbed in the near future than it was in the

early nineteenth century. Then an ordinary man's grave would have been cut across or reused after only a generation or so. Modern sensibilities and legal conventions require that the dead have a longer lease of their plots and the widespread use of substantial headstones also acts as a guarantor of these rights. For legal and broader notions of the right to undisturbed rest see N. Cantor, *After We Die: the life and times of the human cadaver* (Washington DC, 2010), pp. 34ff.

34   For which see K. D. M. Snell, 'Gravestones, Belonging and Local Attachment in England, 1700–2000', *Past and Present* (2003).

35   http://www.thisisbristol.co.uk/news/LAID-REST-190-YEARS-LATE/article-3448698-detail/article.html [accessed 17.4.2011].

10 *Fiery Resolution*

1   D. Lewis, *The History of Llantrisant* (Pontypridd, 1982), pp. 31ff, 59–61.

2   *Western Mail*, 23 September 1947.

3   William Price has attracted much attention. The fullest recent discussion is in D. Powell, *Eccentric: the life of Dr William Price* (Llantrisant, 2005); also J. Cule, 'The Eccentric Doctor William Price of Llantrisant (1800–1893)', in *Morgannwg: Transactions of the Glamorgan Local History Society*, 7 (1963); R. Hutton, *Blood and Mistletoe: the history of the Druids in Britain* (London, 2009), pp. 283ff. Much of the following discussion of William Price draws on Cremation Society archives, now held by Durham University, which include newspaper clippings dealing with his case. For which see Durham University Library, Special Collections and Archives, CRE/H8, H9, H11, H12, H15, H20.

4   Powell, *Eccentric*, p. 41.

5   *Western Mail*, 17 September 1947.

6   P. C. Jupp, *From Dust to Ashes: the replacement of burial by cremation in England 1840–1967* (London, 1990), pp. 47ff; B. Parsons, *Committed to the Cleansing Flame: the development of cremation in nineteenth-century England* (Oxford, 2005); J. Leaney, 'Ashes to Ashes: cremation and the celebration of death in nineteenth-century Britain', in *Death, Ritual and Bereavement*, ed. Houlbrooke.

7   Parsons, *Cleansing Flame*, p. 101.

8   K. J. M. Smith, *James Fitzjames Stephen: portrait of a Victorian rationalist* (Cambridge, 1988).

9   *Western Mail*, 19 February 1884.

10 *Bristol Mercury*, 24 March 1884.

11 *Pall Mall Gazette*, 1884; Parsons, *Cleansing Flame*, p. 101.

12 C. Bynum, *The Resurrection of the Body in Western Christianity, 200–1336* (New York, 1995).

13 The Catholic Church's prohibition of cremation was relaxed only in 1964 as liberalising tendencies arose in the curia but even then many bishops remained strongly resistant to the practice.

14 Jupp, *Dust to Ashes*, pp. 51–2.

15 On this see Jupp, *Dust to Ashes*, pp. 16–17, 51–2; for the anti-cremation views of Bishop Christopher Wordsworth of Lincoln see his *On Burning of the Body and on Burial* (Lincoln, 1874).

16 Jupp, *Dust to Ashes*, pp. 73–6.

17 Powell, *Eccentric*, p. 107.

18 Parsons, *Cleansing Flame*, p. 101.

19 Powell, *Eccentric*, p. 117.

20 Cule, 'William Price', p. 119 ns 1 & 2.

21 There were earlier cemeteries but their large-scale development was a feature of the nineteenth century and was given a particular filip by the closure of the old city churchyards. See J. Stevens Curl, *The Victorian Celebration of Death* (Stroud, 2000), ch. 2.

22 G. A. Walker, *Gatherings from Grave-yards* (London, 1839). The move to close the churchyards was a cause of considerable opposition, much of it from local people attached to them as burial places. See Harding, *Living and the Dead*, pp. 68ff; J. Rugg, 'Cemetery Establishment in the First Half of the Nineteenth Century', in *Grave Concerns: death and burial in England, 1700–1850*, ed. M. Cox (York, 1998).

23 Curl, *Victorian Celebration of Death*, chs 3 and 4; Colvin, *Architecture of the Afterlife*, ch. 16.

24 *Western Mail*, 15 and 18 September 1947. The newspaper noted that 'last year' there were 50,000 cremations.

25 *Scotsman*, 20 February 1885. As late as 1930, only 1 per cent of the dead were being cremated, as noted in P. Jalland, *Death in War and Peace: loss and grief in England, 1914–1970* (Oxford, 2010), p. 204.

26 Penelopen was present at this too, unveiling a plaque in Llantrisant in memory of her father.

27 On diminishing belief in literal resurrection of the body and figurative reinterpretation see Jupp, *Dust to Ashes*, pp. 108–9; A. Hastings, *A History of English Christianity, 1920–1985* (London, 1987), p. 231.

11 *Beyond the Veil*

1   *Primitive Methodist Magazine*, 7 (1826), pp. 159–62, 246.

2   For the town see I. Dewhirst, *A History of Keighley* (Keighley, 1974), esp. chs 4–6.

3   For what follows, the indispensable guide is L. Barrow, *Independent Spirits: spiritualism and English plebeians 1850–1910* (London, 1986); for broader context also S. G. Green, *Religion in an Age of Decline: organisation and experience in industrial Yorkshire* (Cambridge, 1996). The history of spiritualism in Britain is dealt with in a number of important books: J. Oppenheim, *The Other World: spiritualism and psychical research in England, 1850–1914* (Cambridge, 1985); A. Owen, *The Darkened Room: women, power and spiritualism in late Victorian England* (London, 1989); R. Brandon, *The Spiritualists: the passion for the occult in the nineteenth and twentieth centuries* (London, 1983). For broader continuities of 'traditional' belief in urban settings see Kselman, *Death and the Afterlife*, ch. 2; S. Williams, *Religious Belief and popular culture in Southwark, c.1880–1939* (Oxford, 1999), ch. 3, which explores urban 'folk' religion.

4   B. E. Carroll, *Spiritualism in Antebellum America* (Bloomington, 1997); N. Rubin Stuart, *The Reluctant Spiritualist: The Life of Maggie Fox* (New York, 2005); B. Weisberg, *Talking to the Dead: Kate and Maggie Fox and the Rise of Spiritualism* (San Francisco, 2004).

5   Catherine Crowe, *The Night Side of Nature* (London, 1848).

6   Here I am persuaded by Barrow who argues for an early diffusion of spiritualist ideas in England among the working classes prior to them taking hold among elements of 'polite' society. The genesis and spread of the movement, and much of the detail below, is extracted from the pages of an early spiritualist periodical published in Keighley between 1855 and 1857, *Yorkshire Spiritual Telegraph* (hereafter *YST*).

7   Some accounts suggest that David Weatherhead's father was a grocer rather than a pub landlord.

8   Barrow, *Independent Spirits*, p. 6.

9   Decades later, one of Richmond's obituarists remembered that almost everyone in the hall had been convinced by him. For which see *The Two Worlds*, 4 and 6 March 1891, p. 193.

10   Anon., *Table-Moving Extraordinary* (Keighley, 1953); I. Dewhirst, 'Robert Burns and the Yorkshire Table-Rappers', in *West Riding Magazine*, 9 (1972).

11   The Swedenborgians arrived in Keighley in 1787. For the

movement and its context: McDannell and Lang, *Heaven*, pp. 181–95; Casey, *After Lives*, pp. 337–55.

12   Revelation 12:12.

13   Faraday had proposed that involuntary muscular movements caused the phenomena.

14   *YST*, 1, pp. 33–4, 44.

15   Ibid., 1, pp. 49–50.

16   Ibid., 2, p. 99.

17   Deuteronomy 18:10–11: 'There shall not be found among you any one that maketh his son or his daughter to pass through the fire, or that useth divination, or an observer of times, or an enchanter, or a witch, or a charmer, or a consulter with familiar spirits, or a wizard, or a necromancer. For all that do these things are an abomination unto the Lord . . .' The story appears in a letter from one James Burns of Shacks Court, Milburn Street, Carlisle, for which see *YST*, 2, p. 91.

18   N. S. Godfrey, *Table-Moving Tested and Proved to be the Result of Satanic Agency* (Leeds, 1853).

19   *YST*, 1, pp. 3–4.

20   Ibid., 1, p. 125.

21   Emma Hardinge Britten, *Nineteenth-Century Miracles or Spirits and their Work in Every Country of the Earth: a complete historical compendium of the great movement known as 'modern spiritualism'* (Manchester, 1883), pp. 95–6.

22   A faintly patronising middle-class image of the working-class medium pictured here in Emma Hardinge Britten, *Ninteteenth-Century Miracles*, p. 165.

23   For Owen see J. F. C. Harrison, *Robert Owen and the Owenites in Britain and America* (London, 1969).

24   The story is told through correspondence by Owen for the benefit of the *YST* readership in *YST*, 1, p. 94.

25   *Rational Quarterly Review*, 2 (1853); Harrison, *Robert Owen*, pp. 250–2.

26   *YST*, 1, p. 94.

27   Ibid., 1, p. 70.

28   Ibid., 1, p. 200.

29   For example, a series of articles pitting the principles of spiritualism against the values of classical liberalism.

30   And this at a point when most churchmen said that the age of miracles was past and set their faces against belief in continuing supernatural phenomena, a point made also in *YST*, 1, p. 15.

31 *YST*, 1, p. 70.

32 *The Autobiography of Emma Hardinge Britten*, ed. M. Wilkinson (London, 1900), p. 210. These events took place during a visit in 1865.

33 Emma Hardinge Britten, *Ninteteenth-Century Miracles*, p. 91.

34 Robert Dale Owen, the son of Robert Owen, took a similar view. His *Footfalls on the Boundary of Another World* rehabilitated ghost stories, and even the long-mocked tale of the Drummer of Tedworth seemed believable again to some men and women who subscribed to spiritualism. On the later history of the story of the Drummer see Hunter, 'New Light on the Drummer of Tedworth', pp. 313–14. Others were republishing accounts of the supernatural long out of print. John Aubrey's *Miscellanies* was published in a new edition in 1857. Its reappearance also suggests burgeoning interest in the uncanny. See Powell, *John Aubrey*, pp. 292ff.

35 *Westminster Review* (1862) as cited in G. K. Nelson, *Spiritualism and Society* (London, 1969), p. 142.

36 Emma Hardinge Britten, *Ninteteenth-Century Miracles*, p. 158; Harry Houdini, *A Magician Among the Spirits* (New York, 1972), pp. 17–31.

37 *YST*, 2, p. 98.

38 The quotation described the massed ranks of miners addressed by Mrs Hardinge Britten when she visited north-eastern collieries in Emma Hardinge Britten, *Ninteteenth-Century Miracles*, p. 223.

39 A. B. Davenport, *The Death-Blow to Spiritualism* (New York, 1897), p. 26.

40 Houdini, *Magician Among the Spirits*, pp. 1–8.

41 Nelson, *Spiritualism*, pp. 3–7.

42 Davenport, *Death-Blow*, p. 68.

43 *A Burial Service for the Use of Spiritualists and Others*, printed by D. W. Weatherhead, East Parade, Keighley. (n.d.).

44 The story may well be apocryphal. One Sergeant Thomas said he heard it from Martin and it was recorded in his diary only elements of which survive in the records of Miss Pendered. See Balston, *John Martin*, p. 161; M. Pendered, *John Martin, Painter* (London, 1923).

45 Balston, *John Martin*, p. 247.

46 Both books were products of the 1860s, published first in the United States and then in Britain: E. Stuart Phelps, *The Gates Ajar* (Boston, 1868); W. Branks, *Heaven Our Home* (Edinburgh, 1861).

47 S. Herbert, 'Between Genesis and Geology: Darwin and some

contemporaries in the 1820s and 1830s', in *Religion and Irreligion: essays in honour of R. R. Webb*, ed. R. J. Helmstadter (London, 1992).

12 *A Darkling Plain*

1   Song of Solomon 2: 17.
2   A. Besant, *Autobiographical Sketches* (London, 1885), p. 56; for a full and lively account of Annie Besant's life see A. Taylor, *Annie Besant: a biography* (Oxford, 1992).
3   A. Besant, *Annie Besant: An Autobiography* (London, 1893), pp. 52, 43.
4   Besant, *Autobiographical Sketches*, p. 52.
5   Mrs Burrows, 'A Childhood in the Fens', in *Life as We Have Known It*, ed. M. Llewellyn Davies (London, 1931).
6   Besant, *Autobiography*, p. 115.
7   Ibid., pp. 104–5. To be so close to the dead in houses of the poor was not unusual; surveys revealed horror stories of corpses shuffled from bed to kitchen table as families were obliged to struggle on with life as they waited for the funeral to take place. See J. M. Strange, *Death, Grief and Poverty in Britain 1870–1914* (Cambridge, 2005), p. 68.
8   J. Obelkevich, *Religion and Rural Society: South Lindsey, 1825–1875* (Oxford, 1976), pp. 295–9; for beliefs about the afterlife more generally see R. W. Ambler, *Ranters, Revivalists and Reformers: Primitive Methodism and Rural Society, South Lincolnshire 1817–1875* (Hull, 1989), pp. 52–5; R. W. Ambler, *Churches, Chapels and the Parish Communities of Lincolnshire, 1660–1900* (Lincoln, 2000).
9   Ambler, *Ranters, Revivalists and Reformers*, p. 52 n. 32.
10 Besant, *Autobiography*, p. 99; T. Hoppen, *The Mid-Victorian Generation, 1846–1886* (Oxford, 1998), p. 469.
11 Besant, *Autobiographical Sketches*, p. 56.
12 Ibid., p. 51.
13 Besant, *Autobiography*, p. 88.
14 The ground floor has been refitted with large glass windows; the upper storeys are still obviously Edwardian.
15 J. Ewing Ritchie, *Days and Nights in London* (London, 1880), pp. 90–116. The 'heartlands' of secularism in London were to be found among the artisan communities of Bethnal Green, Spitalfields, Camden, King's Cross, Shoreditch and Clerkenwell,

as discussed in H. McLeod, *Piety and Poverty: working-class religion in Berlin, London and New York, 1870–1914* (New York, 1996), pp. 29–32.

16   For which see Taylor, *Besant*, p. 71.

17   Ewing Ritchie, *Days and Nights in London*, pp. 90–116.

18   On Bradlaugh see D. Tribe, *President Charles Bradlaugh, MP* (London, 1971); also B. Niblett, *Dare to Stand Alone: the story of Charles Bradlaugh* (Oxford, 2010).

19   Tribe, *Bradlaugh*, p. 26.

20   On this see Rose, *Intellectual Life*, p. 9, pp. 29ff, ch. 1.

21   J. H. Wiener, *Radicalism and Freethought in Nineteenth-Century Britain: the life of Richard Carlile* (Westport, Conn., 1983), p. 46; on the role of sceptical writing and Paine in particular also T. Larsen, *Crisis of Doubt: honest faith in nineteenth-century England* (Oxford, 2006), pp. 239ff.

22   Wiener, *Radicalism and Freethought*, pp. 106–9.

23   Peter of Cornwall, *Liber Revelationum*, cited in R. Bartlett, *England under the Norman and Angevin Kings 1075–1225* (Oxford, 2000), p. 478; S. Reynolds, 'Social Mentalities and the Case of Medieval Scepticism', in *Transactions of the Royal Historical Society*, 6th series (1991).

24   *The St Albans Chronicle: The* Chronica Maiora *of Thomas Walsingham I: 1376–1394*, ed. J. Taylor and W. R. Childs and transl. L. Watkiss (Oxford, 2003), pp. 500–1.

25   K. Thomas, *Man and the Natural World* (Oxford, 1983), p. 122.

26   Almond, *Heaven and Hell*, ch. 2; M. Hunter, 'The Problem of Atheism in Early Modern Europe', in *Transactions of the Royal Historical Society*, 35 (1985); *Atheism from the Reformation to the Enlightenment*, ed. M. Hunter and D. Wootton (Oxford, 1992), chs 1, 4, 5.

27   D. Berman, *A History of Atheism in Britain: from Hobbes to Russell* (London, 1988), p. 201.

28   For George Holyoake, secularism was not atheism as such but rather a philosophy, a way of living, which depended on 'the province of the real, the known, the useful and the affirmative'.

29   Tribe, *Bradlaugh*, p. 94; *The Infidel Tradition: from Paine to Bradlaugh*, ed. E. Royle (London, 1976), p. 63; and for a similar spread of debate into wider society in nineteenth-century France see Kselman, *Death and the Afterlife*, pp. 7ff, ch. 4.

30   See for example the description in Besant, *Autobiography*, pp. 199–200.

31   According to T. P. O'Connor, Irish journalist, in *T.P.'s Weekly*,

21/8/1903, as cited in 'Annie Besant', in *New Dictionary of National Biography*.

32 The remark was made by Thomas Cooper in 1854, who went rather further than George Holyoake wanted to go with the secularist manifesto. See *Infidel Tradition*, ed. Royle, p. 85.

33 B. Hilton, *A Mad, Bad and Dangerous People: England 1783–1846* (Oxford, 2006), pp. 339ff.

34 Ewing Ritchie, *Days and Nights in London*, p. 105; T. Larsen, *A People of the Book: the Bible and the Victorians* (Oxford, 2011), pp. 68–82.

35 A. Besant, *On Eternal Torture* (London, 1874).

36 Ibid., p. 23.

37 J. Furniss, 'The Sight of Hell', in *Books for Children (and Young Persons): for first communions, missions, retreats, Sunday schools* (Dublin, 1860–2), pp. 6–7; G. Rowell, *Hell and the Victorians: a study of the nineteenth-century theological controversies concerning eternal punishment and the future life* (Oxford, 1974), pp. 171–3.

38 Rowell, *Hell*, pp. 17, 20–1.

39 M. Wheeler, *Heaven, Hell and the Victorians* (London, 1994), pp. 175–87; P. Jalland, *Death in the Victorian Family* (Oxford, 1996), pp. 265–83.

40 *Hymns Ancient and Modern*, cited by D. Rosman, *The Evolution of the English Churches, 1500–2000* (Cambridge, 2003), p. 269; on the broader changes, Hoppen, *Mid-Victorian Generation*, p. 469.

41 Wheeler, *Heaven, Hell and the Victorians*, p. 176; there were early modern and even medieval antecedents for these kinds of ideas. See Almond, *Heaven and Hell*, ch. 3.

42 And was attacked by Annie Besant for doing it in Besant, *Eternal Torture*, p. 8; and for the general point about the endurance of the 'common view' see Wheeler, *Heaven, Hell and the Victorians*, pp. 175–87. For Spurgeon see Rosman, *Evolution of the English Churches*, p. 269; Larsen, *People of the Book*, pp. 247ff.

43 Jalland, *Death and the Victorian Family*, ch. 6.

44 G. J. Holyoake, *The Logic of Death: or, why should the atheist fear to die?* (London 1874), p. 7.

45 Ibid., p. 9.

46 This was the conclusion of the secularist leader George Foote, though he acknowledged that such people also had little inclination towards secularist philosophies either. See E. Royle, *Radicals, Secularists and Republicans: popular freethought in Britain, 1866–1915* (London, 1980), p. 296.

47 S. Budd, *Varieties of Unbelief: atheists and agnostics in English society,*

1850–1960 (London, 1977), pp. 35ff; and still a pattern in some working-class communities into the 1970s, as observed in E. Roberts, 'The Lancashire Way of Death', in *Death, Ritual and Bereavement*, ed. Houlbrooke.

48   Examples are discussed in Budd, *Varieties of Unbelief*. The horrible death of a blind unbeliever is described in a Christian moralising tract: C. J. Whitmore, 'Blind, Body and Soul', in *Seeking the Lost: incidents and sketches of Christian work in London* (London, 1876), pp. 239–40; see also T. H. W., 'The Conquered Infidel', in *British Workman*, September 1872, p. 131; a further case is 'The Smuggler's Deathbed', in *British Workman* (1856), p. 62.

49   Holyoake, *Logic of Death*, p. 3.

50   G. W. Foote, *Flowers of Freethought* (London, 1893), vol. 2, pp. 28–30; Berman, *Atheism*, p. 201.

51   J. M. Clarke, *London's Necropolis: a guide to Brookwood cemetery* (Stroud, 2004).

52   Bradlaugh's monument was originally topped by a bronze bust of him. When delegates of an international secularist congress made a pilgrimage to his grave in 1938 they discovered that thieves had come by night and stolen the bronze, seemingly to make a point rather than for material gain.

53   G. W. Foote, *Infidel Deathbeds* (London,1886), pp. 14–15.

54   The Burial Laws Amendment Act of 1880 allowed a Nonconformist minister to take a funeral without observing the Anglican rite but it also permitted burial without a religious service of any kind. On this see Jupp, *Dust to Ashes*, pp. 62–3.

55   This was the requirement of his will of 1884; it was not reiterated in a later will but appears to have been thought by Hypatia to still have been her father's preference.

56   Hypatia viewed Annie as still in thrall to her middle-class upbringing. See Tribe, *Bradlaugh*, p. 263.

57   Niblett, *Dare to Stand Alone*, p. 321; note here M. Bevir, 'Annie Besant's Quest for Truth: Christianity, Secularism and New Age Thought', in *Journal of Ecclesiastical History*, 50 (1999), which portrays Annie as far from being a slave to shifting emotions but, rather, engaged in a reasoned search for a viable philosophy in a world beset by destabilising change. Contrastingly, William Ewart Gladstone had seen at work her 'violent contrarieties' and argued accordingly in his 'True and False Conceptions of the Atonement' [a review of Annie Besant's autobiography], in *The Nineteenth Century*, 211 (1894).

58   Besant, *Autobiography*, p. 121.
59   Ibid., pp. 24–7.
60   Ibid., p. 25.

13 *The Glorious Dead*

1   J. Wolffe, *Great Deaths: grieving, religion, and nationhood in Victorian and Edwardian Britain* (Oxford, 2000), pp. 259–64.

2   R. Blythe, *The Age of Illusion: England in the Twenties and Thirties, 1919–1940* (London, 1963), pp. 1–14. A version of the idea had also been trailed in 1919 by the *Daily Express*, which proposed that the 'dust' of an ordinary man who had laid down his life in his country's service should be buried so as to consecrate the nation's memorial.

3   G. L. Mosse, *Fallen Soldiers: reshaping the memory of the World Wars* (Oxford, 1990), p. 45.

4   M. F. Snape, *The Redcoat and Religion: the forgotten history of the British soldier from the age of Marlborough to the eve of the First World War* (London, 2005), pp. 210–11; M. F. Snape, *God and the British soldier: religion and the British Army in the First and Second World Wars* (London, 2005).

5   There is a very striking memorial for the fallen of the Boer War at Bury St Edmunds in the Market Square, not far from where John Baret had his house. It features a helmet-less soldier in desert fatigues seated on a rock and was dedicated in 1904.

6   J. Bourke, *Dismembering the Male: men's bodies, Britain and the Great War* (London, 1996), ch. 5.

7   A small number of dead soldiers, kin of wealthy families, were brought home early in the war until the practice was forbidden. The decision that the dead must not by repatriated even by private means was reaffirmed on 29 November 1918.

8   Quoted in Bourke, *Dismembering the Male*, p. 250.

9   The others were Lord Methuen and Sir Henry Wilson and Generals Lord Horne, Lord Byng and Albert Farrar-Gatliff.

10   A copy of the order of service is at: http://www.westminster-abbey.org/our-history/people/unknown-warrior.

11   A. Gregory, *The Silence of Memory: Armistice Day, 1919–1946* (Oxford, 1994), pp. 184–5; B. Bushaway, 'Name Upon Name: the Great War and remembrance', in *Myths of the English*, ed. R. Porter

(Cambridge, 1992), pp. 148–9; Snape, *Redcoat and Religion*, p. 182, for earlier uses of a language of sacrifice.

12   *Daily Mail*, 12 November 1920.

13   Ibid., 13 November 1920, describing the scenes at the Cenotaph. Most of those who made the journey visited both of these emerging shrine-sites.

14   *Daily Telegraph*, 12 November 1920.

15   D. W. Lloyd, *Battlefield Tourism: pilgrimage and the commemoration of the Great War in Britain, Australia and Canada* (Oxford, 1998), p. 82.

16   The words are those of the Liberal politician C. F. G. Masterman and are quoted a little more fully in Jalland, *Death in War and Peace*, p. 61.

17   Jack Lawson, *A Man's Life* (London, 1932), pp. 10–19, 240–1.

18   The Graves Registration Committee, the precursor of the Commonwealth War Graves Commission, announced the availability of such photographs in August 1915.

19   Jalland, *Death in War and Peace*, pp. 63ff.

20   Wilfrid Ewart, *Scots Guard* (London, 1934), pp. 174–80.

21   See also the pilgrimages of the middle-class Bickersteth family discussed in Jalland, *Death in War and Peace*, pp. 63ff.

22   D. Cannadine, 'War and Death, Grief and Mourning in Modern Britain', in *Mirrors of Mortality: studies in the social history of death*, ed. J. Whaley (London, 1981), pp. 196ff.

23   G. Gorer, *Death, Grief and Mourning in Contemporary Britain* (London, 1965), p. 1.

24   Bourke, *Dismembering the Male*, pp. 222–36.

25   Ibid., p. 216.

26   The working classes of the early twentieth century often seemed to historians inarticulate in the face of loss, even in 'ordinary' circumstances, but recent research has shown that silence was not a mark of 'feelingless-ness' among working people innured to death. Rather silence and 'doing' rather than 'talking' was a way in which many men and women confronted loss. In these circumstances, the suspension of the usual rituals made deaths even harder to bear.

27   See Jalland, *Death in Victorian Family*, pp. 307–17.

28   *A Soldier of England: memorials of Leslie Yorath Sanders*, ed. A. Sanders (Dumfries, 1920).

29   M. Warner, *Phantasmagoria: spirit visions, metaphors and media into the 21st century* (Oxford, 2006), p. 244; J. Harvey, *Photography and*

Spirit (London, 2007), p. III. I am grateful to Andrew Jarvis for drawing this book to my attention.

30 J. Winter, *Sites of Memory, Sites of Mourning: the Great War in European cultural history* (Cambridge, 1994), pp. 73–6.

31 Jalland, *Death in War and Peace*, p. 27.

32 Sir Oliver Lodge, *Raymond: or, Life after death, with examples of the evidence for survival of memory and affection after death* (London, 1916), pp. 22–4, 31, 44–6, 65. See also J. M. Winter, 'Spiritualism and the First World War', in *Religion and Irreligion*, ed. Helmstadter; J. Hazelgrove, *Spiritualism and British Society between the Wars* (Manchester, 2000).

33 Lodge, *Raymond*, p. 31.

34 Ibid., p. 10.

35 Ibid., pp. 98ff.

36 Ibid., pp. 197ff, 160, 230–6.

37 Ibid., p. 192.

38 Ibid., pp. 205–7, 218–19.

39 Countless copies still circulate, some inscribed with words of comfort. My own copy, the tenth edition published in November 1918, has a message in black ink on one of the opening leaves which reads 'To my mother with love, Xmas, 1918'. There are no clues about the circumstances in which this gift was given.

40 Such as Rylstone Fell in Yorkshire, which has a memorial on the summit, for which see A. Borg, *War Memorials: from antiquity to the present* (London, 1991), p. 87.

41 War memorials tended, as Jay Winter has shown, to be traditional in design, forms which, he contends, had more power to console than modernist expressions, which were better suited to conveying pain, dislocation, irony, despair. See Winter, *Sites of Memory*, ch. 4.

42 Such shrines often appeared in areas from which 'pals' battalions were recruited; when such formations suffered heavily at the Front pools of concentrated grief formed around the streets from which they had been drawn. See Bushaway, 'Name Upon Name', pp. 150ff.

43 Officers would not be distinguished by any more elaborate form of memorial; each stone also had limited space for an inscription. Mosse, *Fallen Soldiers*, pp. 85ff.

Epilogue

1   Although composed by Dean Ryle, it seems probable that he had an eye to recent controversies about the place of Christianity in the business of national remembrance. The Abbey authorities later had to contend with at least one letter of complaint pointing out that the man buried beneath the slab need not have been a Christian and may have belonged to another religious tradition entirely.

2   As recently argued in S. Bruce, 'Secularization, Church and Popular Religion', in *Journal of Ecclesiastical History*, 62 (2011).

ACKNOWLEDGEMENTS

Many debts have been incurred during the writing of this book. Magdalene College under the mastership of Duncan Robinson remains the most congenial of places to think and to write. Among my colleagues there I owe particular thanks to Eamon Duffy, with whom I have enjoyed many teaching trips exploring East Anglian churches, and to Tim Harper, with whom pints of beer and conversation allowed thoughts to be explored in the happy confines of the Castle pub. Faculty colleagues too have been of enormous help, particularly David Pratt, who listened to ideas and sharpened them, and Rosemary Horrox, with whom I have spent many cheerful years teaching a bleak-sounding undergraduate course, 'Death in the Middle Ages'. She generously read the manuscript of the book as it neared completion and improved it immeasurably. Students who took that same paper also contributed – not always realising it – by asking perceptive questions that sent me back to the texts and made me think about them in fresh ways.

My agent, Peter Robinson, helped me to hammer unformed ideas into a proper project. Will Sulkin, Kay Peddle, Gemma Wain and their colleagues at Bodley Head have turned the sometimes vexed business of writing into a pleasure with their genial efficiency, editorial care and forbearance during those long moments when the author was awash with teaching and administrative duties and so neglecting his email. The proprietors of the Black Swan, Oldstead, helped me in a different way, with the topography of the moors around Byland. They let me see the landscape with a native's eye. Meanwhile Annette and Margaret Jones offered refuge in the north east during research there (received with especial gratitude when the trains were paralysed by snow or signalling calamities). My mother, ever-supportive and ever-generous, offered hospitality during expeditions to the Midlands. Friends Hester Lees-Jeffries and Tom Penn talked over the plan of the book many times, read draft material and helped me improve upon the original design. A special debt is owed to Dan Wilton for travelling with me on the journeys that make up *The Undiscovered Country*.

Tracing the stories that are the book's threads has taken me to many libraries, record offices, museums and art galleries. Mention must be made here of Cambridge University Library, the Minster Library at York, Lincoln Record Office, Palace Green Library at Durham, the British Library, the Laing Gallery at Newcastle, the Bristol Record Office, Keighley Public Library, Truro Record Office, St Ives Museum and the British Museum's Department of Prints and Drawings. In all these places I was met by helpful, knowledgeable staff who smoothed the path of my researches.

INDEX